Domestic Work in Postcolonial Tanzania

Domestic Work in Postcolonial Tanzania

Gender, Learning and Unlearning

Paula Mählck

BLOOMSBURY ACADEMIC
LONDON • NEW YORK • OXFORD • NEW DELHI • SYDNEY

BLOOMSBURY ACADEMIC
Bloomsbury Publishing Plc
50 Bedford Square, London, WC1B 3DP, UK
1385 Broadway, New York, NY 10018, USA
29 Earlsfort Terrace, Dublin 2, Ireland

BLOOMSBURY, BLOOMSBURY ACADEMIC and the Diana logo are trademarks of Bloomsbury Publishing Plc

First published in Great Britain 2025

Cover design by Holly Capper
Cover image © Coprid/Adobe Stock

A catalogue record for this book is available from the British Library.

Library of Congress Cataloging-in-Publication Data
Names: Mählck, Paula, 1972- author. Title: Domestic workers in postcolonial Tanzania: gender, learning and unlearning / Paula Mählck. Description: New York: Bloomsbury Academic, 2024. | Includes bibliographical references and index. Identifiers: LCCN 2024013306 (print) | LCCN 2024013307 (ebook) | ISBN 9781350277038 (hardback) | ISBN 9781350277076 (paperback) | ISBN 9781350277045 (epub) | ISBN 9781350277052 (ebook) Subjects: LCSH: Women household employees–Tanzania–Economic conditions–21st century. | Women household employees–Tanzania–Social conditions–21st century. | Women household employees–Tanzania–Colonial influence. | Social structure–Tanzania. | Labor economics–Social aspects–Tanzania. Classification: LCC HD6072.2.T34 M345 2024 (print) | LCC HD6072.2.T34 (ebook) | DDC 305.436404608209678–dc23/eng/20240326
LC record available at https://lccn.loc.gov/2024013306
LC ebook record available at https://lccn.loc.gov/2024013307

ISBN: HB: 978-1-3502-7703-8
ePDF: 978-1-3502-7705-2
eBook: 978-1-3502-7704-5

Typeset by Deanta Global Publishing Services, Chennai, India

To find out more about our authors and books visit www.bloomsbury.com and sign up for our newsletters.

Kwa wadada wote wa kazi wa Dar es Salaam

Contents

Figures

Tables

Acknowledgements

I could not have written this book without the trust and time devoted by the individual women who have shared with me their work-life stories. I have become friends with some of the women I interviewed in my research. They may not agree with all my conclusions. However, I hope that I managed to make my analysis as transparent as possible and my respect for their experiences visible. I offer tremendous gratitude to all the women for their generosity and for sharing their (work) lives with me. This book could not have been written without them!

I am particularly grateful to Rusi Samweli Kabinga (the name is a pseudonyme) , who shared with me her knowledge and experience and took the time to discuss various phases of the project with me. My gratitude also goes to the Rafiki Network (the name is a pseudonym), which allowed me to take part in their activities. I am also grateful to the members of the network of the Diplomatic Spouses and Corona Tanzania, who took the time to explain to me the role and functioning of their networks.

Academic writing is quite a lonely activity but, fortunately, there are many colleagues who have shared their thoughts with me. During my stay in Nairobi, I became affiliated with the African Women's Studies Centre at the University of Nairobi and I was able to present early drafts of my research at their yearly conferences – thank you for your constructive comments and lively discussions! Thank you Dr Marygorety Akinyi Otieno for answering my many questions about African feminisms. My deepest gratitude to librarian Esther K. Obachi at the University of Nairobi for her excellent help in finding literature and patiently answering my questions. I also presented my research at the Department of History at the University of Dar es Salaam – the Isaria Kimambo History Seminar (IKHS) – thank you for taking time to discuss my work. My deepest gratitude goes to Dr Salvatory S. Nyanto for organizing the seminar and Professor Frederick J. Kaijage and Professor Marjorie Mbilinyi, who read and gave detailed feedback on my historicizing chapter. Dr Samwel

Mhajida – thank you for helping me to research the archives and for your thoughtful advice and discussions on various historical documents!

Numerous are the academic friends and colleagues who have contributed through reading and discussing various versions of this manuscript: Professor Fataneh Farahani, for taking time to read several chapters and for being a feminist friend in academia. Professor Nora Räthzel and Professor Keith Pringle, who discussed early ideas for this book and whose intellectual work and political commitment always have been a source of inspiration to me. Thank you, Professor Carl-Ulrich Schierup, Professor Anders Neergard, Professor Aina Tollefssen and Professor Khayaat Fakier, for sharing various interesting reading suggestions with me. I am also grateful to several colleagues who read early versions of different chapters – Associate Professor Sofie Thornhill, Associate Professor Paula Mulinari, Associate Professor Åsa Broberg, Associate Professor Rebecca Adami, Dr Shamal Kaveh, Dr Christer Langström, Dr Anki Bengtsson, Professor Eva Reimers, Professor Anders Gustavsson, Professor Ann-Louise Silfver and Professor Jorge Garcia-Arias.

I had the opportunity to participate in a workshop on Social Reproduction at the Pufendorf Institute at Lund University – a particular thank you to Associate Professor Catia Gregoratti for organizing this event and for interesting discussions.

I am also grateful to The Pluralising Social Reproduction Approaches collective, particularly Professor Shirin M Rai, Professor Stephanie Wöhl, and Associate Professor Laura Horn, for discussing my research.

My colleagues at Remeso, Linköping University, welcomed me and this project. I had the opportunity to present my research at Remeso's research seminar. Thank you for the lively discussions and comments on possible directions to take.

I am thankful for the Sociology of Education and History seminar at the Department of Education, Stockholm University, for interesting discussions of an earlier draft of the historicizing chapter. I also thank the anonymous reviewers for valuable comments. While I have received support from friends and academics in Sweden, Tanzania and Kenya, the responsibility of this work rests on me.

Jenny Money did a fabulous work editing this book – thank you, Jenny, for your patience and good spirit. Thank you, too, to Olivia Dellow, my editor at

Bloomsbury Academic, for believing in this project from the beginning and for waiting patiently while I recovered from Covid-19 infection. The research presented here has received funding from the Swedish Research Council (VR) and from the research council into sustainable development (FORMAS).

If academic writing can be lonesome, the remaining part of my life is not. Thank you, friends in Sweden and beyond for good laughs and good meals. In particular, Kristin Andersson, for walking along the coast line of Msasani and Resarö with me. Last but not least, thank you to my dear partner, Måns, who kept insisting that I should 'Finish the book – you have something important to say!'; to our children – TovaLisa, Malva and Love – for giving me time and love; and to my four-legged companions, Alija and Lassie, for silent strolls in the woods.

Preface

My research interest in the working life and, in particular, women's work life dates back two decades to my undergraduate and, later, postdoctoral studies. There, the research focus was critical investigations into gender and power dynamics in women's everyday working lives in varied contexts, ranging from academia to the heavy motor industry. Originally, this project started off from a similar viewpoint – that is, investigating women's positionalities at work. However, as I became more involved in the fieldwork, new questions emerged. I realized that one of the main components that constructed women's positionalities in this research was the particularity of the work they were doing – domestic and care work in expatriate private households. As the project developed, I began to realize that domestic and care work were sometimes not seen as work – as was the case when the privileged women expatriate employers performed domestic and care work – and sometimes as work – when subaltern Tanzanian domestic workers performed the tasks. The shared experience between these groups of women whom I have interviewed is that their work was hardly (if ever) recognized and was poorly paid. In addition – and should not be underestimated – are the vast differences between these groups of women in terms of their access to power and resources. In this respect, learning to do domestic and care work in expatriate households in many ways implies learning and learning to negotiate – in other words, to unlearn or learn to cope with racism, sexism and coloniality. How do women learn this work – which often remains unnoticed until it is not done – and what is the historical emergence of learning to perceive and do domestic and care work in this particular way? By researching the complexities of domestic and care work in expatriate households, I saw a window of opportunity to investigate relations such as work, gender, migration, care and intimacy and their interlinkages to global power dynamics related to patriarchy, colonialism and capitalism and possibilities for change.

> The study of domestic service is not a trivial sideshow to the grander subjects of social analysis. It is one which demands reflection on the great debates of social theory: on theories of development, of gender and class and of the metanarratives through which these used to be addressed. (Bujra 2000: 3)

Researching processes of learning, unlearning and learning to cope share an analytical interest with interrogating historicizing processes through an interest in examining processes of change, individually, collectively and with the spacio-temporal context for action. In this book, the historicizing perspective became a means for finding ways to change the future. In this respect, the research presented here marks a beginning rather than an end, and the final chapter discusses what bearing the results have for prefigurative politics, in other words, the collective work of imagining a future we do not know. However, political change is always a collective endeavour and therefore the readers are encouraged here to continue the messy, complicated and necessary work of re-imagining life's work. Collectively. Now.

> The search for new ways of being – at the individual, collective and global levels- and the knowledge to support political, economic and cultural changes required would not take place without the capacity to imagine such possibilities and an ability to act on them in the first place. (Pereira 2002: 9)

1

Introduction

Dar es Salaam, August 2017

The clock is ticking. It is past 2 pm in the afternoon and the sun stands high in the clear blue sky. Sweat is pouring down my back as I sit in the shade, watching the perfectly cut emerald green football court of the 'International School of Tanganyika'. In the corner of my eye, I see the gardeners in their blue working gear, bending under the scorching sun. It is my son's second week at school and my first visit to watch his football practice when I overhear a conversation between two women sitting just behind me in the shade.

- *I need a new dada,*[1] *can someone recommend one?*
- *I know a good one.*
- *What does she do?*
- *Ah, she does all sorts of things; cleaning, laundry, shopping . . . But I am sure you can make her do all sorts of things – I mean, she is really good, she never stops working, she just loves working.*
- *How much does she cost?*
- *I pay 300,000 for her but I am sure you can make her work for less; she really loves to work.*

I stare at my feet, unable to move. 'How much does she cost?' and 'I pay 300,000 for her'. I later find out that this is a common monthly wage for a domestic worker; however, at the time of the incident, this way of talking sounds like echoes from the transatlantic slave trade to me. Who talks like that today? I raise my head and turn around. Two white women in their late 30s, in shorts and T-shirts. By their accents I can tell that English is not their first language; my guess is that they come from different European countries. I recognise the bright-coloured shorts they are wearing – they are from H&M. I tried the model on at the mall in the northern suburbs of Stockholm a few weeks ago. I remember the occasion. I was excited, the kids and I were to travel with my husband to his new work post at the UN, Dar es Salaam. New shorts were part of getting ready for the big adventure. When the women see my face, they stop chattering. 'Hi! Are you new here? Do you fancy a coffee?' The woman in the bright shorts hands over a mug to me with a big smile.

The autoethnographic incident outlined above is chosen as the introduction to this book as it exemplifies the volume's focus, which is to interrogate domestic work taking place in the everyday as a process of learning. The incident shows how the exploitation of female domestic workers is normalized in a contemporary and everyday situation. Both the women who used these expressions and I – who became involuntarily integrated in the conversation – belong to the privileged transnational and mobile elite. Later in the discussion, I learnt that the female domestic worker who was brought up as a possible employee is Tanzanian. What I did not realize when this incident occurred was that the female domestic workers whom I later came to know and spend time with during the fieldwork for this book would be Tanzanians and rural-to-urban migrants – just like the female domestic worker mentioned in the incident. The privileged female expatriate employers that I was lucky enough to meet and hang out with – some became my friends – were transnational privileged migrants and the trailing-spouses of international businessmen and diplomats, just like the two women whose conversation I overheard. Importantly, many of the trailing-spouses had left their careers in their home country to follow their husbands and to take care of the family during their spouse's new posting in Dar es Salaam. This had meant not only upward-class mobility for most of the women but also decreasing control – economic, social and legal. While they navigate at different ends of the economic stratum in Tanzanian society, the women's lives are brought together by their relation to paid and unpaid domestic work. In other words, the situation presented above exemplifies how contemporary gender regimes and past and present colonial orders construct domestic-work relations and the migration trajectories and positionalities of the women involved. This involves the ways in which the devaluation of (gendered, classed and raced) domestic and care work is constructed, together with the women who perform such work, paid and unpaid.[2] As this book will show, these processes are not identical for the women involved but, instead, comprise layers of dependency which may counter – as well as reinforce – various forms of inequality and hierarchy, both between women and between women and men in the household. Therefore, the relation between female domestic workers and privileged female expatriate employers, as well as these women's access to power and resources, is dynamic, changing and under constant negotiation.

The focus of the research presented here is to interrogate the gendered, racialized and classed processes, relations and positions that are central for learning domestic and care work in expatriate households in Dar es Salaam, Tanzania. Importantly, this involves interrogating how learning domestic and care work involves learning, coping with and unlearning gender, race and class. Learning involves meaning-making processes of domestic and care work. Meaning-making processes refer to thinking and understanding – as well as doing – domestic and care work. Learning, coping and unlearning refer to different processes of meaning-making that are closely interrelated in complex and sometimes ambivalent ways. As I argue throughout this book, what binds these processes of learning together is an emphasis on agency, transformation and, sometimes, change.

Ways of knowing and learning are not arbitrary but are, instead, forged in history and relations of power. For this reason, an important part of the aim of this research is also to investigate continuities and changes from the British colonial era in East Africa – in particular the 1920s–1960s – and contemporary ways of learning domestic and care work. This perspective on historicizing learning is guided by an interest in how a temporal perspective on learning domestic and care work can contribute to the collective labour of 'prefigurative politics' (Monticelli 2022). In other words, how we can learn from history as we dwell in our present and imagine a future we do not know. The field of prefigurative politics is diverse. Of relevance for the research presented in this book is research into knowing (Pereira 2002), learning (Freire 1998; Dinerstein 2022) and scholarships of hope (Bloch 1986; hooks 2003), which will be further elaborated in the final chapter.

Alongside with the theme of interrogating learning is a research interest in interrogating pedagogies of unlearning in this volume. Unlearning means seeing or doing things in ways they are not usually understood or done. Pedagogies of unlearning runs like a thread in all chapters, theoretically, methodologically and empirically. More specifically, in the historicizing chapter I discuss how it is possible to historicize differently and emphasize alternative narratives. From the perspective of Tanzanian domestic workers and privileged female expatriate employers respectively, examples of unlearning domestic and care work – and aspect of Life's Work – from the everyday are analysed. And finally I let autoethnographic extracts introduce the different chapters which means that the research presented in this book is part of a critical discussion of decolonizing qualitative research method, in particular for Western scholars who do research in the non-West. In the final chapter of this book I let the methodological, empirical and theoretical research findings presented in the various chapters supplement a discussion of how pedagogies of unlearning from the everyday can contribute to imagining differently and working towards a future we do not know: prefigurative politics.

The remaining parts of the chapter are outlined as follows: first, a description of the overall analytical framework of this book is provided. The theoretical assumptions made in an analytical framework is closely connected to methodological decisions. These are presented in Chapter 2. In the outline of the analytical framework presented here, I will discuss how the aim is situated, theoretically and empirically, in relation to previous research in the field of domestic work and domestic workers. Secondly, the context of research is outlined. Thereafter, main theoretical conceptualizations that taken together constitute the overall analytical framework is presented. This section comprises three main blocks: the conceptual frameworks for interrogating learning, unlearning and learning to cope are outlined. In addition, the conceptual framework for interrogating continuity and change is described before; finally, the theoretical umbrella of variegated social reproduction, which highlights the importance of analysing nuances and complexities of social reproduction (SR) across geographies and colonial histories, is set out. A fourth section presents previous research into domestic workers and female employers. The chapter ends with a short outline of the different chapters of this volume and a reading instruction on how they should be read.

A framework for analysing connections

The aim of the research – to interrogate domestic and care work as a process of learning gender race and class – is situated at the heart of a complex grid of connected relations of power – oppressive and at times subversive. Central in this framework is the understanding that colonialism impacted on the metropole as much as on the colony. From this perspective analysing how histories are connected and how this have impacted on contemporary ways of organizing life are central. Rather than falling into the trap of endless relativism this is a perspective that puts alternative voices at the centre and analyses *how* voices connect, overlap or at times partly converge (Bhambra 2014). This is an analytical framework that resists the disciplining functioning of disciplines and combines sociology with anthropology, and in this volume sociology is connected to historicizing and educational perspectives and literary-informed studies – indeed, this opens for processes of learning from each other. A research analysis of connections often focus on spatial or temporal relations. The latter drawing from research from postcolonial research perspectives and the former from cultural geographic research perspectives. In this book I am inspired by recent theoretical research on care and domestic work (Gutiérrez Rodríguez 2021), which combines both perspectives in a bid to understand the situation of migrant domestic workers in private households located in Europe. Gutiérrez Rodríguez (2021) emphasizes that it is pivotal that postcolonial perspectives are put in conversation with spatial and gender relationalities. From here local articulations of global inequalities can be analysed through spatio-temporal connections. Analytically, this implies historicizing 'place-making' (Lefebvre 1991). The relevance of 'historicizing place-making' for the research presented in this book is that expatriate households, that is the work*places* of domestic workers, are conceptualized as work*spaces*, and doing domestic and care work as gendered (and racialized and classed for that matter) work processes that are continuously produced from the colonial era and still today. In particular and from the perspective of privileged female employers and Tanzanian female domestic workers respectively, different chapters in this book will focus on how domestic and care work is hierarchically and unevenly produced. While the analysis departs from the expatriate households in Dar es Salaam, narratives on the metropole, colonial and contemporary, linger in the background and impact on the many ways in which domestic work is learnt and instructed onsite, that is the expatriate households in Dar es Salaam, Tanzania. Moreover, how domestic and care work is produced across different scales which are connected, such as the private household and state, are conceptualized here through individuals' (with different citizenship) relation to the state. Moreover the connection between bodies and built space is articulated through the design of households. In other words, in this book an analytical framework of analysing connections means that the analysis of continuities and changes in learning domestic and care work during the British colonial era of East Africa, in particular the 1920s–1960s, and current conditions for learning domestic and care work in expatriate households is connected with an analysis of spatial and gender relations.

Emphasizing on connections in the analysis of domestic and care work is not new. 'Global Care Chains' is a well-established conceptual framework which theorizes the link between the conditions for work and migration (historical, economic and social, all of these being gendered, classed and racialized) in the sending and receiving countries (see, e.g., Hochschild 2000; Lutz 2011, 2017, 2018; Parreñas 2015; Parreñas, Kantachote and Silvey 2020; Romero 2018; Yeats 2012). The investigation presented here is inspired by this prior research but does not have an identical framing of connectivity. In this respect, my investigation is inspired by research by Anderson (2015), which highlights the necessity of analysing the migration–citizenship nexus from the perspective of migrant domestic workers in private households in Britain rather than going into detail about the conditions in the sending countries. In the investigation presented here, the migration–citizenship nexus is the reverse; in other words, it is the female employers who are transnational migrants and the domestic workers who are Tanzanian citizens. The intention is not to erase this crucial difference, which would be to neglect the gendered, racialized and classed consequences of colonialism.

In this book, investigating how power relations are connected means paying attention to the complexities, continuities, disruptions and transformations in three different but interrelated research dimensions of learning domestic and care work.

First, a research interest in interrogating *continuity and change*, I have interrogated learning domestic and care work through particular mechanisms for colonial domination that creates a link between modernity and colonialism (Weiner 2018). These mechanisms make it possible to analyse the exploitation of subaltern workers and how their work contribute to the wealth of the metropoles. More specifically, the ways in which women's learning, unlearning and coping with domestic and care work have evolved and transformed or remained the same – from the colonial household to the contemporary and postcolonial expatiate household. In particular I have investigated the division of labour in the household: the role and functioning of various types of contracts or lack of contracts and a particular dependency relationship between domestic workers and expatriate employers. This results from subaltern domestic workers taking loans from their privileged expatriate employers. My focus is to analyse how contemporary domestic workers and expatriate employers understand and negotiate the loans that the employers frequently give to their staff, as the salaries that they offer to workers are too low for the latter to survive on. Loans instead of decent salaries are not new in the cultures of the expatriate community in Dar es Salaam. In this context, I discuss what contemporary loans between subaltern domestic workers and privileged expatriate employers produce – and the differences from and similarities to the system of indenture, first put into practice by the British colonial administration in different parts of the world (see also Chapters 5 and 6). My reason for linking back to this system is because central in it was the organization of labour and labourers around debt and dependency vis-à-vis their employers. Historicizing loans, debt and dependency between subaltern domestic workers and privileged expatriate employers implies expanding and *nuancing* the analysis of debt and dependency – which often is framed in dichotomous ways and with an economistic emphasis on the productive sphere – and, instead, shedding light on the overlaps between social oppression, economic exploitation and social reproduction (see also Gore and LeBaron 2019). Importantly integral to analysing mechanisms for colonial domination is the examination of co-existing narratives of how subaltern domestic workers and privileged expatriate women have negotiated, coped with and, at times, unlearned preferred ways of understanding and doing domestic work and the positions and relations that follow from this work. As mentioned before, an interest in discussing the results of unlearning from the perspective how they can contribute to a prefigurative politics of domestic and care work.

Secondly, a research interest in analysing *connections between the everyday and wider societal structures and institutions for processes of learning domestic and care work*. In the research presented here, I use a broad conceptualization of the state. This means an understanding of the state which centre the individual's relation to the state as it is mediated by gender, race and class, including the analysis of the absence or weakness of connections. Chapter 4 presents an analysis of how domestic work in expatriate households in Tanzania has evolved in tension with state-regulated narratives and narratives from the everyday. Using various texts, the chapter weaves together fictional and archival narratives on migration, colonialism, patriarchy and alternative subaltern narratives with an emphasis on power and resistance. Chapters 5 and 6 focus on processes of learning and possibilities for unlearning domestic and care work in everyday life in expatriate households but do not end there. Central here is the analysis of the cheapening of domestic work and workers that takes place in expatriate households and how cheapening is negotiated and at times unlearned. Cheapening involves various processes of lowering the value of domestic work and workers and will be explained in detail later in this chapter.

Finally, a research interest in making *theoretical connections as a means of moving towards a decolonial take of social reproduction theory (SRT).* To accomplish this goal I have initiated a conversation between intersectional research on social reproduction (SR) and theories of critical education. In particular, I draw from research that analyze SR from a geographic lens, from Black feminisms and African feminisms and critical education as I discuss various theoretical connections between these bodies of theories and through these connections, discuss the potential for a decolonial take of SRT.

Situating the research

Who are the employers of domestic workers? In mainland Tanzania, there are three main categories of employers of domestic workers: international businessmen, upper- and middle-class Tanzanians and diplomats and development workers (ILO 2016). In this book, I focus on expatriate employers in Dar es Salaam – in particular, diplomats and international businessmen. The difficulty of finding previous research on the contemporary expatriate group in Tanzania is well known and described in research (Smiley 2010). In this context, the ILO (2016) has identified some insights: in households with an income level of over 1 million TZ shillings (around 380 euros), 75 per cent of domestic workers get regularly paid. The lower the income of the employer, the less likely the domestic worker is to receive payment. Among the group of employers who earn up to 900,000 shillings per month (*c.* 350 euros), 58 to 73 per cent of the domestic workers report that they either do not get paid at all, in monetary forms, payment is late, or their payment is given to a third party. This information supports the interview findings in this book. Here we see that domestic workers express a preference for working for the expatriate group (as compared to national households) as they can be more certain of getting paid, and also where the working conditions are better and their salary is higher.

It is estimated that there currently are 67 million domestic workers worldwide (ILO 2016). Knowledge about their lives and labour conditions has improved over the past twenty years and, currently, abuse and exploitation are well documented within the sector (ILO 2015). Mainland Tanzania (excluding Zanzibar) is no exception; currently it is estimated that there are approximately 1.8 million domestic workers nationwide. This figure includes workers that are working in various informal arrangements. A situational analysis made by ILO (2016) focuses on workers who self-identify as domestic workers and reports that there are 883,779 domestic workers, representing 5 per cent of the national work force. The majority (67 per cent) are females aged fourteen to nineteen years, of whom 68 per cent are internal migrants from poorer rural areas who have migrated to the urban region of Dar es Salaam. Only 0.19 per cent of the domestic workers are international migrants. In 2016, 70 per cent worked more than 14 hours a day and 70 per cent were never given annual leave (ILO 2016: 6). Grassroots movements of domestic workers – for example the ILO Convention 189 – have successfully lobbied for greater recognition of this largely unrecognized and isolated workforce (ILO 2016). However, the Tanzanian government has not yet ratified the convention. Despite an overall positive social and economic development since the 1990s, 49 per cent of the population is currently living below the income poverty line, compared to the population of neighbouring Uganda, with its lower share of 41.7 per cent.[3] Here, it is worth noting that the majority of the population in Tanzania lives in rural areas (65 per cent). In terms of gender inequality, Tanzania can be found at the lower end of the range – 130th out of 160 countries – but it is still above the average in the Southern African group.[4] The majority of workers are employed in the informal sector (71.8 per cent) with only 14.5 per cent conducting 'waged and salaried work'.[5] Around 82 per cent of total employees are in precarious employment and the figure is higher among women (Human Development Report 2020).[6] Despite Tanzania's overall positive economic development over the past two decades, Human Rights Watch have noticed that violations against human rights, including women's rights, are increasing in the country (Human Rights Watch 2019). The World Bank estimates that Covid-19 will cut GDP growth by at least half and increase poverty in Tanzania (World Bank 2020a). Globally, there have been reports of the increasing exploitation of domestic workers and violence against women in general (Pattanaik 2020). While these are important and daunting figures, the research presented in this book will not delve into the consequences and dilemmas that have been accentuated by the pandemic, the reason being that this is a research topic of its own.

My research focuses on expatriate households located on the Msasani Peninsula in Dar es Salaam, where the majority of embassies and expatriate households are located. The location of these households has historical roots, as the colonial administration deliberately concentrated their offices and households in this space in order to facilitate practical domestic life as well as to enhance security. Even today, security is a main argument for the expatriate community to choose to live here instead of other neighbourhoods, despite the fact that Dar es Salaam scores very low in terms of crime risk (Smiley 2010). It is worth mentioning that the domestic workers who have found work in expatriate households on the peninsula belong to the top of the hierarchy in terms of salary and prestige among domestic workers. In spite of this, many of the domestic workers I interviewed described harsh working conditions and hierarchical relations. From a different perspective, the privileged expatriate female employers recalled feelings of insecurity and sometimes a lack of safety caused by having strangers in their homes or leaving their children with strangers.

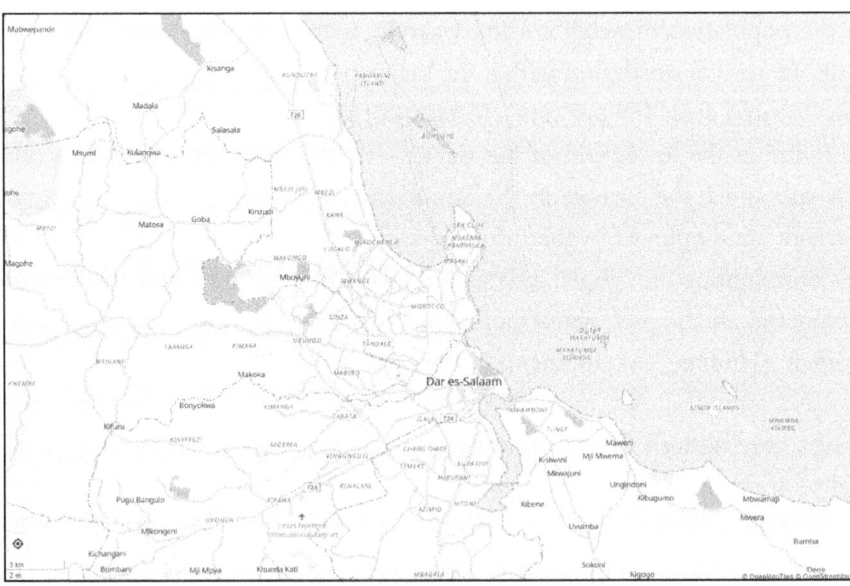

Figure 1.1 Dar es Salaam. *Source*: OpenStreetMap. Data is available under the Open Database License/ https://www.openstreetmap.org/copyright

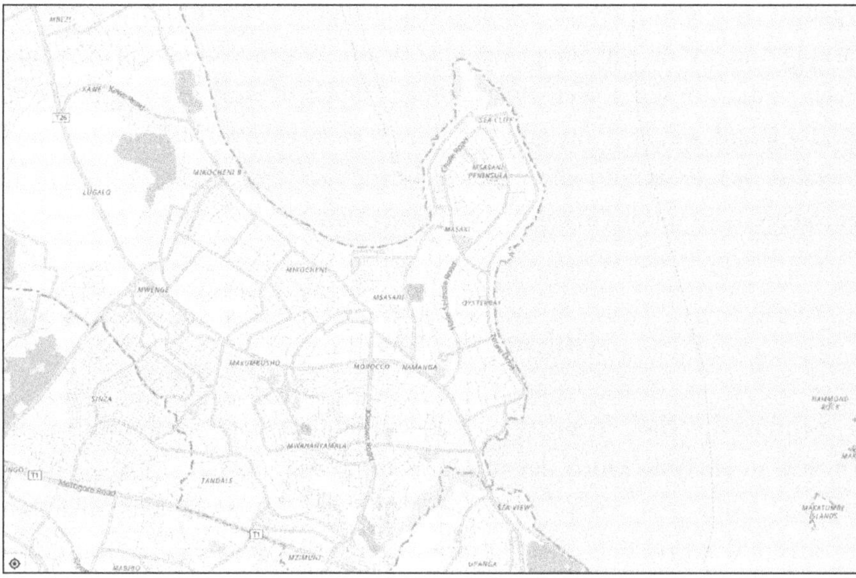

Figure 1.2 Msasani Peninsula. *Source*: OpenStreetMap. Data is available under the Open Database License/ https://www.openstreetmap.org/copyright

Why investigate domestic work as a process of learning?

The learning perspective in this book shares a similar research interest as previous research (see, e.g., Andersson 2000; Bujra 2000; Cock 1984; Kiaga 2007; Killias 2018; Lutz 2011; Parreñas 2015) in investigating how domestic-work relations between employers and workers are built and negotiated, as well as the importance of situating domestic work in time and space. For example, other researchers, such as Nicola Constable (2007), have applied the concept of 'disciplining' to investigate how the labour conditions of migrant domestic workers in Hong Kong are constructed, negotiated and sometimes resisted. Lan (2006) makes another contribution by focusing on processes of 'boundary making' in households. A learning perspective differs from these prior accounts through its focus on transformation, continuities and change.

A learning perspective contributes to denaturalizing the power relations that construct dominant ways of understanding, doing and valuing – or devaluing – domestic and care work as well as the women who perform this paid and unpaid labour. In particular, it means investigating the meaning-making of power relations and complexities in the everyday when we look at gender, race and class. In this respect, change is central for theories into learning and, as we will see in the historical emergence of labour relations. When we denaturalize the everyday doing of domestic work as something that we have learnt, we can contribute to a critical analysis of something that could otherwise be seen as naturalized labour. In addition, this implies destabalizing naturalized conceptions of gender, race and class.

Unlearning and coping

As mentioned earlier, focusing on learning domestic and care work means centring an analysis which denaturalizes the power relations that construct domestic work as a site of oppression and subordination. In similar but not identical ways, it is therefore possible to investigate how oppressive practices and relations can be challenged, that is unlearned. Contrary to the straightforward, deliberate and planned processes of affirmative action, the work of unlearning refers to subtle processes of thinking, seeing or doing things in ways that they are usually not done.[7] Therefore, the concept of unlearning is another analytical cornerstone which allows a focus on the dynamics of several, sometimes dual, perspectives concerned with doing and negotiating power relations in the everyday, individually (see, e.g., Biesta 2013) and collectively (hooks 2003).

In relation to the lead theme of this book, which is investigating learning and unlearning domestic and care work, I suggest that coping in all its diverse and complex forms – such as, for example, enduring, or simply doing nothing – can be theorized as a form of resistance under conditions of oppression (see also Chapter 5). Whether and how this contributes to or prevents social change needs to be empirically investigated.

The divisions between learning, unlearning and coping are not clear-cut. Instead processes of learning, coping and unlearning are complex and ambivalent. What binds them together is a focus on agency and change – first, from the perspective of how subjects – individually and collectively – learn, unlearn and cope and, secondly, how they do so within the context of action (Biesta and Tedder 2007; Emirbayer and Mische 1998). From this perspective, a learning analysis is integral to analysing change which involves but is not limited to individual processes. This means that processes of learning, unlearning and coping are situated at a complex intersection between structures and individual meaning-making.

Unlearning, much less researched than learning, is related – but not identical – to non-learning.[8] Where non-learning refers to misunderstandings of a particular content, it differs from the much subtler process of unlearning. Another main distinction between non-learning and unlearning is the emphasis on transgression. In other words, unlearning emerges from what individuals pick up from transgressing established knowledges, perceptions or practices (Biesta 2013) (see also Chapter 3 in this volume). Making an intervention in the field of lifelong learning, Biesta (2017) emphasizes the necessity of interrogating processes of emancipation that do not involve learning in the sense of 'learning to do what you are told'. While Biesta's critique of lifelong learning has mainly centred the concept in policy contexts, his philosophical underpinnings which, to a great extent, draw from Foucault are relevant for the theoretical framework presented here. In particular, two philosophical pillars are important: first, the understanding that knowledge and truth are impossible to divide and, instead, that subjects are always operating within a knowledge–truth nexus. Secondly, how this philosophical point of departure produces a plurality of truths. From this it follows that, while critique and change are possible from such a viewpoint, this does not include an understanding of emancipation as an escape from power or by revealing the truth about power. Instead, emancipation takes the shape of eventalization when it focuses on how it is possible to complicate and to pluralize our understanding of events and to make visible taken-for-granted elements, relations and domains of reference. In short, eventalization has the ambition of showing that things can be different and takes the shape of a practical critique:

> It is an instrument for those who fight, those who resist and refuse what it is. Its use should be in processes of conflict and confrontation, essays in refusal. It doesn't have to lay down the law for the law. It isn't the stage of programming. It's a challenge directed to what it is. (Foucault 1991: 84 cited in Biesta 2017: 255)

Change is central in critical education, one of the most well-known analyses of change being presented in Freire's (1998) pedagogy (see Chapter 3). As outlined in Biesta's understanding of eventalization, there is a difference in how the latter emphasizes the pluralization of processes of transgression rather than learning. From this it follows that central in eventalization is not how subjects can learn from their lives but how systems of oppression have operated and from this process regain their dignity (this would be a Freirean perspective). Instead, at the forefront, are processes of transgression and the pluralization of truth – in other words, it is what subjects pick up from these processes which constitutes what Foucault called eventalization (1991), Biesta has labelled 'emancipation-without-learning' (2017), hooks (2003) has labelled transgression and what I call processes of unlearning. Here I wish to add that the extent to which unlearning brings about political change is dependent on subjects' access to power and resources; in addition, it is an empirical question.

Another feature that distinguishes the analytical framework presented here from prior research into domestic work is the conversation between intersectional research on SR and critical education, in particular theories into learning, which is presented in more detail in Chapter 3. Intersectional research on SR in various, different and critical ways, is inspired by Marxist feminisms which place the analysis of inequality and materiality at the centre of paid and unpaid domestic work – an aspect of social reproductive labour – as further elaborated on later.

Continuity and change

In the context of discussing SR from the perspective of learning, a specific focus on the materiality of social relations and how they *transform* over time is merited. The following quotation from the preface to the introduction to *Capital* (Marx 2018) gives important insights into what a perspective on historical material dialectics could bring to our discussion:

> The one thing which is of moment to Marx is to find the law of the phenomena with whose investigation he is concerned; and not only is that law of moment to him, which governs these phenomena, insofar as they have a definite form and mutual connection within a given historical period. Of still greater moment to him is the law of their variation, of their development, i.e., of their transition from one form into another, from one series of connections into a different one. This law once discovered, he investigates in detail the effects in which it manifests itself in social life. (Marx 2018: 13)

The historical material dialectic method provides a helpful model for thinking about process and change and is also central in research into learning (Carpenter and Mojab 2017). When this perspective is reworked from the perspective of Marxist feminisms labour studies, it makes possible an intersectional analysis of how hierarchies of gender, race and class are integral to the division of labour:

> Historical materialist dialectics [. . .] examines the *historical* conditions that produce and bring about material contradictions, such as the social division of labour that produces 'sexualization' and 'racialization' and the wage-labour and capital – i.e., *class* relations – on which this division of labour is founded, as well as the development of material conditions which can lead to their collective transformation. (Cotter 2020: 54, Italics in original)

This perspective is quite the opposite of a positivist perspective in historical research, which has the ambition to trace the emergence and retreat of entities. Instead, to historicize means to investigate how learning domestic and care work has evolved through history, with a particular focus on change, materiality, hierarchy and power. Of relevance for the argument in this volume is how Shivji (2019) in his discussion on Tanzanian labour relations links ahistorical scholarship with producing and maintaining neo-liberal economic and political practices in contemporary ways of organizing relations of production – 'The contemporary neo-liberal discourse has one fundamental blind spot. It treats the present as if the present has no history' (Shivji 2019, cited in Tamale 2020: 2). While Shivji's critique makes a decolonial contribution to historical research, it is less effective when it comes to theorizing gender and women's agency.

Lugones (2010) presents a decolonial feminist critique of historicizing that implies opposing a world view which is atomic, homogenous and consists of separable categories. This critique reveals the colonial construction of gender and gender relations, heterosexual relations and normative ideas around family. Moreover, it is a critique of a historical narrative which has not only constructed the white Western bourgeois man as 'the human par excellence' but, moreover, constructs the white woman as an inversion of the white man and indigenous people as lesser humans (closer to animals) – as dehumanized women and men. In addition, it has a focus on the various ways in which resistance is formulated. Focusing particularly on processes of historicizing labour and labour relations, feminist decolonial critiques oppose the view of a historical narrative which reduces 'indigenous females [. . .] to instrumental vehicles for the reproduction of race and capital' (Tamale 2020: 4). Instead, what is needed is an analysis which connects the ideological dots of racism, colonialization, capitalism, sexism and heterosexism in the analysis of gender and labour and which focuses on power and resistance (Tamale 2020: 6). From this follows an emphasis on historicized, relational and localized knowledge. Localized, in the meaning of being context-specific without losing sight of structural power relations and hierarchies. In the African context, this means that a shared structural logic refers to the fact that 'the vast majority of the continent shares a common history of slavery, colonialism and oppression' (Tamale 2020: 7). For the purpose of researching domestic and care work in expatriate households, this requires linking the analysis of the meanings attached to domestic work and workers with context-specific histories of the interplay between colonialism, capitalism and patriarchy, in all its intersectional and variegated meanings.

Variegated social reproduction

The gender division of domestic and care work has long been at the centre of feminist research (for an overview, see Ferguson 2020). From the 1960s on, the research debate intensified, however, mostly centring on conditions in the West. It is within the recent intersectional conceptualization of social reproduction, which takes into account geographic, postcolonial and intersectional theories (Bakker and Gill 2019, Bhattacharyya 2018) and intersectional research from the perspective of Black feminisms (Davis 1983, Stewart 2021, Davis et al 2022) and African decolonial feminisms (Fakier and Cook 2009 Ossome 2021a, 2021b; Tamale 2020) that the research presented here will make a contribution. Broadly defined, social reproductive labour comprises not only the everyday domestic and care work of raising children, cooking and cleaning but also the broader work which people do to sustain themselves and others. In other words, working in societal institutions such as schools, prisons or hospitals is also social reproductive work (Ferguson 2020). Moreover – and as outlined in Chapters 3 and 4 in this volume – a focus on relations to land and processes of finding livelihoods are central features in African feminism's decolonial[9] contributions to SR research. From this perspective social reproductive work is not only structured by sexism but by social oppression in general – such as racism and postcolonialism (Mbiliniyi 2016; Ossome 2021a, 2021b). I elaborate on this in Chapters 3 and 4.

For the investigation presented here, an intersectional perspective on labour means that distinct oppressions such as on gender, race and class are not reducible to each other and are context-bound; however, at the same time, their differences are expressed through structural logics, in the context of the research presented in this book relations such as colonialism, patriarchy and capitalism are important structural logics (Mies 1986, Bhatthacharyya 2018). This is not to say that wage-labour relations construct gender or race oppression – gender and race oppression are sometimes predated to class-based oppression. Moreover – an additional complexity – sometimes domestic work exceeds capitalist relations of production as, for example, in home-making.[10] In this context, the relevance of situating and contextualizing social reproductive labour becomes pivotal, and here the plurality of theories and perspectives under the Marxist feminism*s* umbrella becomes visible.

Feminist postcolonial critiques make important contributions by highlighting how colonialism was interlinked not only with the drive for capital accumulation but also with the quest for modernity, as shaped and defined in the metropole (Katz 2001a). In these processes, social reproductive labour, which involves the maintenance and reproduction of life and the means of life, becomes a distinguishing factor based on racialized differences. It is for this reason that this book understands social reproduction work as Life's Work (Mitchell, Marston and Katz 2004) as it captures various forms of labour which extend beyond wage labour. Conceptualizing social reproductive work as Life's Work implies centring social agents in their everyday lives. Through detailed investigations of everyday lives it is possible to conceptualize the state through subjects various relations to the state, including when these relations may be absent or very weak. This perspective carries with it a particular spatial perspective where Life's Work is produced 'through the practices of social agents at work, at home, and in other quotidian spaces' (Mitchell, Marston and Katz 2004, p.18). Naturally, paid and unpaid domestic work is therefore understood as an aspect of Life's Work. This perspective implies that social reproduction is variegated (Bakker and Gill 2019). Foundational for an analysis of variegated social reproduction is the view that global capitalism operates along variegated geographies of social reproduction that are systematically uneven and internally differentiated and that are more or less subjected to global and disciplinary structures. This perspective stands in contrast to perspectives where subjects emerge as bearers of structures predefined by systemic logics. While it is important to nuance and decentre Western-centred meanings of social reproduction, I here argue that it is important not to lose sight of structural relations which may articulate differently depending on the context but which, nevertheless, share important logics. One example of such structural logic is what Ray Patel and James Moore (2020) call cheapening. In their book *A History of the World in Seven Cheap Things*, they depart from a historical framework of colonial relations and capitalism for understanding cheapening. Focusing specifically on care and care work, Patel and Moore (2020) disclose the relation between colonial discourses of domesticity and the organization of domestic work along gendered, racialized and classed hierarchies. This means that colonial discourses of domesticity have conveyed preferred ways of learning domestic work which implies its naturalization and suggested most women and subaltern workers as better disposed to doing this work. Importantly, this involves a division of labour within domestic and care work where subaltern workers are assigned work that is considered dirty or constructed as low-skilled, often under harsh and sometimes demeaning conditions (Patel and Moore 2020; see also Hall 2007). Patel and Moore use the concept of cheapening to analyse the lowering of the value of domestic work and of workers that perform this work. Moreover, cheapening involves the exclusion of most women – indigenous, colonized and slaves from society as well as from being human – hence they were constructed as part of nature and they were *cheapened* (Patel and Moore 2020: 24). A main constituency of processes of cheapening is the naturalization of work and workers – in other words, cheapening comprises the view of the inseparability of bodies and labour (Patel and Moore 2020: 24). Central in my book is therefore investigating how the cheapening of domestic work and domestic workers in expatriate households was learnt during the British colonial era in Tanganyika – in particular during the 1920–1960s – and how these learning processes are currently produced. In other words, how are these learning processes transformed, contested or coped with and what are the continuities and changes?

Madam and maid

Intersectional research[11] has challenged the universal claim of 'woman' and contributed by exposing differences and inequalities among women (Crenshaw 1991; Mohanty 2003). Employment relations between women in private households are particularly clear examples of the inequalities that exist within a group of women. Romero has described the relationship between two such women not as 'a bond of sisterhood' but as 'a bond of exploitation' (Romero 1992, cited in Lan 2006: 3). Race and the class division of labour in domestic work offer certain specific positionings, are often tied to images around slavery and colonialism and are at the core of postcolonial research into domestic work (Bujra 2000; Cock 1984; Glenn 1992; Phyfer, Durrheim and Murray 2020; Romero 1992). In other words, postcolonial research centres on linkages between past and present forms of exploitation of women's paid and unpaid domestic work. Complementary to postcolonial research is that of studying domestic work and women's migration. The migration of female domestic workers is part of a global solution to privileged women's dual workload in world economic system, as Shellee Colen (1995) has pointed out. In this context, migrant domestic workers leave their own families behind in exchange for financial aid (Lan 2006: 4). Scholars have labelled this development 'The global nanny chain' (Hochschild 2000) or 'the international division of reproductive labour' (Parreñas 2015). Importantly, the migration routes and destinations for domestic workers are no longer exclusively from the Global South to the Global North but are within regions of the Global South. In particular, the 'new domestic world order' (Hondagneu-Sotelo 2001) has been investigated through the demand for domestic workers in regions such as the Gulf States and Asia. These migration patterns nuance the image of the white madams and Black female domestic workers and, instead, expose the inequalities among women in the Global South. The situation of domestic workers in Africa, with the exception of South Africa, is still under-researched. The groundbreaking book *Maids and Madams: A Study in the Politics of Exploitation* (Cock 1984) presents a detailed investigation of the work conditions and employment relations between white South African female employers and Black South African domestic workers. The historical perspective shows how the development of the domestic-work sector in South Africa is integral to the development of the apartheid state and its migration regulations. Contrary to its development in Tanzania, domestic work was never male-dominated in South Africa. Instead, the workpool of Black African women was secured through the apartheid state migration regulations to and from homelands. In her analysis of the development of the domestic-work sector in Tanzania, Bujra (2000) showed how the growth of the sector is interlinked with rural-to-urban migration, the rise of the middle class and the shift from a male- to a female-coded occupation. Kiaga's (2007) doctoral thesis focused on the recruitment of domestic workers, work relations and identity formations of female employers and workers in contemporary Tanzanian households. Her research points to the complexities within the recruitment system *Undugu* – which is built on kinship and social relations – and how it reproduces gender inequality through domestic service. In this respect the research in this book differs from that in Kiaga's as it focuses on expatriate households. Despite the rich findings presented earlier, there is still no solid investigation into how domestic work – both paid and unpaid – and the women who perform it came to be understood in this particular way. In other words, there is a shortage of research into the everyday and the naturalized and taken-for-granted mechanisms of learning and doing domestic work and the perceptions of women who perform this, whether paid or unpaid. To address this deficiency, I have designed this research to include the perspectives of both privileged expatriate female employers and Tanzanian female domestic workers. I situate the analysis at the household level and the everyday meaning-making and doing of domestic work, as well as in relation to broader social and cultural contexts, including the politics of postcolonial racism, gender relations in family lives and class relations. Last but not least, I apply a historical lens to analyse changes and continuities in contemporary ways of carrying out domestic work with conditions during the colonial period and ask how it is possible to imagine it differently.

Outline of the book

While the analytical framework for analysing connections (i.e. continuities and changes, the everyday and institutional and moving towards a decolonial take of SRT) is a thread that runs through the various chapters of this book, it is important to underline that each chapter has a distinct functioning in this web. Each chapter focuses on different aspects of learning and possibilities for unlearning domestic work – an aspect of Life's Work. This means that different chapters focus on historicizing domestic-work relations, sociological analysis of learning in the everyday in contemporary households and theoretical elaborations of SRT respectively. For this reason, each chapter is designed as a single piece and this design makes it possible to read them as separate pieces. I use the allegory of a prism to exemplify: each chapter can be likened to a facet grinding in a prism. When a beam of light hits a specific grind, a pattern appears that reflects a larger unit. Taken together, these patterns produce a deeper understanding which is informed by historical, sociological and theoretical analysis of domestic work. Having said this, and as mentioned before, the different chapters are not completely separated but are inspired methodologically and analytically from an overall framework of making connections (Bhambra 2014). Regardless if the chapters are read as separate pieces or one after the other, the chapters through their various and differing emphasis on history, theory and sociological analysis of learning contribute to further our understanding of and possibilities for re-imagining domestic work. The final chapter discusses the results with a particular focus on unlearning and digs deeper into imagining differently, so-called prefigurative politics (Monticelli 2021).

Chapter 2 is a methodological chapter which presents overall methodological considerations made before embarking on and during a multimethod and multilayered research investigation. Chapter 3 presents a theoretical conversation between critical education and intersectional research on SR – in particular how it is possible to draw from African decolonial feminisms and Black feminisms and research that apply a geographic lens on SR and move towards a decolonial take of SRT. Moving on to the work of historicizing, Chapter 4 makes a methodological contribution to historicizing domestic-work relations in expatriate households and weaves together different narratives of domestic work, gender and migration in Tanzania. These narratives depart from earlier historical research and my research from the archives[12] and extends to analysing a fictional novel. Chapter 5 interrogates continuities and changes – from the colonial era and contemporary households – in how domestic workers learn, learn to cope and unlearn preferred ways of doing domestic work in expatriate households. Continuities and changes are the main themes in Chapter 6 which focuses on how privileged expatriate women learn domestic and care work. The chapter makes a contribution by theorizing ambivalences and complexities of how oppression and privilege are constructed and, in this respect, move beyond predefined perceptions of who can be oppressed and who can become the oppressor. The final chapter – Chapter 7 – situates the main results from the research presented here in the framework of prefigurative politics (Monticelli 2022). More specifically in this chapter I discuss how pedagogies of unlearning that emerge from methodological, empirical and theoretical findings from the research presented here can inform the work of imagining domestic and care work in a future we do not know.

2

Tales of the field

In social-constructivist research, it is well known that the social positioning of the researcher influences what is considered to be a relevant research topic or data. Moreover, the ways in which data are collected and interpreted are perceived as a relational social process. In other words, how the informants perceived me and the research project also impacted on how they chose to answer my research questions and, therefore, on the research process and outcome (Best 2003; Lan 2006). This means that a reflexive account of a research process not only reveals the power relations between the researcher and the informants but also brings to the surface the wider historical and social context in which they are both located. In the fieldwork carried out for this book – doing interviews, searching for literature in archives or attending meetings or social gatherings – I was frequently reminded of the wider historical and social power relations of this project. For example, when I conducted my interviews, whether in private households, cafés or public spaces, I never saw a white woman serving under a Black woman. There might have been situations where Black women were in a management position but, when this did occur, there would always be a Black man or woman serving under her. These tales have left an imprint on the research focus of this book; investigating how mundane domestic work is learned and how this process also implies learning gender, race and class and the continuities and discontinuities of these learning processes from the colonial to the postcolonial era in Dar es Salaam.

Connected histories – Connected Life's Work

The methodological framework in this book revolves around three sets of connections which will be outlined next. The first connection refers to recognizing that colonizers and colonized are at least as affected by colonialism. In other words, the necessity to recognize that (post)colonial societies have been built on both sides. Denying this means an implicit acceptance of the cultural superiority of colonial powers (Bhambra 2007: 19). In the context of the research presented here, this implies a research interest in analysing the historical (material and contradictory) conditions that bring about the division of labour in expatriate households in Tanzania – and which produce race, class and gender – as well as the conditions that can lead to the collective transformation of labour relations (see also Cotter 2020).

The second connection is between historical narratives and contemporary narratives. This means that the analytical focus is not only on how learning processes present themselves in today's world but also on their historical emergence, with a focus on hierarchy and power. The analysis of continuity and change in ways of learning domestic and care work in Chapters 5 and 6 is the opposite of a positivist historical perspective, which aims to trace the emergence or retreat of entities. Instead, as stipulated in the introductory chapter a historicizing perspective focus on processes of continuity and change. This methodological grip is inspired by the regressive-progressive method (Hess 2000: XV; Rönnlund and Tollefsen 2016: 187) applied in Chapters 5 and 6. This method draws from Marx's understanding of the historical, material, dialectics method (see Chapter 1). In short, this method departs from a detailed investigation of a contemporary phenomenon and traces it backwards in order to understand continuity and change and to find openings for the future. Chapter 4 shares similarities with Chapters 5 and 6 but is not identical in its methodological framing. It has an explicit historicizing focus and is similar to Chapters 5 and 6 as it shares an interest in interrogating how processes and relations connect. In addition, Chapter 4 differs from Chapters 5 and 6 as it places more emphasis on analysing connections between different narratives, in particular narratives that are subaltern and have received less attention in the colonial archives. Moreover, its design is aligned with historical postcolonial research which follows non-linear trajectories and theorizes 'backwards' and 'forward' (Bhambra 2007).

The third connection refers to an interest in *how* colonial narratives are connected to contemporary narratives. In this volume, colonial narratives are connected to contemporary narratives through an interest in relations.

In this respect, the methodological framework for this book is inspired by oral history in a broad sense.

> oral history is a work of relationships; in the first place, a relationship between the past and the present, an effort to establish, through memory and narrative, what the past means to the present; then, a relationship between the interviewer and the interviewee, and between the oral form of the narrative and the written or audiovisual form of the historian's product. (Portelli 2009: 21)

The focus on relationships articulated in the quote above is here translated into a research interest that extends beyond asking what happened historically; instead, it asks, 'What does it mean?' In other words, what does it mean that domestic work is narrated in this particular way in colonial documents? What does it mean that servants' quarters are displayed in this particular way in the colonial archives? And how does it relate/not relate to the ways in which domestic work is narrated in contemporary interviews with privileged female expatriate employers and Tanzanian domestic workers? In other words, different texts are interlinked to the work-life interviews of the women since a main component of oral history is the investigation of individuals in their particular social and historical context. Oral history is particularly suitable for analysing historical relations which have not usually attracted much research interest before, as these relations were considered to be too mundane (Portelli 2009). Another main feature of oral history is that it is the narrator who is at the centre of the account. This means that oral history distances itself from seeing interviews as a testimony or a witness. Instead, the subjective element is seen as an additional layer of data (subjectivity is something to which I return later in the chapter).

Circuit of culture

This section of the chapter will dig deeper into how different texts are connected. In this book, colonial texts – that is guidebooks and cookbooks intended for colonial settlers, archival texts and contemporary texts, guidebooks for contemporary privileged expatriates and a contemporary fictional novel as well as contemporary interviews – are all analysed as related societal narratives that impact on how domestic work and domestic workers are conceptualized and how these workers understand their positionalities (see also Hall 1997 and

Chapter 5 in this volume). From this perspective, a personal diary, cookbooks or handbooks can be seen as additional layers of representation to other texts such as interview transcripts. This methodological grip for analysing how cultural representations are connected is labelled 'circuit of culture' and points to how layers of representation are interconnected (Hall 1997). This way of analysing representations indicates that cultural expressions such as cookbooks can be understood as texts which inform the behaviours of readers (Jansen 2019: 5). Against this backdrop, colonial household books – more specifically, the instructions and recipes intended for colonial households – or contemporary handbooks and glossy lifestyle reports are interesting to analyse as they are not purely utilitarian 'but rather a way to understand work, lives, and relationships in a given place and time' (Blackett 2019: 85). In other words, these texts can be used to gain insights into preferred ways of organizing imperial lives whose habits were intended to replace those that already existed. It is in this way that the analysis of colonial and contemporary texts supplements the analysis of how contemporary expatriate women learn, cope and unlearn domestic work in expatriate households in Dar es Salaam.

The false consciousness debate

A common critique of the historical material dialectic perspective is that it is privileging an analysis of structural domination at the expense of a subject's agency (Carpenter and Mojab 2017). In this context, a feminist, historical, material, dialectic perspective on learning domestic and care work merits attention being given to conceptualizations of ideology and, in particular, to the false consciousness debate. Nora Räthzel (1997) has theorized the role of ideology in how people think and act. I found her argument useful for analysing ideology in learning processes and how this analysis moves away from that of 'false consciousness'. The argument of Räthzel (1997) concludes that ideology is not false consciousness; instead, ideology should be understood as a consciousness that understands the world according to the unmediated experiences of everyday life. In other words, consciousness is what subjects learn from their everyday practices. In this book, my ambition with the analysis is therefore not to change subjects through correcting their false consciousness but, instead, to analyse how subjects learn from their everyday lives, while keeping in mind that learning takes place within structures that are multiple and sometimes contradictory. This is not to say that structures and economic relations determine the way in which subjects learn, because subjects live under various structures simultaneously and develop multiple and various, sometimes contradictory, ways of knowing, doing and learning. Even if there are dominant ways of knowing and learning, there are also ways of knowing things differently, other ideas to learn (Räthzel 1997). However, as Gramsci (1971) rightly pointed out, the subjects that are marginalized are rarely those whose ideas are made central in societal institutions and structures.

Researching the everyday through extreme situations

The research presented here draws from my interest in domestic work as articulated in 'everyday situations'. However, in the context of the research presented here, diplomatic and international businessmen's households in Dar es Salaam are not exactly 'ordinary' households but, instead, represent a privileged and mobile, economic, cultural and social elite. How can extreme contexts help us to understand ordinary situations? Here, I lean on previous feminist research which suggests that studies of exceptional circumstances are particularly suitable for analysing relationships between individuals and between individuals and their context, since they stand out more clearly compared to situations which are 'quieter'. Moreover, for researchers interested in social change, these situations also tell us something about human possibilities and the ability which people have to transform themselves and the conditions in which they live (Räthzel 2018).

Situating myself in this research

My understanding of oral history is influenced by Portelli (2009), who perceives the subjective dimension in research to be an additional layer of knowledge which is part of the analysis rather than an obstacle that needs to be overcome. This approach applies to the work-life narratives which the women involved told me about but has also been useful for making sense of my personal experience of living as a privileged diplomatic spouse over a period of three years (2017–20). During this period, I worked part-time on my university work in Sweden and part-time in charge of domestic and care work for my family. My university work had, until now, focused on researching racism and sexism in academia in Sweden and beyond.

Sweden is a country which has a history of race eugenics and a contemporary profound grammar of colour-blind racism and whiteness in academia (Mählck 2012, 2013). To research racism in a colour-blind context means negotiating – from my position as someone of mixed-race and middle class – processes of being racialized, exoticized and, in the beginning of my career as a young woman, sexualized. I also have experiences of being excluded from Black academic communities for not being 'black enough' (Mählck 2013). This means that I have, from my earlier studies, experiences of researching from below, interviewing mainly white academics with higher professional statuses compared to mine. I have also experiences from class-belonging in academia given my middle-class background. Through my international and comparative research in South Africa and in East Africa, I have learned how my position as a racialized Other in Swedish academia changed during fieldwork. The subject positionality I have had to negotiate was of someone who could pass as white and, sometimes, being constructed as a representative for colonial power. This means that when I started the research for this volume, I had embodied experiences of negotiating simultaneous privilege and subordination and I also knew and had felt how these processes change during transnational research, creating complex, dual and translocal 'insider-outsider' positionalities (see also Farahani 2015, experiences from within Swedish academia). While I was prepared to negotiate gender and race relations in my new life as a part-time academic and part-time trailing-spouse, I had not, prior to 2017, experienced such profound class privilege, *on a daily basis*. This experience created a dissonance with my habitual feminist research identity which, in addition to knowing how to design critical research projects, also meant doing and acting in feminist solidarity and against multidimensional relations of oppression in academia on a daily basis. Sometimes this feminist labour has been successful, sometimes it has been more challenging and sometimes I have not succeeded at all, despite my good intentions.

The encounter with a privileged everyday life as an expatriate – and how this way of organizing everyday life was taken for granted by most members of the diplomatic and international business community – triggered my research interest. From a messy and complicated position of privilege and disadvantage, both insider and outsider, I realized that my personal experiences are important sources of information. For this reason, every chapter in this book starts with an extract from my diary which is analysed from the perspective of autoethnography. Yet, as hooks (1994) has taught us, personal experiences cannot be the only source of information. For this reason, the extracts – selected as they point to incidents from the everyday that have been contradictory and complex – have been analysed, with the ambition to highlight how personal experiences connect to political practices which are not arbitrary but, instead, deeply embedded in temporal and spatial relations of coloniality. This research grip resonates with analytic autoethnography (Anderson 2006) where autoethnographic data is analysed to gain insights into a broader set of social phenomena than those provided by the data themselves. This is different from evocative autoethnography where the researcher reflects on their feelings towards a particular topic with the ambition to make the readers connect to these feelings (Anderson 2006: 377). The incidents from my diary are chosen as they reveal how the everyday is as being far from neutral but, instead, constructed of situations which are loaded with power relations and asymmetries and which have no simple solutions (Smith 1987). This means that my observations of my involvement in everyday situations are analysed with a particular focus on making connections visible; between subjects and objects of research, epistemologies, geographies and relations of power. A scholarship which views the everyday as a 'feminist sociological problematic' (Smith 1987) allows us to acknowledge how domestic and care work is constructed through everyday mundane relations of learning and how it is possible to unlearn and, hence, to undo relations of oppression produced through dominant narratives. Domestic and care work is variegated and hierarchically produced in different geographic spaces. The site I have chosen for my research, expatriate households in Dar es Salaam, is an empirical site where gender relations, postcolonial hierarchies and different migration trajectories, transnational and rural-to-urban, meet and clash. For this reason, the expatriate household is a perfect site for analysing the uneven conditions of domestic and care work and, moreover, how it is possible to rework the everyday through processes of critique and affinity, as complicated, contradictory and ambiguous as this may be (this is further outlined in the concluding chapter).

We resided first in Dar es Salaam (Tanzania) for one year and, later, in Nairobi (Kenya) for two years. In our households in Dar es Salaam and then Nairobi, we employed Tanzanian domestic workers and Kenyan female domestic workers respectively and a male driver, who all worked for us and helped me to organize and carry out the domestic and care work. One of the female domestic workers in our household in Dar es Salaam chose 'Rusi' as her pseudonym in this book, and she played a tremendously important role in introducing me to various domestic workers there as well as discussing possible interview themes with me (see Appendix on methodology and participants profile). These years represent an embodied fieldwork experience of inhabiting as a privileged researcher from the West doing research in the non-West and, in particular, of experiencing a positionality as a privileged female expatriate (who could sometimes pass as white) and a diplomatic employer. This means that I have lived, battled and negotiated the power imbalances involved when a Western researcher does research in the non-West, together with the privileges and contradictions involved in a diplomatic spouse's life. There are enormous economic and racial privileges. Let me give one example – one regular trip to the shopping mall or the hairdresser would mean spending the equivalent of a month's pay for a Tanzanian domestic worker. Having said this, it is important to remember how this life experience also implies a decrease of control – economic, social and legal – for the spouse, control which is directly passed on to the family provider, the husband. One such example refers to the legal sphere: some of the spouses I interviewed told me that they needed their husband's written consent to travel out of the country with their children. I have not been able to verify this latter information but I mention the travel restrictions here to exemplify the feelings of dependency, vulnerability and unfreedom that these women wanted to share with me. In this context, it is worth underlining that these feelings of vulnerability are experienced from a privileged class position and, as such, at a different level from the vulnerabilities experienced by the domestic workers in their everyday work lives.

Ethics

Women were contacted through snowball sampling, where they were asked to recommend other women whom I could interview. Importantly, the group of domestic workers would have been impossible for me to reach without the help of the *Rafiki* group[1]. *Rafiki* is a Kiswahili word meaning a friend, which signifies what the group is about. It is an informal and loosely compiled circle of female Tanzanian domestic workers who meet occasionally to support and look after each other. My knowledge of and reference to the *Rafiki* group made it possible for me not only to find but also to gain the confidence of the domestic workers. At the initial stage, perhaps longer, some domestic workers perceived me as a representative for employers, which was a misunderstanding I had to address both before, during and after the first interview. With some domestic workers, particularly after we had met a few times, I felt that we could, despite the language, race, class and postcolonial barriers, reach moments of closeness during our interviews. However, with other domestic workers, these barriers were always present and I would feel a degree of suspicion on their part. From some of the domestic workers, I could also detect a sense of them seeing this project and me as a possibility for improving their situation. Here, I would explain that I, personally, could not offer economic help but that my ambition with the project is for the results to be used to change the workers' situation for the better.

The privileged expatriate female employers, on the other hand, felt more at ease with the interview situation and with me. They did not ask for anything in return and, with one exception, I had the impression that they agreed to meet with me without fear as they were used to moving freely in public spaces. Often, the privileged expatriate female employers offered me access to their domestic workers as a way of helping me in my research. This offer reveals a lot about the power dynamics between the female employers and the domestic workers. Here, I should mention that the domestic workers were very keen to ensure that their employers never found out about their meeting with me. Naturally I never, for ethical reasons, accepted the trailing-spouses' offer. For similar ethical reasons, I was keen to keep the groups of domestic workers and female expatriate employers separate and ensure that they did not belong to the same household. Importantly, the domestic workers, with two exceptions, were day workers and did not live in the same area or even close to the employers.

Writing from a feminist perspective means paying attention to power imbalances during the research process and I strived to make the interviews and fieldwork as transparent and comfortable as possible for the women involved. This was done by handing out written information about the project in English and, when necessary, in Kiswahili. I have been keen to choose extracts from my diary that represent ordinary situations and do not risk exposing the identity of the persons involved.[2] I offered to meet at places where the women felt safe and arranged for secure transportation when necessary. Moreover, in many other more subtle ways, I tried to , even out any power imbalances during the interview situation.

The research presented in this book is not merely a reflection of the opinions of the interviewed women. Nor is it the result of my experiences only. Instead, the research focus and the framework of inquiry presented above are the result of analytical work, which means that the women involved may not always agree with my conclusions. I nevertheless hope that my respect for their experiences and my gratitude for their cooperation are visible in the text.

3

Pedagogies of unlearning

Dar es Salaam, September 2017

My neck hurts after hours of computer work. As I walk along the narrow and shady corridor, I bend to pick up socks and schoolbags. My breath burns against my hand when I wipe sweat from my forehead; the air-conditioning must have been switched off. I call her name gently. Only the echo from my footsteps in the empty stone house answers me.

I find her in the hot and steamy outdoor laundry area, sitting on the floor. Sheets are hanging out to dry; freshly ironed clothes are neatly piled on the ironing board. When she sees me, she hurriedly stows away her plate of Ugali.

- ***Rusi:*** *I am having my tea. Did you need me?*
- ***Paula:*** *Why are you sitting here?*
- *She follows me into the dining room and we finish our meals while I try to make conversation. After a while she looks me straight in the eyes.*
- ***Rusi:*** *May I go now? I'm here to work.*

The above conversation is from my diary on the first day that Rusi Samweli Kabinga,[1] a domestic worker came to work in our household in Dar es Salaam. Later, during our many conversations, Rusi will tell me that many domestic workers have been instructed by their employers not to remain in the main house during lunch breaks and how this involved instructions not to use chairs or sofas without permission. She will also tell me how domestic workers are frequently told that air conditioning can only be used by members of the household, thus making them work in rooms where temperatures could be well over 40 degrees Celsius. Moreover, she mentioned that many domestic workers are afraid to drink water or take food from the fridge in case they are charged afterwards by their employer. Considering the low wages which domestic workers receive, it is very difficult for them to pay for food, water or electricity (for air conditioning).[2]

The above passage illustrates clearly how relations of production – that is, paid and unpaid domestic work as well as gender, race and class – are intrinsically connected. Paid and unpaid domestic and care work in private households offers a particularly clear example of the connection between private and public spheres of production, the complex work relations and positions of power, privilege and subalternization and the various forms of resistance that may occur separately or simultaneously. The overall focus of this book is to interrogate domestic and care work as a process of learning gender, race and class. Integral to this is investigating how these are resisted through processes of unlearning and learning to cope, as well as continuities and changes over time.[3] While the results from the interviews and archival research are presented in Chapters 4, 5 and 6, the aim of this chapter is to present a conversation between intersectional research contributions that discuss social reproduction and critical education and through this dialogue move towards a decolonial take of SRT. Central in this process is what I call an ontology of transgressions and pedagogies of unlearning. This implies pluralizing approaches to social reproduction and an emphasis on the link between unlearning and undoing. The latter is much more discussed in postcolonial and decolonial studies. SRT has received increased attention during the past decade and is currently described in the research literature as a theory with many fractions (Luxton 2018). There is also an ongoing debate on the complexities between SRT and intersectional research on social reproduction, in particular on the grounds of their different understandings of the origins of oppression (Stewart 2021). Recognizing this debate, I will primarily focus on intersectional research that discuss social reproduction and discuss these contributions from a critical education lens. Importantly, the division between SRT and research on SR from an intersectional perspective is done for analytical reasons. This means that I recognize that the divide between these theoretical approaches is much more fluid than I suggest here. Moreover, I posit that engaging with theories at the global margins can be a fruitful beginning towards a decolonial take of SRT. With theory at the global margins I refer to critical theory from the West and the non-West that have not been at the centre of SRT or critical education: notably feminist postcolonial and decolonial contributions. The reason for choosing to situate the discussion of paid and unpaid domestic work in this chapter within intersectional research contributions to SR – in particular those from Black feminisms, African decolonial feminisms, and research that applies a geographic lens on SR and conversation with critical education, is their mutual interest in emancipation and transformation from within and from below.[4] A note on language is merited here. I see domestic and care work as an aspect of Life's Work (further elaborated on below) and the framework of Life's Work being in dialogue with SRT.

Let me return to my diary notes to further explicate the necessity to initiate a conversation between intersectional research that discuss social reproduction and critical education.

At first glance, the autoethnographic incident outlined above may seem like an example of colonial power and racialized, gendered and classed subordination only. Instead, the incident also reveals resistance articulated from different positions of power; from the perspective of Rusi, the domestic worker, resistance is articulated by her refusing to chat with me over lunch as friends, which would obscure the employer–employee relationship. For my part, as incomplete as this act may be, I tried to make a gesture of an evening out or undoing the hierarchical employer–worker relationship by offering her lunch in the dining room. I here outline this incident, as it highlights a feminist 'problematic' (Smith 1987) which can be researched, analysed and changed in future practice.[5] It is in this respect that processes of resistance are connected to practices of unlearning dominant ways of doing domestic-work relations in expatriate households, something that will be elaborated on later in the chapter. In addition, the field note signals the importance of recognizing what subaltern pedagogies can bring to our discussion on how to decolonize SRT and, moreover, how this can be a conversation which allows pluriversality – that is a world where many worlds fit: 'By recognising the existence of multiple ontologies, the modern misconception of the existence of only one world and multiple cultures is thus challenged' (Mendoza 2018: 118).[6]

Taking a critical stance, Mendoza (2018) notes how, too often, subaltern perspectives are glossed over or, worse, co-opted without being recognized by scholars in the West – in other words, intellectual theft. Another example of co-optation is when indigenous knowledge is read from an inverted lens 'whereby indigenous cultures save the modern world' (2018: 119).[7] In this context, 'critical moderns' – Mendoza includes decolonial and postcolonial scholars here – seek salvation from the subaltern (instead of the usual colonial saviour complex). In a broader perspective, this means that critical moderns use indigenous knowledge to hide and redeem their own complicity in colonialism produced over time. Graness (2019: 163) largely sympathizes with this critique and makes an addition: the necessity of avoiding romanticized conceptions of indigenous knowledge as well as one-dimensional conceptions of the West. Instead, it is necessary to recognize the plurality of critiques that exist in the West:

> It is very important to determine whether there are alternative values and concepts that can be mobilized today to counter the negative effects of the ones spread through modernization and colonization from the West to the rest. One must recognize, however, the inner plurality of every culture, every knowledge system.

Bearing these critical remarks in mind, the main outcome of the dialogue between intersectional research that discuss social reproduction and critical education presented in this chapter will result in a move towards a decolonial take of SR which draws from theory developed in the West as well as from the non-West, moreover from non-Western scholars trained in the West. In particular I draw from arguments which rely on intersectional research from Black feminisms and decolonial African feminisms and contributions to research on SRT developed from a geographic lens. The contributions from critical education theory included in this chapter deal explicitly with ways of knowing and how this is interlinked with ways of living and possibilities for change. Against this backdrop, the dialogue presented in this chapter should be read as the beginning of a conversation rather than the end. Now that we have established the focus of this chapter a reading instruction is merited.

The move towards developing a decolonial take of SRT is outlined in four steps. Step one: I will begin with presenting a brief overview of early foundations of SRT, contemporary debates and how I situate the research presented in this chapter in these debates. Thereafter, I move on to clarify how I bridge theories which have different ontological origins. Step two: through a survey of recent literature, in particular intersectional research on social reproduction made from the perspective of Black feminisms, African feminisms and contributions which applies a geographic lens on research on social reproduction, I discuss the potential for pluralizing approaches to social reproduction research, a precondition for moving towards a decolonial take of SRT. Step three takes us into the field of critical education. Here, various contributions that centre learning from the everyday and how unlearning is possible are presented. The fourth and concluding part of this chapter presents the result from the dialogue between intersectional research on social reproduction and critical education and how this dialogue contribute to a move towards a decolonial take of SRT. A main result from this dialogue is what I call pedagogies of unlearning. At the centre of pedagogies of unlearning is a conversation about an ontology and pedagogies of transgressions. The plurality of transgression*s* reveals various interlinkages and connections between different worlds and worldviews while emphasizing an analysis of power and resistance. Moreover, it highlights the necessity to reconstruct current ways of learning domestic and care work – 'Life's Work' (Mitchell, Marston and Katz 2004) – in ways that signal respect for humans, community and nature.

Foundations and current debates in SRT

Lise Vogel's theoretical work *Marxism and the Oppression of Women* (1983, revised edition 2013) is often described as an early landmark in SRT (Rodríguez-Rocha 2021). In particular, Vogel problematizes earlier Marxist feminism theories of a dual-system of oppression where patriarchy and capitalism work as separate spheres in the oppression of women. Instead, Vogel (1983 revised edition 2013) argues for a perspective which treats capitalism and patriarchy as a single entity. Such approach makes visible how oppression of women works through their involvement in wage labour and in unwaged labour in households.

Another early landmark in SRT can be found in the works of 1970's Marxist feminisms, notably Mariarosa Dalla Costa, Selma James and Silvia Federici. Their ideas were central in the international movement 'Wages for housework'. Here, feminists demanded that the sphere of reproductive work should enter the analysis of production – the 'Wages for Housework' movement is one such example. Arguing that 'Wages for Housework' is a perspective and not simply a demand for monetary compensation, Federici (2012) explains how this movement would be a first step, a basis or a perspective from which to start a struggle with a broader goal: 'we do not struggle to enter capitalist relations, because we have never been out of them.

We struggle to break capital's plan for women' (Federici 2012: 19–20). In other words, the broader goal was not to transform women's positions within capitalism but, instead, to get rid of the wage system and formulate a critique of capitalism.

These early contributions to SRT outlined above differ in their approach to value. More specifically, if they consider socially reproductive work as value-producing or not. The former perceiving socially reproductive labour as a precondition for capitalism but not in itself value-producing. The latter proclaiming a perspective which perceives social reproductive work as value-producing *and* being fundamental for capitalism. Contemporary SRT contributions often draw from both strands (Rodríguez-Rocha 2021).

Another contemporary and broad definition of the analytical scope of SRT reads as follows 'SRT is concerned with the activities and relations involved in producing and maintaining life' (Gregoratti and Tornhill 2023: 3). Closely aligned with this definition is the importance of reflecting on how, under conditions of capitalism, the division between work and non-work is entangled with racial and gendered hierarchies and modes of exploitation (Bhattacharya 2017). In this aspect, this definition adds an important contribution to SRT as it brings unpaid domestic work – currently much less theorized than paid domestic work – back to the centre of attention in SRT.

As we can see from the brief outline here, learning has not typically been at the centre of analysis in SRT. Having said this, it is important to note that educational perspectives have not been completely absent from SRT or in intersectional research on SR. Important previous contributions emphasize the role of socialization for producing and maintaining a gender division of labour or the processes where different value is ascribed to labour (Davis 1981). Another example refers to how skills or qualifications are connected to practices that reinforce already existing differentiation between paid and unpaid labour and between those who are considered to be able to advance and those who will be left behind: processes that are highly racialized and gendered (see Haug 1997). A more structural approach to theorizing learning in SRT centres processes of the historical emergence of contemporary labour relations and as such connects reproductive work to societal processes of continuity and *change* – a concept which is core in pedagogical research (Carpenter and Mojab 2017). Despite these crucial insights, placing learning processes at the centre of is still an underdeveloped theme in SRT.

Relations of production and Life's Work

Another research debate refers to critically discussing the terminology of *Social* in SRT, highlighting the importance of developing a perspective that diverges from the view which conceives of both domestic and care work and non-domestic and care work as the very same activity, or *vice versa*, the two being completely separate. 'Instead, it poses the fundamental challenge to occupy and further develop the concept of the relations of production to make it useful for feminist questions' (Haug 2020: 11). This perspective suggests that there are two forms of production – the production of life and the production of the means for life – but that they should be analysed together. This will reveal both the specificities in each form of production and how they interact. Integral to this is the view of gender relations as forms of production (in the broadest sense, such as in norms, cultures, values, language etc.) and not an addition to them. Paula Mulinari (2020: 141–2) explains further:

> One of the strengths of Marxism-feminism is its ability to explore the links between different spaces such as private and public, reproduction and production, which have been described as separated, to maintain and naturalize power relations.

In this context, Haug (2020) emphasizes the centrality of analysing gender division and caring practices, home and family relations, and how this, by necessity, also entails a critical discussion of paid labour. Here I suggest that an analytical focus on relations of production aligns with a Life's Work perspective (Mitchel, Marston and Katz 2004). Life's Work is a theoretical concept and at the same time an analytical framework of inquiry for investigating, broadly defined, labour relations. At the most fundamental level, Life's Work is a framework for investigating the 'messy fleshy' (Katz 2001a: 711) components of material everyday lives. In other words, it challenges the socially constructed division between private and public spheres of life and a narrow view of work as waged work only. Instead, a theory about Life's Work and the subjects involved is investigated as Life Workers (Mitchell, Marston and Katz 2004). This means investigating how particular groups are constituted as workers – waged or non-waged or so poorly waged that it is impossible to live on. Moreover, of interest is also the difference between institutions and their relative degree of importance for constituting a differentiated labour force daily and over the long term.

Integral to this is paying attention to subjects' differing access to power and resources and how power relations related to gender, race and class at times intersectionally, and sometimes separately, constitute conditions for Life's Work. The latter being particularly important for understanding how racialized distinction and hierarchy of workers, mostly women, who perform paid and unpaid domestic and care work, is produced. Finally, and as mentioned in Chapter 1 in this volume, understanding social reproductive labour as Life's Work implies bringing a spatial perspective to research on social reproduction.

Working with theories with different ontological origins

Because of its ontological origin SRT has sometimes been understood as being impossible to combine with more poststructural perspectives (Rodríguez-Rocha 2021). Recent developments of SRT have worked in the direction of finding affinities between poststructural theories that can productively pluralize SRT in intersectional and geographic directions (Bakker and Gill 2019; Rodríguez-Rocha 2021). This is crucial for better understanding the differentiation between bodies, workers and communities on a world scale (Mitchell, Marston and Katz 2004, Strauss and Meehan 2015: 1). A geographic lens makes visible the importance of geographic location/place for the production of variegated social reproduction. Let me give a few examples from my interviews: employers have told me how different Tanzanian domestic workers are to them, stressing differences in educational and cultural backgrounds. These differences are thereafter used to legitimize harsh working conditions: conditions that employers admit would never be acceptable for domestic workers in the West, not to mention how unthinkable these conditions would be for privileged female expatriate employers as they do unpaid domestic work and care work in their own households. This example points to how domestic work is hierarchically and unevenly produced in different geographies and within particular locations.

Another example, in my interviews and fieldwork, domestic workers tell me how they are not the mere recipients of these instructions but negotiate and navigate these different demands in their everyday work lives. For example, one domestic worker told me how she, if she was left without water, planned to replace a little bit of the contained water with tap water so that the employer would not see that she had been drinking clean water while she had left the house. Usually contained water is kept in the kitchen area, making it easy to replace with tap water. The kitchen area is where the domestic workers often dwell in the household, bringing a spatial dimension to how the domestic worker navigate this instruction. This incident is narrated to me with an emphasis on how afraid she is of drinking tap water as she is worried she would become unwell. Moreover, the domestic worker emphasizes that she is not paid a decent salary, in addition, clean water is expensive and this being the reason for the employer giving her tap water to drink instead of clean water. While she does not use the words 'processes of cheapening' I interpret that she is navigating the employers processes of cheapening of her as beeing the intended meaning of her narrative. As mentioned in the introduction chapter, processes of cheapening is an analytical lens which explicitly theorize the exploitation of domestic workers and how this originates in perceptions of domestic workers as naturalized, less than human, which was common during colonialism (see Chapter 4 for more examples).

Moreover, the latter example taps into the research tradition of Black feminisms which has a long tradition of departing from material experiences from the everyday as they theorize and actively resist exploitation, individually and collectively (Stewart 2021). Taken together, these examples point at how processes of learning and unlearning from the everyday extends beyond the household and align with relations of colonialism, ecology- here relations to water, economy and geography. It is in this aspect that recent developments of SRT, intersectional research on SR and critical education are ontologically aligned through their connection to poststructural epistemologies recognizing the materiality of practices, while at the same time insisting that the world we experience is always already socially constructed and is continuously produced over time (Hennessy 1993).

This is important to keep in mind as the theories in critical education, and in particular the theories in learning I draw from in this volume, often – not always – draw from Foucauldian-inspired poststructural approaches, which at first glance may seem as being at odds with SRT and intersectional research on SR.

Intersectional research on SR

The early fundaments of SRT which placed women's unpaid domestic and care work in the private sphere at the centre of the analysis have been critically discussed from the perspective of Black feminisms (Mohanty 2003, Davis et al 2022). Davis (1983) points out how this research focus reinforces the idea that SRT is white and bourgeois women's feminism. In other words, making unpaid domestic work the main site of struggle against capitalism reveals a partial and ahistorical perspective on women's oppression. This perspective obscures race and class relations within the group of women and how contemporary women's differing positions and relations to the labour market are not arbitrary but are, instead, interlinked in various and complex ways to larger historical relations related to colonialism and capitalist expansion (Davis 1983; Mies 1986; Bhattacharyya 2018; Davis et al. 2022). In this sense, denaturalizing domestic work not only implies criticizing it as a form of work that is particularly suitable or natural for women but also contests the view of women as an ontological category more generally. As mentioned in the introductory chapter, this argument entails a view that it is necessary to talk about variegated social reproduction that has evolved differently over time and in different geographic locations, notably without losing sight of grander narratives of oppression (Bakker and Gill 2019).

Drawing on statistics on a world scale, Alessandra Mezzadri (2020) points out that the main labour force is employed under informal or informalized conditions: 85.8 per cent in Africa, 71.4 per cent in Asia and the Pacific, 68.6 per cent in the Arab States and 53.8 per cent in the Americas. This means that the total informal employment for the whole emerging and developing economies bloc is 69.6 per cent and, with the extension into the precarization of work in the Global North, 61.2 per cent at a world level. From this, Mezzadri concludes that 'our entire planet primarily labours *informally*' (2020: 156). Drawing on the Wages for Housework movement (outlined earlier), Mezzadri suggests that this theoretical stance contributes in important ways to intersectional research on SR by theorizing the role of wagelessness under capitalism. Mezzadri (2020) proposes three examples in which social reproduction directly shapes the labour surplus value process. First, the housing arrangements for informal labourers are co-constitutive of labour relations. In particular, the many dormitory arrangements where workers sleep shape whole industries and often reflect historical and colonial plantation lines. Secondly, the role of labour circulation – in particular, how villages and extended families absorb the labour power of workers and subsidize capital by taking care of workers during the lean seasons of production. This resembles the role and functioning of housewives in bourgeois families, who had as their main responsibility that of a caregiver for family members as compared to the (often male) breadwinner who was cared for. The third example is where labour surplus value is subsumed through the labour of homeworkers. A focus on these latter shows the impossibility of separating productive and reproductive activities 'Indeed, whenever I encountered women garment homeworkers, they laboured on the batch of clothes provided by the contractor while cooking, cleaning or caring for their children or elderly, all in the single space of their dwelling' (Mezzadri 2020: 159).

African feminisms' decolonial research on SR

Sylvia Tamale (2020) reminds us that African feminism's decolonial critiques are *not* one but diverse and focus on areas related to the practice of law (Tamale 2020), knowledge relations and research methods in the academy (Mama 2011; Oyěwùmí 1997), the field of gender research in African universities (Pereira 2002) and eco-feminism (Britwum 2009; Fakier and Cock 2009; Kelleher 2019) to mention but a few. What binds these diverse contributions together is an analysis of the intersectional dynamics of the forces of racialism, capitalism and patriarchy with the ambition to ensure that 'Europe's colonialization of Africa is not tucked away as part of a distant receding history but instead viewed as a living reality and legacy' and in this narrative to emphasize power and resistance (Tamale 2020: 9). What follows looks deeper into a few specific contributions which are relevant for interrogating domestic and care work as a process of learning.

Lyn Ossome (2021a, 2021b) makes a contribution to research on SR by highlighting the necessity to expand the understanding of labour (2021a: 558). She suggests that labour relations should be expanded from the traditional Marxist perspective (producing surplus value) to discussing the importance of land in social reproduction – that is livelihoods – or, in other words, labouring to survive. This critique makes two important contributions: first, it brings the legacies of colonialism and slavery to the forefront of the analysis and, secondly, its focus on agrarian relations highlights cultural relations which are often underestimated from a Marxist economic perspective. This is important for understanding women's ascribed power (as compared to achieved power) and involves theorizing women's roles as bearers of tradition, mediators of capital and reproducers of family. This perspective is essential for understanding 'the historical transition of any society' (Ossome 2021a: 561). Jocelyn Cock (1984) shows how the apartheid state deliberately undermined Black domestic life and, moreover, how Black South African women had often been carrying out paid domestic work in white households. In other words, this research highlights how the state organization of land and labour intersected with race relations, patriarchy and colonial capitalism. Continuing this line of thought, Fakier and Cock (2009) contribute to debates around 'the crisis of social reproduction', much discussed in the West, which refers to diminishing welfare systems and women's dual roles as family caregivers and income-providers (see, e.g., Lutz 2011, 2018). In particular, the contribution from Fakier and Cock (2009) shows the importance of locality for theorizing crises in social reproduction; drawing from the South African context, their research shows that, while there is a growing crisis in social reproduction globally, it is the most acute in the South. For example, climate change impacts more directly on livelihoods in the Global South. Another example is how the global pandemic of Covid-19 has deepened global inequalities, resulting in harsher working conditions in the informal economy in the Global South (Amnesty International 2021/22; Roy 2021).

Reconnecting to the discussion around land, Ossome (2021a) contributes to research on SR by situating the discussion of sex/gender categories and relations to land and labour in the context of East Africa. In so doing, she also makes a contribution to broadening the geographic and ontological scope of SRT. She does so in two steps: drawing from Amadiume's (1987) research which theorizes the sexual division of labour and labour ideology among the Nnobi people in relation to ecological factors. From this position, Ossome shows how Western conceptions of gender can be destabilized. This is done through highlighting concepts such as 'Male daughters' or 'Female husbands' – biological sex/gender categories and their role in the allocation of land and power. For example, the concept of 'Male daughters' refers to women who, in the absence of brothers or fathers, return to their home which they have inherited from their fathers (Amadiume 1987: 34). Following this line of thought, Ossome writes that 'Amadiume's work helps us to think through the sexual division of labour and [. . .] the ways in which gendered relations around land took on a materiality conceptually defined by social embeddedness' (2021a: 561). Ossome's second analytical step draws from an analysis of agrarian reform in Zimbabwe. This reform began in the year 2000 as a part of a land redistribution policy. In her analysis, Ossome shows the importance of processes of decommodification of land for analysing social reproduction. Another example from a Ghanaian context centres on women's dual roles as workers in the coastal fishing industry and being mainly responsible for livelihoods at the household level (Britwum 2009). From a detailed mapping of women's roles and positions in relations of production, Britwum calls for historically sensitized intersectional analysis rather than discussions that depart from a gender division of labour only. From this perspective, it is possible to analyse gender dynamics between women and men as well as between women. In addition, Britwums research point at how relations of production are shaped by cultural norms, climate change and state regulation of the fishing industry. Taken together, these discussions on SR which include ecological and livelihoods perspective contribute to unsettle and pluralize SRT. A focus on livelihoods is used in this book in Chapter 4, which focuses on historicizing domestic-work relations. In particular, a broad understanding of labour relations points at how women have played an important role in the production of livelihoods through sewing, weeding and harvesting (Giblin 2005). In addition, the same chapter stresses the importance of including a perspective which stresses relations to land as this is pivotal for analysing the alliance between the colonial administration and local patriarchies that were put into practice to control women's labour and mobility (Mbilinyi 1988, 2023).

Geographies of SR

Feminist geographers (Katz 1991, 2001a, 2001b; Mitchell, Marston and Katz 2003) add an important dimension to elaborating on the role of spatial relations for social reproduction. More specifically, an emphasis on the spatial makes explicit how bodies, institutions and places are not arbitrary constructs but are, instead, intrinsically connected and sometimes mutually constituted. Thinking about bodies and spaces, how they mutually produce each other and how this is integral to learning domestic and care work may appear abstract. Therefore, I include here an example from my fieldwork which points to the interface between bodies, the built environment and space. In the context of the empirical site for this book, where outdoor temperatures are over 40 degrees Celsius and where power breakdowns are frequent, making air conditioning unstable, it is not difficult to imagine how hot it is in front of a gas stove with several pots and pans boiling and frying or standing next to steamy irons. In the households I visited, the kitchen and laundry areas were frequently designed *without* air conditioning and the steam from boiling pans or hot irons would mix with sweat from hard-working bodies. The kitchen and laundry areas are usually arranged for bodies that are standing, walking, working – in other words, being in motion. In other rooms, the furniture is specifically arranged – in living rooms, the chairs are usually placed around a table and coffee tables are put close to armchairs or sofas which have a view of beautiful paintings or flower arrangements. These spaces are arranged for socializing, interacting and resting comfortably. In the household there were several spaces where family members or their guests could withdraw to rest privately. Significant here is the interior design of bedrooms – large beds and tables next to the bed so that small items could be reached without having to get out of bed. For example, remote controls for the air conditioning or the security alarm for the local police station or private guards could be accessed while in bed. Usually bedrooms had bathrooms *en suite*. Most houses also had so-called servants' quarters, where live-in domestic workers, guards and/or gardeners had their accommodation. Servants' quarters were sometimes located in a separate small house close to the main house. However, they could also be separate rooms in the basement or at the far end of a house (see Chapter 5). As pointed out earlier, we know from the literature on global work relations how the location and architecture of the dormitories where workers live and sleep are central for re-constituting labour relations (Burawoy 1985; Pun and Smith 2007) and that contemporary housing arrangements often recall colonial arrangements – barracks arranged in lines mirroring colonial plantations (Mezzandri 2020). From this perspective, learning (paid and unpaid) domestic work also involves learning to manage bodies and spaces. This includes the various ways in which women negotiate and sometimes resist these built-in instructions (see Chapter 5).

At first glance, it seems almost contradictory to talk about agency in relation to the built environment as the built environment is, at first sight, seemingly immobile. In the context of learning, the built environment signals the importance of materiality for processes of learning. This comprises two interrelated processes: how subjects learn and negotiate built-in instructions and, moreover, how educational relations regulate the design of buildings to achieve particular learning outcomes. Central for both aspects of learning the built environment is agency, which is at the core of critical education theory which is outlined next.

Learning from the everyday

At the beginning of this chapter, I outlined how intersectional research on SR, recent elaborations of SRT and critical education are ontologically connected through their relation to poststructural epistemologies and to intersectionality. Moreover, these frameworks are connected through an interest in analysing concrete inequalities as they manifest in the everyday. In other words, the elements of routine and repetition which constitute a major way of organizing the everyday can form a radical point of departure for individual, collective and structural change. In the following, I will highlight particular examples of critical education that have been selected on the grounds of their emphasis on theorizing knowledge relations in the everyday and how this can be part of processes of emancipation and change. I begin with outlining research contributions which centre everyday learning and thereafter move on to outlining the fundaments of unlearning.

Recognizing that the everyday has been theorized from various perspectives, I have chosen theoretical contributions from Paulo Freire, Dorothy Smith, Sara Motta and Charmaine Pereira because these scholars, from their different epistemological and geographic locations and in different ways, connect learning from the global margins with social movements, in particular feminist and decolonial struggles for changing Life's Work under conditions of capitalism. This analytical grip reconnects to the claim outlined in the beginning of this chapter which pointed at the necessity of recognizing the plurality of worldviews and knowledges rather than deciding beforehand where, how and by whom theoretical contributions developed to critically interrogate capitalism can be formulated.

Paulo Freire's most read work – his chapter entitled 'Pedagogy of the Oppressed' in his (1998) *Paulo Freire Reader* – refers to a set of ideas or a philosophy that is concerned with the political nature of education, in particular education for emancipation and social transformation. In Freire's (1998) pedagogy, learning from the everyday and from the historical emergence of the present is crucial. More specifically, from a class perspective, it centres on the everyday work experiences of peasants and the urban poor in various non-Western contexts and extends the meaning of learning through the concept of literacy; simply put, Freire was concerned with the idea of learning the world through the word (1998). It is in this respect that the pedagogical grip of 'learning the world from the word' is closely linked to how Dorothy Smith (1987) uses the concept of 'problematic' to introduce an analytical perspective as well as a tool for emancipation, which departs from and centres learning from the everyday. More specifically, the term 'problematic' is transformed from its original philosophical meaning to a practice-oriented tool for critically interrogating taken-for-granted experiences and power relations in women's everyday lives:

> The concept of problematic is used to relate the sociologist and the sociological inquiry to the experiences of members of a society as knowers located in actual lived situations in a new way. It is used here to constitute the everyday world as that in which questions originate. The term 'problematic' is ordinarily used to talk about matters at the level of concept or theory rather than at the level of experience and action (it should not, incidentally, be confused with the concept of problem). As it is used here, we follow the procedure of going from a social actuality to develop a conceptual apparatus disclosing and explicating its properties. The problematic is property of the social organization of the everyday world. The concept of problematic explicates the property of the everyday world as a focus for sociological work. (Smith 1987: 91)

Centring on North American contexts, Dorothy Smith's framework around the everyday as a feminist sociological problematic is perhaps one of the most straightforward Western feminist theories which include learning and the social organization of the everyday: that is labour at the same time. In so doing, Smith extends the meaning of learning as well as the meaning of work from the standpoint of Western women. The everyday world as a sociological problematic lays the basis for Smith's (2005) book *Institutional Ethnography*, the research for which is designed to denaturalize how power relations are produced and reproduced through everyday and mundane relations and practices. This research framework involves analysing the rules or regulations or 'Relations of Ruling'. An important element of this work comprises the analysis of text and how text organizes human relations, experiences and ways of knowing. In other words, I here suggest that Freire's work on literacy and Smith's concept of 'problematic' are methodologically aligned.

Charmaine Pereira (2002) discusses the relation between knowing and transformation from a slightly different angle compared to Smith and Freire. More specifically, Pereira focuses on how African feminist research has pointed to ways of transcending an often assumed separation between knowing and imagining and suggests that these are in fact connected: 'knowing is itself dependent on the exercise of imagination. This recognition requires us to bring together the intellectual and personal parts of our being, of what we think it means to be human and the practices that expand or inhibit that expression' (2002: 9). It is from this argument which *'bring together the intellectual and personal parts of our being, of what we think it means to be human and the practices that expand or inhibit that expression'* that I connect Pereira's work with that of Freire's and Smith's emphasis on learning from the everyday, from within and beyond academia. This argument points to how undoing patriarchy, colonialism and capitalism in the everyday, as variegated, differentiated and complex these processes may be, by necessity, is accompanied by processes of knowing and imagining differently in the everyday as well as in academic research. These are arguments that resonate with unlearning developed later in the chapter. In addition, Pereira notes how for African feminists, this endeavour comprises a double challenge 'of critiquing the scholarship produced by African men for its gender blindness, while sharing the concerns of African male colleagues with the imperialist, colonialist and racist connotations of mainstream constructions of Africa' (2002: 32).

In this respect, Freire (1998), Smith (1987) and Pereira (2002) from their differing positions make visible the connection between learning from the everyday and critical social movements (i.e. women's liberation and decolonial struggles in the Global South).

Having said this, it is pertinent to theorize subjects who are unwilling to change and who are not interested in solidarity. In 2013, Sara Motta made an important contribution by theorizing how capitalist practices are sometimes internalized and how this reinforces the view of systems of oppression as self-reproducing. Integral to this is theorizing how privileged and subaltern subjects are complicit in these practices – albeit not erasing the hierarchy and differences in their positionalities. In this context, Motta's (2013) theoretical contribution is valuable, as she highlights how the transcendence of oppression is not a given but a possibility. Central for learning about oppression *and* the transcendence of oppression is agency. For this reason, the following sections will dig further into that.

Agency and learning

It is difficult to imagine learning or unlearning without agency. Drawing from the work of Emirbayer and Mische (1998), Biesta and Tedder (2007: 136) conclude that agency is not an individual capacity. Instead,

> Agency should, rather, be understood as something that has to be *achieved* in and through engagement with particular temporal-relational contexts-for-action. Agency, in other words, is not something that people *have*; it is something that people *do*. It denotes a 'quality' of the *engagement* of actors with temporal-relational contexts-for-action, not a quality of the actors themselves.

So, if agency is theorized as *engagement* rather than something that subjects possess, how is engagement achieved? The main components in theories of agency are routine, purpose or judgement. Emirbayer and Mische (1998) suggest that these three components should be theorized together, with a particular focus on how they interplay (sometimes in the same direction and sometimes in contradictory or opposite ways) in various contexts in processes of learning. From this, it follows that agency should be understood in a three-dimensional way which is constructed by configurations from the past, orientations for the future and engagement with the present (Biesta and Tedder 2007: 135). Importantly, agency is achieved in transaction with a particular context-for-action, within a particular 'ecology'. The focus on the spatio-temporal or – in Emirbayer and Mische's (1998) terminology – the ecological highlights that it is important to theorize learning not only through agency in the everyday in the life course of the individual but also in relation to how the context for action, that is the spatio-temporal context, conditions the agentic practices. This will make it possible to analyse whether and how female employers and domestic workers act in some situations in their everyday lives or over their life course and not in others. Whether this brings about change or emancipation in practice in a person's life depends not only on orientations and engagements with the present but also on the available resources and on engagement with contextual and structural factors (Biesta and Tedder 2007). The following section digs deeper into a conceptual framework of unlearning and how it is connected to a feminist and decolonial critique and, moreover, how these pedagogical relations carry with them a particular spatial dimension of speaking from the margins.

Unlearning as a practical critique

Biesta (2013) draws on the Foucauldian concept of 'eventalization' – not for theorizing how subjects can learn differently – as in the meaning of revealing false consciousness. Neither does 'eventalization' generate a deeper knowledge which can be useful for escaping oppression and formulating formal instruction manuals for emancipation. Instead, what is implied is a *practical critique* which takes the form of a transgression. This means illuminating the pluralities of social conditions, events and domains and imagining that things can be different – and that things are not necessarily the way they have to be:

> Thus, the emancipatory potential of transgression lies in the possibility 'of no longer being, doing, or thinking what we are, do, or think', and, in precisely this sense, Foucault (1984: 46, cited in Biesta 2013: 12) suggests, 'it is seeking to give a new impetus . . . to the undefined work of freedom'.

This means a perspective where emancipation is not seen as an escape from power but, rather, as a practical critique of the way things are organized and represented and the pluralization of truth. From this perspective, learning for emancipation is what subjects pick up from the processes of transgression rather than the other way around. While these perspectives on unlearning are valuable for the research presented here, I also underline the necessity of theorizing the historical emergence of the context-for-action, here expatriate households in Dar es Salaam. For this reason, I here turn to the field of feminist subaltern pedagogies.

Subaltern pedagogies

Feminist subaltern pedagogies brings postcolonial, gender, race and class relations to the centre in processes of unlearning (Keyl 2017). For this book, which is concerned not only with learning subalternization or privilege but also with how these positions can be subverted, how privileged expatriate women and Tanzanian domestic workers unlearn becomes crucial. The term 'subaltern' originates from postcolonial studies – so-called subaltern studies which sought to counter the colonial historical narrative of India from below and from within. Essential in a subaltern pedagogy is a view of knowledge as based on 'a twofold ontology linking dynamically and dialectically the social and historical dimensions of individual and societal development' (Soja 2010: 70). In important aspects, subaltern pedagogies build on Freire's 'Pedagogy of the Oppressed' in his (1998) *Paulo Freire Reader*. More specifically, it is used to counter white-saviour complexes by emphasizing the necessity of learning from the participants' everyday experiences (as compared to banking education which means a one-way direction of learning where teachers are senders and students receivers) and for re-reading the everyday (1998). The influence of Global South feminism and postcolonial studies on subaltern pedagogies refers to the critical stance on Western feminism, in particular that of Gayatri Spivak (1988). Her work centres on the representation of the Other in Western intellectual discourses by critically interrogating the neglect of the very same voices. Moreover, this perspective challenges a Western-centric white-saviour complex and/or fetishizing the 'other' (Kapoor 2004).

Learning from the margins

Subaltern pedagogies place subjects in spatial relations – in other words, a critical spatial perspective refers to the ontological and pedagogical processes of the subaltern as they enter new spaces, whether geographic, social or political. It is from these liminal spaces – more specifically, the gaps created by the juxtaposition of the local and 'the other' – that subaltern processes of unlearning are created (Keyl 2017). A similar but not identical perspective on unlearning can be found in bell hooks' (1989) 'speaking from the margins'. She asserts that taking on the perspectives of margins is therefore a political decision rather than something which is inherited or given in educational practice and research. She asserts that marginality can be a central location for the production of counter-hegemonic discourses as it nourishes a person's capacity to resist (hooks 1989). I highlight hooks' work here as her thinking on learning and unlearning not only theorizes from the margins but, as Keyl

(2017) points out, hooks' argument has a spatial dimension. Let me elaborate on this thought: resisting the marginal and acting on the experience of living otherness and giving it new meaning are examples of knowledge which is spatially produced. In her works *Teaching to Transgress: Education as the Practice of Freedom* (1994) and, later, *Teaching Community: A Pedagogy of Hope* (2003), bell hooks develops the link between transgression (ontologically and spatially) and learning from a feminist pedagogical and intersectional perspective. Central for hooks' understanding of learning from transgression is the importance of partial perspectives and changes in perspective – that is, the value of experiences of dislocation: when we move (willingly or by force) a new perspective emerges and 'dislocation is the perfect context for free-flowing thought that lets us move beyond the restricted confines of a familiar social order' (hooks 2003: 21). While hooks does not explicitly talk about unlearning, I find that hooks' theory of learning from transgression resonate with how Biesta understands eventalization as a practical critique of what is – what I call unlearning. In this context it is important to underline that hooks never perceived that experience should be given epistemic monopoly but felt, instead, that it is one form of knowledge. In other words, hooks presents a theory for researching and understanding learning from transgression from an intersectional perspective. This perspective on learning embraces a view of learning as both specific and universal. She connects the idea that people must choose between the subjective or the universal when they learn to a dominant discourse of white male-supremacist-based Western dualism. Here I suggest that hooks (2003) shows – from a transgression standpoint – how it is possible to theorize unlearning as individual *and* as a social process without losing sight of present structures and their historical emergence that confine current social orders.

Closely related to collective dimensions of unlearning is hooks' emphasis on learning through dialogue, which goes beyond face-to-face communication in the classroom and, instead, refers to learning with social groups as well as 'the great things' of the world and with 'the grace of great things' (hooks 2003: xvi). The latter referring to a spiritual dimension in hooks' work, often being glanced over in feminist discussions. I here, on the contrary, suggest that spirituality – in the aspect that working collectively for change requires hope which has an element of spirituality in it – is an integral part of unlearning collectively. Closely aligned with this line of thought is the theoretical contribution from

Pereira (2002) outlined previously. As stated earlier in this chapter, Pereira stresses on the relation between knowing and imagining and states that imagination is essential for being able to search for knowledge which can bring about change, not only for individuals but also for collectives, 'Without imagination we cannot search for the kind of knowledge [. . .] that allows us to move from where we are to where we would like to be even before we get there' (Pereira 2000: 9).

In this respect, hooks' (2003) theory of learning from transgression and Pereira's work on knowing and imagination add a feminist, postcolonial, collective and spiritual/hopeful and political dimension to Biesta's understanding of eventalization.

The postcolonial as decolonial learning

Postcolonial educational perspectives can be criticized for dealing too much with the past (and applying an elitist perspective from above). Rather than totally dismissing postcolonial research, McCoy, Tuck and McKenzie (2016) underline how decolonial educational research needs to put educational theories in dialogue with indigenous knowledge and global activism and 'how education [. . .] might better account for the history, present and future by attending to its embedded issues of colonialism [. . .] (2016: 2). Continuing this line of thought, Tamale (2020: 171) elaborates on what she calls a 'pedagogy of unlearning'. This pedagogy, in important ways, means conscientization – which originates from Freire's (1998) pedagogy of hope. At the core of conscientization is a unity between reflection and action and being aware of the reasons behind what you do (Freire 1998: 237–8). Reverting back to Freire's pedagogy of the everyday as a site for struggle and emancipation, Tamale expands on Freire's line of thought 'Unlearning or Conscentisation not only requires exposure to knowledge and understanding of the historical processes of colonial domination and Western modernity, but also to the gendered ordering of human relations' (2020: 171). From this, it follows that, rather than dismissing postcolonial scholarships per se, a critical interrogation into the historical origins of contemporary coloniality, as context-specific, different and variegated as these processes may be, is crucial for developing a decolonial critique of how we come to understand Life's Work under conditions of capitalism. In this aspect, Tamale adds a feminist and decolonial lens to Freire's original work on conscientization. While not theorizing labour explicitly, Tamale's emphasis on ways of knowing and understanding '*the gendered ordering of human relations*' which, I here underline, is essential for understanding Life's Work. This lays the ground for developing further the pedagogies involved in formulating a decolonial take on SRT.

Pedagogies of unlearning: Towards a decolonial take of SRT

In this chapter, I have presented a dialogue between intersectional research on SR and critical education with the ambition to move towards a decolonial take of SRT. In this final and concluding section, I outline the outcome of such conversation, recognizing that this debate is ongoing and unfinished.

In the context of moving towards a decolonial take on SRT, I here suggest that hooks' (2003) conceptual framework around transgression presented earlier in this chapter is useful. However, here transgression*s* – in its plural form – will be applied as it refers to the plurality of relations involved in unlearning Life's Work under capitalism. Departing from the everyday but not limited to it (see the earlier examples from Freire, Smith and Pereira), the ontology of transgression*s* can form a platform for developing local and contextual sensitizing theoretical contributions and methods. Moreover, I suggest that an ontology of transgression*s* makes possible a focus which allows for a pluriversality of perspectives and world views – one such example is the issue of livelihoods, which has received less attention in SRT. In the African context, reproductive labour is intimately connected to land and working for a living which often extends beyond working to produce surplus value, it also involves challenging Western conceptions of gender. The ever-increasing ecological crisis and the precarization of workers are all revealing how the local and the global, the West and the non-West, are interconnected in hierarchical ways. From these perspectives, transgression*s* imply pluralizing SRT: they point to the interconnectedness of the human and nature, the local and the global and the West and the non-West, both in terms of how these relations of production function in processes of exploitation and how imagining differently is possible. The framework of variegated social reproduction is in line with this theoretical stance; however, here a learning perspective adds an additional layer of complexity as it explicitly focuses on continuity and change. An ontology of transgression*s* points at the entanglement of spatial and temporal relations involved in Life's Work and how Life's Work has evolved differently – yet not completely separated – in different locations. Therefore, the ontology of transgression*s* makes possible a practical and political critique of the lack of them as this has evolved over time. The lack of transgression*s* means perceiving Life's Work from an ahistorical and universalizing perspective – put bluntly, it is a lack of seeing, knowing or acting beyond standpoints of privilege. As such, transgression*s* centre care as we move towards pluralizing SRT which is a precondition for developing a decolonial take of SRT and re-inscribe *care*ful transgression*s* as a condition for unlearning in solidarity.

The pedagogical dimensions of an ontology of transgression*s* become apparent when theorized intersectionally in the everyday – paying attention to the various and sometimes mutually constituted and contradictory ways of seeing and doing domestic and care work in the everyday. This perspective also reveals the many dual and shifting positions of simultaneous privilege and subalternization. The ontology of transgression*s* can, therefore, inform and contribute to pedagogies of unlearning, which can be used for imagining how domestic and care work could be organized differently and shared equally, both between women and between women and men – but also how this labour extends beyond individual or labour relations in the household. More specifically, recent critiques from Black feminisms, decolonial African feminisms and feminist geography place positions, perspectives and knowledge (in other words, processes of unlearning, which emerge from liminality, subalternity, materiality and spirituality/hope) at the centre of a decolonial take of SRT. As such, pedagogies of unlearning make a critique of how global capitalist relations, to various and different degrees and in a plurality of localized and contextual ways, have entered relations – such as love, care, family or kin relations, and moreover relations to land and water which were not capitalist from the beginning. In other words, pedagogies of unlearning refer to doing, knowing, critiquing and re-imagining, as well as the pedagogical work involved when meeting, discussing with and negotiating subjects who are not interested in change or in solidarity.

4

Learning from the archives

I look at the crowd as the car moves slowly toward the entrance of the archives. I search through my mind for public holidays or announcements of demonstrations. 'Why is there such a crowd?' The taxi driver and I look at each other through the rear-view mirror. 'These are casual labourers, Madame, they are looking for work'.

Inside the archives it smells of dust that comes from old books.

> The study of domestic service is not a trivial sideshow to the grander subjects of social analysis. It is one which demands reflection on the great debates of social theory: on theories of development, of gender and class and of the metanarratives through which these used to be addressed. (Bujra 2000: 3)

Notes from my fieldwork and a quotation from Bujra (2000) are chosen as the introduction to this chapter for two interlinked reasons. The quotation from Bujra highlights how domestic-work relations are not limited to households but are, instead, at the core of analysing wider social transformations in society, related – but not limited – to migration, labour relations and colonialism. The reference to knowledge politics, more specifically reflecting on the positions from where knowledge claims are being heard in Bujra's quotation, makes a connection to my field notes, which highlight the importance of recognizing the locality from where subjects manage and negotiate representations (Foucault 1989; Haraway 1996). Choosing an incident where I communicate with the taxi driver through the rear-view mirror is not arbitrary. Instead, the rear-view mirror is used as a pedagogical example of how the reflection in the mirror represents us *and* the position from where we observe. In the example above, this is the most clearly outlined in our different understandings of the crowd. In this situation, the crowd appears in a part of the city which is widely represented to upper-class white expatriates as an unsafe area and the general advice to tourist and expatriates is to stay away from there. Research shows that the representation of unsafety is produced within a discourse of racialized, classed and gendered assumptions of the place and the people who are staying in that place – so-called spatial stigmatization (Keene and Padilla 2010: 1216). The difference in our – the taxi driver and mine – various classed, gendered and racialized relations to the place and how the place previously has been represented to us, shape how we perceive the crowd and reveal how we are simultaneously both insiders and outsiders (Farahani 2015; Corbin Dwyer and Buckle 2018) in the making of the representation of the crowd as we observe. This does not mean that the hierarchical, racialized, classed and gendered labour relations that connect us have ceased to exist. In research, the construction of the place of observation has historically been interlinked with the project of colonial power. From this viewpoint, the ordering of representations of bodies in spaces, including the space of the observer, is what creates appearances and 'the hierarchy of truth' (Mitchell 1991: 63). I here make visible the places of observation, with all their complicated and messy intersectional power relations, as part of a politics of destabilizing knowledge hierarchies in an endeavour to historicize domestic work.

Being particularly interested in ways of knowing and learning about – as well as processes of ignoring – racialized inequality, Ann Laura Stoler (2010: 249) frames her investigation of the colonial archives around learning what it takes to live an imperial life:

> what people were *disposed to do*, were inclined to believe, thought they could intuit, or could choose to ignore. Imperial dispositions are composed of *trained habits of attention* channelled through principles of plausibility and rules of relevance. These are politicized cognitions and practices that distinguish sensory overloads from sensible acts. (italics in the original)

Stoler includes official texts as well as pieces of ribbon, a pencil drawing, newspaper clippings, a pressed flower, a child's drawing or a wisp of hair in her analysis as she points to how the personal and official are being separately organized in colonial archives, yet 'In content, the filaments and phrases that join them are strong yet elusive' (2010: 241). From the perspective of Tanzanian everyday family lives as articulated by Tanzanians, rather than how Tanzanian lives are represented in the colonial archives, Giblin (2005) develops an analytical framework that centres the tensions between dominant state-centred narratives and thought, beliefs, social relations and practices in everyday life. In this context, Giblin interrogates the making of Tanzanian family relations in both the colonial and the postcolonial state and argues for the importance of drawing from non-linear or fictional sources for understanding history – 'not History but the story, the fable, the rumor as opposed to times, dates and places are important' (Walcott 1998: 219; cf. Giblin 2005: 6). Inspired by this view, this chapter includes literary texts and newspaper articles that go beyond scholarly historical work and original texts retrieved from the colonial archives to gain 'a thick understanding' (Mies 2010) of learning and unlearning domestic work in expatriate households. This methodological grip is part of the main analytical theme of this book, which is to interrogate processes of learning domestic and care work in expatriate households as well as possibilities of unlearning dominant narratives. An important part of this theme is to include additional narratives from within and from below. Central here is the view that texts and practices are closely aligned; in other words, one type of text, such as archival texts, informs the understanding of other types of text such as the fictional novel and the imaginations of readers (Hall 1997 and Chapter 2 in this volume). From this it follows that the ambition here is to historicize domestic work relations in expatriate households from the perspective of learning rather than providing a historical account of them. As outlined in the introductory chapter to this book, a learning perspective brings two important aspects to the analysis of domestic work: first, it challenges the idea that women and subaltern workers are naturally better disposed to conduct domestic work compared to Western men. The second aspect is an emphasis on transformation and change. This chapter thus proposes a theoretically driven and empirically grounded methodological contribution to historicizing domestic work. In this way, the research presented here will contribute to the ongoing work of decolonizing the archive (Sawyer and Osei-Kofi 2020; Swaby and Frank 2020). The methodological contribution presented here builds on two main pillars that are interconnected – learning *in* the archives and learning *from* the archives. Historians of education have a long tradition of interrogating the link between educational relations and colonialism through archival documents (see, e.g., Mitchell 1991). Other research has focused on how coloniality is put into practice by emphasizing the link between colonialism, capitalism and educational systems; this is done by analysing the negation of knowledge that already existed (Santos 2014) or the location of schools and the division of labour within the educational system and, in addition, the division of labour produced through educational systems (Gerrard, Sriprakash and Rudolph 2022). In other words, these prior studies have interrogated processes of learning *in* the archives. Learning *from* the archives revolves around how various narratives are organized in the archive applying a perspective from within and from below. This is further developed in the concluding section.

How to historicize

In the field of subaltern historical studies, Dipesh Chakrabarty (2000: 254) distinguishes between the 'analytic narrative' and the 'affective narrative' while acknowledging how these narratives are held in tension with each other. The analytical narrative centres the critique of capitalism as it is operating on a world scale while the affective narrative explores the diversity of social relations and practices in the societies that have been incorporated into capitalist economies. The view that both narratives are indispensable is central in my book as well as in the organization of this chapter. This means that the narratives of domestic-work relations that are brought together here are seen not as freestanding – or completely subsumed for that matter – but, instead, as representations that are in tension with the state. The analytical focus here is on unpaid or very badly paid domestic work in expatriate households as a form of largely unrecognized labour. Learning and unlearning this labour are interesting concepts to interrogate as these learning processes have, in various and stratified ways, contributed to building and maintaining and sometimes resisting British colonialism in East Africa. In this respect I have been inspired by Patel's (2021: 6) understanding of a global history of coloniality as 'something that can be unraveled from the values and norms institutionalized in everyday life, within the family system and marriage alliances, within sexualities, in education, its pedagogies, and its philosophies'. This resonates with the perspective of variegated social reproduction outlined in Chapter 1. More specifically, this perspective implies that domestic work – an aspect of Life's Work – is unevenly produced in different geographic spaces, within societies and households and that these processes cannot be understood as freestanding from a global history of coloniality. Marjorie Mbilinyi (2023) reminds us that the labour history of Tanzanian women is complex and diverse. It includes the educated elite, leaders of the nationalist movement as well as the poor majority of peasants, beer brewers and prostitutes. The focus on interrogating domestic work in expatriate households limits the scope of this chapter and prioritizes the women and men who were likely to be employed in this sector as well as the processes and movements that underpinned this development. From this follows that this chapter includes research contributions from the field of women's history and gender history.

The 1990s are chosen as a starting point for historicizing domestic work because the economic transformations taking place during this decade in various ways lay the groundwork for contemporary domestic-work relations in Tanzania. Let me elaborate on this: the notion of the 1990s as the era of privatization and neoliberalization of the economy taking place at a global scale had immediate and harsh consequences for labour relations in Tanzania (this is further developed in the next section). In addition, the effects of adjustment programmes were highly gendered; while there may have been commonalities in experiences of particular categories of women and men, there exist important inequalities between most categories of women relative to men in the same social standing (Pereira 2002: 14). In other words, in Africa 'the implementation of these programs resulted in a crisis of reproduction' (Imam 1988 cited in Pereira 2002: 14) indicating the necessity to analyse how labour is gendered and how relations of production intersect and are mutually constituted. For this reason, I start from the 1990s and historicize back and forth in time, with a particular interest in understanding connections and linkages. Moreover, this historicizing chapter analyses paid and unpaid domestic work in expatriate households in Dar es Salaam through the narratives of the 'division of land and labour', 'women and internal labour migration', 'the organization of domestic workers' and 'colonial discourses around domesticity' in Tanzania. These narratives form the main pillars in the chapter because they have been highlighted in the field of women and labour studies in Tanzania (see, e.g., Bujra 2000; Mbilinyi 2016). Moreover, these aspects of labour history also resonate with the recent African feminist research on social reproduction which emphasizes colonialism, informal labour and relations to land for the production of livelihoods (see Ossome 2021a, 2021b and Chapter 3 in this volume).

A note on language is warranted here. I use various concepts such as developing and developed countries, the Global South and the Global North and the non-West and West in this chapter. The reason for this is because these labellings appear in the different data sources that I have analysed, indicating the cross-disciplinary approach to analysing domestic work applied in this book as well as a conceptual development in the field of global sociology. I use these concepts interchangeably as they focus on different and hierarchically situated positionalities rather than on fixed geographic locations. These positionalities indicate the different means of access to power and resources, the latter being in a position of domination over the former.

Tanzania and the 1990s

Webster, Britwum and Bhowmik's (2017) research on the formality and informality of labour relations makes at least two remarks which are important here; first, they point to the 1980s and the early 1990s as a landmark period for understanding the contemporary precarization of labour and, secondly, posit that the changes taking place were different in the developed and the developing worlds. From this it follows, they underline, that the history and legacy of colonialism as well as the policy of liberalization have impacted on the Global South in ways that are quite different from that of the Global North (2017: 4). Moreover, when labour is defined broadly, this tendency is stronger:

> It is not only that there has never been a 'golden age' of decent work in the colonial workplace (Scully 2016). When one goes beyond the workplace into the hidden abode of reproduction – the household and the community – these differences become clear (Lee and Kofman 2012: 393). In the Global South, the crisis is not simply over jobs; it is a crisis over the very reproduction of society itself. (Webster and Von Holdt 2005; Webster, Britwum and Bhowmik 2017: 4)

The early 1990s was a period of political change as well as economic depression worldwide. Among the crucial changes taking place during this decade, there was the breakdown of the Soviet Union, several new European countries entered the European Union and protests in South Africa resulted in the freeing of Nelson Mandela, not to mention the blockage of the GATT trade liberalization meeting in Uruguay which could have helped developing countries (Bujra 2000). For African countries, this political and economic situation implied that international donors in the West were now in a stronger position than ever and could increase pressure by attaching strings to their donor funding (Mbilinyi 2023). This political economy would, in substantial ways, shape the organization of labour and damage the work conditions for labourers across the continent.

Analysing a series of articles in the *Daily News* published during the 1990s in Tanzania is part of the archival research I have done for this chapter. These articles critically discussed the world economic situation, focusing on how donor demands went hand-in-hand with both the decentralization and the privatization of the economy, often involving multinational corporations. The articles also discussed how international donor demands for political and economic transformation stirred development in several nearby African countries such as Kenya and Zambia. At the centre of these critical journal debates were discussions on the abolition of state subsidies as well as political changes which referred to 'among other things, the reduction of corruption and an end to one-party rule and military dictatorships' (Ingram1992). These debates reflected a political discourse which placed Tanzania in a global perspective: 'Tanzania is not an Island but needs to move with time' is a dominant theme in the speech made by the party chairman, Ndugu Mwinyi (Ally 1992), in which he urged delegates from all over the country to vote for a transformation from a single political party system to a multi-party system in 1992. Importantly this transition should

> ensure the change from a single to a multi-party system brings peace, tranquility and political solidarity in the nation [. . .] they should not be parties based on division of the people or the nation on either side of the Union, tribalism, religion, race or creed. (Lupatu 1992)

Despite strong support for the transformation, political leadership in Tanzania remained a critical gaze on an equation between a plural-party system and democracy:

> True democracy is a matter of people willing to work together on the basis of mutual respect, toleration of different views and free to discuss issues [. . .] it must conform to the norms of a particular society [. . .] it was not a commodity like Coca-Cola which simply could be imported. (Mawalimu Nyerere, in Ally 1992)

From the overview above we note how the years around the 1990s were turbulent and in particular with regards to the increased pressure from international donors. As displayed in the latter quotation, the local response comprised a move towards a multi-party system yet remained critical towards too much steering towards a neo-liberal system. In order to understand the turbulent times of the 1990s we need to dig into the early independence years. With a particular focus on gender, the next section digs deeper into this.

The early independence years

One of the first things that the postcolonial government removed was the colonial government's specific labour and land laws and regulations to support access to cheap migrant labour for corporate-owned plantations and settler farms (Mbilinyi 2023). State subsidies for the small-scale peasant production of cash crops were followed by *ujamaa villagization*[1]policies in the 1970s and 1980s, being an important part of this politics (Mbilinyi 2023). After gaining independence in 1961, the new government made important changes designed to transform gender relations which had deepened during colonialism. Landmarks in these political imperatives refer to changing inheritance laws for widows (Mbilinyi 1994: 174), encouraging education for girls (Mbilinyi 2016) and making incentives for women's and men's equal participation in the 'villagization' programme to name but a few (2023). While these actions revealed a political desire to emancipate women, it is debated how well this ambition led to subsequent changes in gender equality, as exemplified in this quotation by Geiger (1982: 46):

> the Government policy in Tanzania has not seriously challenged the basic structures of gender relations, although the rhetoric of leaders emphasizes the need to change women's roles. Inequality between women and men still remains rooted, manifested and perpetuated in the sexual division of labour.

Referring specifically to the Arusha declaration, the first five-year development plan in 1964 and the policies both before and after these main policy documents, Kiaga (2007: 38) supports this critique:

> In my examination of development policies since independence, for example, I found that neither gender relations nor women were consistently integrated in their formulation or implementation.

However, research into the gender equity efforts in the villagization programme has shown ambiguous patterns. Mbilinyi (2016) suggests that women were able to benefit from the restructuring of land that followed from the Ujaama period, in particular their access to land and the product of their labour. Moreover, the women created cooperative farms, shops and maize mills which provided employment and income (2016). Nevertheless women's increased access to land during this period, the economic crisis of the 1980s and the effects of the Structural Adjustment policies led to a crisis of employment in the formal and informal market, a large portion of which consisted of women (Mbilinyi 2023). The next section situates the situation of domestic workers in Tanzania during the 1990s in a global context.

Domestic workers in global perspective

The growth of domestic workers in the West in the 1990s is associated with the growth of households in which both partners worked full-time (Lutz 2011). In this context, employing a domestic worker became a way for women who worked outside the home to cover their own domestic responsibilities since their partner's equal participation in domestic work simply did not materialize (Bujra 2000; Lutz 2011). The growth of domestic work is also visible through the increase in labour migration to the West from non-Western societies. The driving forces behind this are often described as the uneven distribution of economic wealth at a global level and the development of a global market for cheap domestic workers, migrants' need to find work in their new country and non-Western societies' need for remittances (see also Enloe 2006; Lutz 2011).

In her work, Enloe (2006) points to the mutual responsibility of states and transnational agencies, particularly highlighting the work of the International Monetary Fund (IMF), for engineering and facilitating processes of labour migration. In rapidly industrializing countries in Asia – such as Indonesia and the Philippines – the state introduced policies particularly designed for the labour migration of domestic workers (Killias 2018; Parreñas 2015). In Malaysia, the rapid growth of migrant domestic workers associated with the state's modernity project and the growing middle-class consumption of goods and services is seen as a symbolic personal and national progress (Chin 1998).

For newly industrialized countries, such as Malaysia, the rise in industrial growth led to an increase in the employment of migrant domestic workers. For many developing countries, like Tanzania, the growth in the number of domestic workers was associated with the opposite – a lack of industrial growth and of available household equipment. Domestic workers were employed precisely because the industry could not provide labour-saving devices and imported goods were too expensive for majority of the population (Bujra 2000: 38). To avoid a simplistic and over-polarized narrative of differences between the West and the non-West, a cautionary note is necessary here: during the 1990s, women's participation in paid labour increased in Tanzania and therefore also an increased demand for paid domestic workers in Tanzanian households. From this perspective, development in Tanzania shares commonalities with development in the West (Mbilinyi 2023).

In South Africa the situation is more complex; here industry was able to produce domestic-work devices such as cleaning and washing machines but the transformation into households that were using these instead of domestic workers was disrupted by the state-constituted labour segregation which conserved a reservoir of cheap Black South African workers (Cock 1984). Frequent in the African context is also the involvement of young people or even children through various forms of apprenticeship – some of which are involuntary and take the shape of forced servitude, such as modern slavery. Currently, child labour in the domestic sector is considered to be Tanzanians' main trafficking problem and often takes place in the guise of apprenticeships which have roots in the precolonial labour organization and was further exploited under the colonial state (ILO 2016). The link between female and child workers exploitation has historical roots: the labour of women and children was regulated under the same Ordinances during the German and, later, the British colonial administration.[2] Looking closer into this, we find that the conditions for domestic workers, women and children were less regulated compared to other sectors such as industry.[3] Moreover, from my archival research, I found that the conditions in which child domestic workers had to labour were often noticed but not dealt with.[4]The next section digs deeper into colonial efforts to control women's labour and how women in various ways have negotiated these attempts.

Women and labour

While documentation on gender and work during the precolonial era is scarce, there are some historical writings which support the idea that women's participation in work outside the home was complementary to men's labour. Drawing on oral transcripts, Nyerere (1966: 9, cited in Kiaga 2007: 28) stated:

> In African societies . . . traditionally we lived as families, with individuals supporting each other and helping each other in terms of equality. We recognized that each of us had a place in the community, and this place carried with it the right to whatever food and shelter was available in return for the use of whatever abilities and energies we had. The old and the sick, or those whose crops had been destroyed by natural disasters, were not left alone in their suffering. Other people shared with them and did so without feeling on either side that this was 'charity' from the better-off, or involved any loss of human dignity for the one who was (though not fault of his/her own) in need . . . the community was a unity in which every individual was important and among which goods available were shared without too great inequality.

Gender research on precolonial as well as colonial Tanzania has stressed the work identity of women, which includes multiple work arenas, whether as a weaver, a cultivator or a trader (Giblin 2005; Mbilinyi 2016). In line with this research, Kiaga (2007: 28) emphasizes the importance of applying a broad perspective on labour to avoid simplistic conclusions around women's participation in work. Following this perspective, Kiaga (2007) found that the complementary view of the organization of labour between women and men during the precolonial era, as displayed in Nyerere's text, resonates with how the division of labour between women and men is displayed in research focusing on the early years of the country's independence:

> Men are almost universally responsible for initial heavy clearing and stumping of the new fields. But from that time women progressively share or take over the work of sawing, weeding and harvesting. (UNECA 1975: 50, cited in Kiaga 2007: 29)

The view of women's labour as complementary to men's is not undisputed in research, and Giblin's (2005) study of family relations in colonial and postcolonial Tanzania stressed that patriarchal structures were part of precolonial societies, although this does not mean that women were without agency. He shows that women played an important role in the production of livelihoods and states that 'In spite of patrilineal exclusivity and clan hierarchy that prevailed in the world of chiefly politics, the daily lives of women involved networks of paternal and maternal relatives, spouses' kin and neighbors'

(2005: 87). Continuing this line of thought, Mbilinyi (1988) interrogates the tension between oppressive gender regimes and women's agency through the lens of labour relations under the British colonial administration.[5] Mbilinyi (1988) points to how the colonial administration increased its efforts to control women's labour by maintaining three colonial labour regimes: labour migration, casual labour and peasant labour. All three regimes depended heavily on female labour, which led the colonial administration to try to control women's mobility by limiting the spaces where unmarried women could reside or work. For example, only married women could travel or else they needed mandatory documents. Another example, single women were not allowed to reside or work in larger towns or in labour camps. For this reason, so-called customary marriages – which usually involved decisions made by elderly chiefs or parents and involved a dowry – were encouraged by the colonial administration (Mbilinyi 1988). There are several examples of how women resisted these 'customary marriages':

> Wife Timu admits quite frankly not only that she committed adultery with Anyimike in the manner described but that she [did] so often that she cannot count the times. She did it because she liked him. She has also done it since that case began but nowadays does not do so because her husband and she have moved to another village. (ibid/f422, PC appeal 29/1945 in Mbilinyi 1988: 8)

According to court practice in 1945, a marriage was consider broken if the wife had committed adultery several times with the same man (a woman could not divorce a man on the grounds of adultery). Thus, committing adultery had become a method for women to divorce from an unwanted marriage. In her research into the colonial archives, Mbilinyi (1988) found reports which display collective actions of resistance:

> It even happened in some chiefdom or another that girls made a kind of conspiration not easily to become married. They then refused so long until the chief himself ordered the young men to carry their fiancées off by force. So, there were times where mass marriages were forced upon certain districts. (Paul Rother f11.A 24.5.40 cited in Mbilinyi 1988: 24)

At the centre of Mbilinyi's argument is a patriarchal alliance: 'Colonial and imperial governments gave men control over women, particularly wealthy men or Native Authorities, as a new form of security or pawn in exchange for male obedience and cooperation' (1988: 26). Moreover, the significance of casual and peasant labour has risen relative to migrant labour and these patterns persisted in the years after the independence: 'the regulation of female labour in production and reproduction is therefore as significant a problem for capital today as it was yesterday' (1988: 26).

Focusing on the growing middle class, Kiaga (2007) stresses that the view of African women as oppressed has been heavily over-emphasized in previous research; Mhajida (2021) shows how middle-class women during the 1950s and 1960s negotiated patriarchal gender norms, modernity and motherhood. In this respect, Mhajida's (2021) research nuances the image of professional Tanzanian women as either urban dwellers or migrants. Moreover, it highlights how the conditions for middle-class women's careers during the 1950s and 1960s were shaped by inherited colonial gender, race and class relations and women's negotiations of the same (2021). As pointed out in the theoretical Chapter 3 of this volume, relations to land and social reproduction are intrinsically connected to the production and reproduction of gender relations, on which the following section will focus.

The division of land and labour

Serving as a main producer of crops for the colony, Tanzania was divided into regions where some were labour reserves and some became designed for commercial peasant production. As a consequence, some regions became more developed than others, which still has consequences for the economic development of the regions today (Coulson 2013).

In Tanzania, processes of domesticity were facilitated by the division of labour put into practice by colonial settlers – taxation and men's labour migration being the main constituents.[6] This process began with the German administration, which created laws[7] which would facilitate wage labour and force Africans into it so that they would pay taxes. From this situation, the British colonial administration developed the Ordinances which regulated the payment of labourers to be in cash only and the requirement for written contracts as well as how workers should be recruited:

> Any operations undertaken with the object of obtaining or supplying the labour of natives who do not spontaneously offer their services at the

> places of employment, or at an office established by Government, or by an employer's organisation with the approval of the Labour Commissioner, for the purpose of receiving applications for employment, and in which 'recruit', 'recruiter' and 'recruitment' have corresponding meanings.[8]

As we can see, a prominent feature of the above citation is the element of resistance on the part of the 'native servant', indicating that the notion of freedom of contract is nothing but a paper construct serving the interests of the colonial administration. The following quotation from Sir Percy Girouard, one of the first governors of the East Africa Protectorate, is an example:

> We consider that taxation is the only possible method of compelling the native to leave his reserve for the purpose of seeking work. Only in this way can the cost of living be increased for the native . . . and it is on this that the supply of labour and the price of labour depends. (Kiaga 2007: 33)

By introducing a tax for men, colonial rule created a labour force for their needs and a division between labour for subsistence and labour for money. This transformation, which brought men into commercial farming and other types of monetary work, also implied a transformation of the value of work. All work that was not compensated for in monetary form lost its value – processes that were highly gendered. In this context, Kiaga notes:

> It seems to me that this commoditization of certain jobs and not others, and valuing monetary elements of work is the foundation of the unequal gender division of labor in Tanzania. (Kiaga 2007: 34)

Kiaga's conclusion resonates well with the analysis made by Giblin (2005), which shows the involvement of the colonial state of East Africa and Tanganyika in the production of the gendered devaluation of women's unpaid work. By examining prior research on the topic, Mbilinyi (2016) supports this conclusion and stresses how the gendered division of labour is the result of changes in the political economy during the colonial and postcolonial periods rather than any '*transhistorical and unchanging traditional gender division of labour*'(Mbilinyi 2016: 18, italics in the original). In this context it is worth taking a closer look at Giblin's research on gender and labour in the colonial district of Njombe. This area was part of a territory in southern and western Tanganyika which provided workers for plantations and mines. Giblin's research resonates with Mbilinyi's (1988) – conducted almost a decade earlier – and he notes how, between the 1920s and the 1960s, men would migrate (willingly or by force) to primarily sisal plantations in central and north-eastern Tanganyika. During the Second World War, men were conscripted to either civilian or military labour and it is estimated that only one-third of men were at home during the season of harvesting (Giblin 2005: 109). Giblin stresses how the absence of men was used by women to negotiate spaces for a livelihood and how family and kin relations became a space for negotiating the involvement of various state formations (2005: 86). An interview quotation from Giblin's research is cited here as it highlights the agency of women and, moreover, women's unpaid peasant labour, which is too often neglected in historical labour research as well as in contemporary debates in SRT (see Chapter 3). 'There was no problem, you just farmed. He had left you a house and given you a hoe, what else would you need? You would just get busy' (2005: 86). Based on the results of a survey carried out by the University of Dar es Salaam, Giblin concludes that men's labour migration provided women with the independent possession of land and other recourses. A survey over land possession near Njombe town in 1949–50 showed that, of 600 landholders, 47 per cent were women (Giblin 2005: 87). A cautionary note is necessary here: the survey also revealed that women owned less cultivated land compared to men, indicating that women had greater difficulty in finding labourers who could assist them in the fields (Giblin 2005: 87). Despite changes in gender relations and labour migration during the 1930s and 1940s, rural households were still mainly dependent on the male income; however, as we will see in the following sections, this will change with the increase in women's rural-to-urban migration in the 1970s.

Women and internal labour migration

Colonial rule imposed taxation on men and through this, sometimes forced, labour migration. Moreover, colonial rule also imposed regulations which prevented the mobility of women and children.[9] Consequently, women's rural-to-urban migration got off to a slow start during the 1950s, before intensifying during the 1980s (Bujra 2000). This means that, in the 1950s, women's migration patterns were linked to their husband's migration trajectory – either by following their husbands, seeking marital status in the urban areas or finding a better way of increasing their livelihoods in the rural area when they were the main family provider. Challenging the view of African women's dependence on men for migration and for livelihoods Aili Mari Tripp (1997) has documented the increase of self-employed women in Dar es Salaam. By the late 1980s more than half of the women in Dar es Salaam (69 per cent) were self-employed and only 9 per cent were waged, which indicates a shift over the years between the 1960s and the 1970s (Trip 1997: 108).

Looking closer at the patterns for women's migration we can see that, from the 1980s onwards, women's rural-to-urban migration began to increase, due no doubt to the economic restructuring of Tanzania's political economy and donor-driven economic programmes (Coulson 2013). The World Bank and the IMF structural adjustment programmes (SAPs) are particularly important to mention here. In exchange for continued donor support, Tanzania rolled back free universal education, health care and water, which was privatized and made accessible through user fees. Mbilinyi (2016) argues that the user fees functioned in a similar way to the earlier colonial taxation system (as previously described in the section on the division of land and labour) as it forced both women and men to intensify their labour in marketed production. In this context it is worth noting that women are currently the main providers of user fees for basic reproduction services (2016: 120).

By combining information from several data sources, Kiaga (2007) is able to show the development of different migration patterns from 1995 onwards. One of the main changes which took place was the increase in female migrants from rural-to-urban areas which, during a five-year period from 1995 to 2000, was higher (0.8 per cent) compared to that of male (0.6). During the same period, the share of migrants in the economically active population increased from 4.1 to 16.2 per cent. Using 2002 census data, the turnover of lifetime migration increased by 46 per cent between 2002 and 2016. Dar es Salaam is the region which receives the most migrants. Here Kiaga (2007) reveals another pattern: circular migration being salient. While not all rural-to-urban migrants would work in domestic service, a majority would be employed in various kinds of service jobs. Who were the domestic workers in colonial and postcolonial Tanzania? The following section takes a closer look at this group.

Domestic workers in colonial Tanzania

Domestic servitude was not invented by the colonial settlers; on the contrary, in the precolonial period, Africans as well as Arabs and Indians had domestic slaves – so-called skivvies. Moreover, non-European groups continued to be part of the employment category during the colonial era. Despite the precolonial existence of domestic servants, the colonial archives exclude Africans as employers. Given this, the statistics presented below need to be viewed with some scepticism.

The number of waged workers was never high in colonial Tanganyika, where most workers remained farmers, and industrialization was only just emerging. Yet domestic workers were significant since they outnumbered many other work groups in the early 1920s. Among waged workers, there were more domestic workers compared to those in manufacturing or mining and the group was only outnumbered by agricultural labourers and those working in the construction industry and transport (Bujra 2000: 7).

In Table 4.1, we see that the wages for unskilled labour remained low and even decreased over the years – this will be further discussed in Chapter 5 – with the Eastern parts and Tanga having the highest wages. In 1926, the number of domestic workers reached 20,000; by the late 1940s this figure had doubled to 40,000 (see Table 4.2). The proportion of domestic workers among wage labourers varied between 7 and 13 per cent, although these figures are likely to be underestimated. Despite the inconsistency in statistics, the colonial archives reveal an interesting gender pattern in which domestic workers are almost exclusively referred to as men. Female domestic workers appeared in the statistics for the first time in 1951, with their number estimated at just 653 workers throughout the country. By the end of the colonial era, female domestic workers made up only 4.5 per cent of the adult domestic work force (Bujra 2000: 7).

From a male to a female occupation

Statistics continued to be scarce in the years after independence. Bujra (2000: 8) draws from the NUMEIST survey, carried out in 1971 by researchers at Dar es

Table 4.1 Wage Rates by Province 1927 and 1940 (TZ Shillings per Month)

Province	1927	1940
Unskilled labour		
Northern	10–30	7–15
Lake	6–24	6–20
Western	7.5–24	5–12
Central	10–18	5–12
Eastern	15–30	6–21
Southern	10–26	8–15
S. Highlands	5–15	6–12
Tanga	15–30	9–18
Semi-skilled labour		
Northern	18–30	15–30
Lake	10–30	9–50
Western	12–40	9–50
Central	15–45	10–30
Eastern	20–60	10–60
Southern	15–40	9–60
S. Highlands	10–45	10–30
Tanga	24–50	10–35
Skilled labour		
Northern	30–80	30–100
Lake	40–120	30–200
Western	20–150	23–80
Central	30–100	20–99
Eastern	20–180	30–100
Southern	25–90	15–100
S. Highlands	30–105	20–150
Tanga	40–120	20–200

Source: Coulson (2013: 75).
Note: The rates for 1927 include an allowance for the payment of rations in kind. In 1940 an amount varying from 3 to 15 shillings per month should be added to make the figures comparable. Current exchange rates are approximately TZ 4,000 = 1.56 euros or 1.30 pounds sterling.

Salaam University, to shed some light on this: a random sample of 5,523 urban residents from the seven largest Tanzanian towns showed that 40 per cent were waged workers, 85 per cent of whom were men. Among these, 144 (6.6 per cent) were employed as domestic workers, of whom 86 per cent were men and 14 per cent women. At 6.6 and 6.5 per cent respectively, men and women were equally likely to become domestic workers. The NUMEIST survey most probably covered a broader sample of domestic workers compared to what was visible in the colonial archives, hence, it covered more ethic groups as well as groups with different income levels. Bujra (2000: 8) shows how the patterns are similar to those found in the archives from the colonial era; the proportion

Table 4.2 Colonial and Postcolonial Estimates of Domestic Work Labourers

Date	Estimated number	Men	Women	Juveniles	Source
1926	20,000	-	-	-	Annual Blue Books
1936	20,000	-	-	-	Annual Blue Books
1940	30,000	-	-	-	Annual Blue Books
1942	35,000	-	-	-	Annual Blue Books
1947	25,500	-	-	-	Census of Native Labour
1948–50	30–40,000	-	-	-	Labour Department
1951	15,342	13,631	653	1,058	Tanganyika Statistical Abstract
1952	20,430	-	-	-	East African Statistical Abstract
1971		86 %	14 %		NUMEIST SURVEY

Source: Bujra (2000: 7).

of domestic workers in the total workforce was similar and men were over-represented. Despite this, it is worth noting that the proportion of female domestic workers in 1971 was three times higher at 14 per cent compared to that in colonial times – 4.5 per cent in the 1950s (Bujra 2000: 8).

As described earlier in this chapter, the increase of female domestic workers coincided with an increase in the migration of labourers from rural-to-urban areas of Dar es Salaam and other big cities. During the 1970s, Tanzanian socialist politics in rural areas continued to push women and men to urban areas although they found few openings for wage labour. So, despite domestic workers receiving low salaries and working long hours, their supply continued to be high. By the 1980s, waged employment had increased – mainly, however, through the expansion of state employees, although great gender disparities existed. In the late 1980s only 3 per cent of women were engaged in paid labour as the majority of women remained in rural areas, making up 75 per cent of the active population in agriculture, which produced 90 per cent of the food requirements of the country. Only 20 per cent of central government employees were women (Kiaga 2007: 39).

The decade of the 1980s was marked by inflation and a drastic fall in wages. Even those with high wages in society could no longer support their families. Under these economic conditions, combined with a state political agenda which proclaimed Tanzania to be a socialist egalitarian state, it is reasonable to believe that the number of domestic workers would decrease. Paradoxically the opposite happened. Meanwhile, urban migration continued and remained at 11.5 per cent in 1988 (Bujra 2000: 10). In the context of a growing and largely feminized and informal sector, it is pertinent now to dig deeper into its organization.

Domestic workers' organization

The organization of domestic workers has been described as taking place in three different phases (Bujra 2000). The first phase commenced with the registration of the African cooks', washermen's and houseboys' association in 1939; a decade before them, the drivers' association was registered in the late 1920s and that of shop assistants in 1930, all of which became unionized. During this period, the first minimum wage legislation was conceded by the colonial administration (Bujra 2000: 156). The national registration of associations followed in 1945 and indicated the beginning of the second phase in 1945–9, during which the registration of associations was cancelled. The third and last phase commenced in the 1950s with the associations' leaders refusing to disband.

Moving to a more detailed description of the first phase, we find that the union's earliest leader was Saleh Bin Fundi, described in the research literature as a night watchman (Bujra 2000: 157). Working outside the household was put forward as the reason for his success in mobilizing workers. His work as a watchman enabled him to avoid surveillance and to create alliances. Under his leadership, members of the African cooks', washermen's and houseboys' association continued to organize themselves and sought alliances with white-collar African groups. Organization across work sectors was also visible in other associations, such as that of dockers (Bujra 2000: 158; Kaijage 2000). While dockworkers did not become unionized until the 1950s, they were crucial for the development of labour organization between different worker groups from 1939 onwards (Kaijage 2000: 318). In this context Cooper (1996) notes that unions were not necessarily at the forefront in workers' struggles. For example, in Nigeria in 1945, unions were pivotal for the organization of workers' protests, resulting in changes in salaries, whereas, in 1939, 1941 and 1945 in Mombasa, Kenya, unions played no significant role. The flipside of this was that, without unions taking the lead, it was difficult for workers to push their demands in a more systematic way. However, the lack of organization could also be positive as the protests could spread beyond particular professions or unions (Cooper 1996: 141; see also Cavallero and Gago 2021 for a contemporary debate on the role of unions and labour relations). For the domestic workers in Tanzania, the first period of unionization was characterized by a number of public meetings to raise support among workers as well as to send petitions to the government requesting better wages and shorter working hours. In addition, early trade-unionism, investigated by Illiffe (1979), shows how a vast amount of activity was also centred around training members in how to conduct collective action and construct group solidarity.

The second phase, between 1945 and 1949, was where various worker associations were demanding better working conditions and higher salaries and were opposing racial discrimination. As an example, a strike begun by the dockworkers in Dar es Salaam on 6 September 1947 differed from prior protests. The strike lasted a month and spread through workers' organizations across labour sectors and geographic regions; Illiffe (1979: 402) referred to this strike as the largest protest against the colonial regime since the Maji Maji Rebellion (July 1905 to July 1907). However, this period was also marked by obstacles in the unionization of workers in Tanzania as well as in other parts of the British colonial empire. Here, it follows an example from Coopers research (1996) on Northern Rhodesia: in 1939 the governor put to one side a bill for workers' unionization, arguing that[10]

> The African workers are not yet thought to be sufficiently advanced to be able satisfactorily to organize a Trade Union and take a proper part in Trade Union activities. (Cooper 1996: 119)

In Tanzania during 1940 to 1945, the African cooks', washermen's and houseboys' association was deregistered by colonial officials. The reason given in the colonial archives was the lack of transparency in the handling of money and registrations (Bujra 2000). Illiffe (1979) contested these archive accounts by showing how the organization of workers stretched way beyond capital investment in various locations in Dar es Salaam as well as in local branches in Dodoma, Kigoma, Chunya, Kilosa, Lindi, Singida, Tanga and Korogwe (1979: 397–8). The letter quoted below is from a worker's perspective, here represented by the union. It is sent from the domestic workers' union (registered in 1945 as the African Cooks, Washermen and Houseservants' Association) and was addressed to 'Her majesty the Queen Elizabeth'; it was also copied to the governor, various African worthies and the governor of New York:

> Now let the Europeans of Tanganyika work without pay and rent their houses and pay their servants with their own money and use their purposes for all purposes as we do: this will make it necessary for them to go away for they will have no profit. We ask [for the removal of] European, Indian and Arab . . . we are tired of your people. (Letter from Special Branch to political Liaison Officer, Dar es Salaam, 21 October 1953, cited in Bujra 2000: 68)

Bujra (2000: 70) proposes that letters such as this can be read as a subversive discourse – since it reveals those in power – rather than as a counter discourse. The reason for this distinction, Bujra (2000) outlines, is the fundamental power inequality that existed between the association and the colonial authorities. Drawing on the processes around how the association was being deregistered (as described above) and how the colonial authorities postponed the re-registration and stopped all attempts by the association to meet with the UN on the grounds that the association was not doing unionism the 'right' way shows how the colonial authority could both define and deal with these voices. It shows how the discourse around 'proper unionism' was produced within an already existing system of colonial power (2000).

The third and last phase shows how Fundi and other members refused to disband, wrote numerous petitions and asked for a meeting with the UN Trusteeship Committee. This meeting was never realized, and, in 1953, Saleh Bin Fundi disappeared from the archives (Bujra 2000: 159). Not surprisingly, the struggle at this time was led and dominated by men, reflecting the gender composition of the workforce (Bujra 2000: 161).

Domestic workers' trade-union formation

Research globally has pointed out the difficulties of forming group protests, stemming from domestic workers being separated in private households

(ILO 2015, 2016). The analysis of previous historical research presented here shows how domestic workers were among the first to be unionized in Tanzania. In 1955, the Tanganyikan Federation of Labor (TFL) was formed to represent the interests of all unions. One of the ten unions that came together under the coalition was the Hotel Workers' and Domestic Servants' Union. In 1956, domestic workers played a vital role in a series of strikes for workers' rights that swept through the country. These protests preceded the new Employment Ordinance(CAP 366 in 1957) which recognized that a contract of employment is a voluntary agreement between the employer and the employee. This dramatic change by the colonial state followed the recommendations made by the ILO on employees' welfare.[11] During this period, my research from the archives shows how domestic workers and trade unions actively worked for better payment and working conditions, as the quotation will display:[12]

> During the month of series of demands have been circulated to employers of domestic servants and hotel workers in the Iringa and Njobe districts by local branches of the Tanganyika Domestic and Hotel Workers Union.
>
> These demands which call for substantial increases in wage rates and improved conditions of service are believed to have originated from the Union's headquarters in Dar es Salaam and they have generally been ignored by local employers. In the meantime it is the evidence that the Iringa branch of the Union is attempting to persuade its members to resort to strike action on the 15th May, 1960, in support of its demands, although at this stage it's difficult to assess the amount of support the strike call is likely command from local members.

A minimum wage was set at 81.90 Tanzanian shillings (approximate equivalent today is 0.035 USD) for which the TFL could take the credit. However, the victory was conditional; it was only to be applied in the capital and for adults over eighteen years and it was only half of what was claimed by domestic workers (Shivji 1986: 130, cited in Bujra 2000: 161). My research from the archive supports Bujra's (2000) conclusions and shows how the organization of domestic workers for their rights took place simultaneously with the general turn against colonialism that swept through the continent at this epoch. The fight for workers' rights was therefore also a fight against colonialism, as this invitation to boycott clearly shows:[13]

> To all citizens European, African and Asian.
> Freedom and hard work 1960.
> Boycott. Boycott. Boycott
>
> We are appealing to all citizens to boycott the business of M/S Dhanan Bros P.O. Box 583 Mawenzi road. The rich miser Indian who has sucked the blood of a certain African by failing to pay his due for the last five months.
>
> Shall the blood of our beloved African Brethren be shed in vain? Shall we forgive and forget our brother who had suffered martyrdom for his sweat? Shall we continue to do business with persons who had sucked the blood of our beloved African Brethren? Let us unite, boycott his business, employment and his social contacts as well: this is the time we must straighten those who are trying to create misunderstandings between racial feeling.
>
> Freedom and hard work.
> Juma Hamisi
> District Secretary
> Tanganyika Domestic and Hotel Workers' Union
> Territorial Union
> (Affiliated to the Tanganyikan Federation of Labour)

The call for boycott is dated 9 April 1960 and, in addition to revealing how the fight for workers' rights is linked to a wider anticolonial struggle, also shows the link between the Tanganyika Domestic and Hotel Workers' Union and the TFL.

After independence in 1961, the TFL was transformed into the National Union of Tanganyika Workers (NUTA) which was affiliated to Tanganyika African National Union (TANU) (Bujra 2000: 164–6). It consisted of nine industrial sections, one of which was for Hotel and Domestic Workers. During this period, the unions used the rhetoric of socialism but, in practice, workers' rights were not expanded. In 1978, the NUTA changed its name to *Jumuiya ya Wafanyi Kazi wa Tanzania* (JUWATA). From having between 3,000 and 4,000 members in 1956, the Hotel and Domestic Workers were the smallest section by 1986, accounting for only 3 per cent of all members (9,964 out of a total of 342, 468) (Bujra 2000: 166). Against this backdrop, the decrease in domestic workers' unionization indicates their complex positionality – the expatriate employers, who paid the highest salaries, were leaving the country and the new employers showed little interest in improving their work conditions. Bujra (2000: 171) suggests that two factors influenced this development: the increased competition for work through rural-to-urban migration and the decrease of the autonomy of unions (see also Kaijage 2000 for a discussion on unionism and workers' autonomy). In this context, it is worth noting that women did get organized in TANU but it is less documented in the colonial archives (see Geiger 1987 for examples that draw from oral history). Moreover, women organized in support groups and networks beyond labour organizations. The Mbiru protest in 1945 serves as an example of women's involvement. Women protested against issues of taxation and multiracialism. As part of the protest, 500 women assembled outside the district headquarters where representatives from the colonial administration were meeting with local chiefs. After several protests and a petition, the government dropped their graduated income tax (Mbilinyi 2023, 10). Women's involvement in nationalist struggles led by Bibi Titi from 1955 onwards is another example. The nationalist struggle on mainland Tanzania was organized by TANU, and here women's micro-level support was crucial for mobilizing and urging women and men to join the nationalist movement (Ibid). In 1979, more than 7,500 women's groups were identified in mainland Tanzania (Kiaga 2007: 42). As already mentioned in the introduction to this chapter, historicizing domestic work in Tanzania is not a linear endeavour and, for this reason, I now turn to the colonial discourses which underpinned much of the development outlined thus far in this chapter.

Colonial discourses of domesticity

The historical legacy of European domesticity was a main pillar in constructing and legitimizing the gendered division of labour and the value of different types of work. Focusing on gender and labour in the Empire, Hall (2007) shows how sexuality has impacted on the division of labour between women and men and between the colonial power and the colonized in similar but not identical ways on the African continent, North America and Asia. Examples from the Middle East are discussed in Farahani (2018). Central in Hall's (2007) study is the hierarchical division between gender and race and how white women gained and maintained their value through their work in constructing the expatriate household as a white and 'civilized' space and by giving birth to white children. With males being the norm among domestic servants in colonial expatriate households, one would have expected this to be an area of controversy. Instead, this was taken for granted and, as such, represented the opposite to the situation in many European countries at the time. In Tanganyika, the domestic servant was expected to be male and it was generally unthinkable to have female domestic workers during the 1940s. At the same time, the domestication of African women was highly celebrated in the media and in official documents (Bujra 2000; Geiger 1987).

By the 1950s, the discourse around domestic servants being males began to change. However, the rationales put forward could sometimes be very different. In her research, Bujra (2000: 66) highlights these different rationales in her analysis of the following conversation between M. J. B. Molohan – senior provisional commissioner – and Lady Twining, the wife of the previous governor of Kenya. The following quote is from Molohan's book *Detribalization*:

> [urban African women] have time on their hands and so become a liability. I have always felt that more encouragement should be given and more facilities made available for women to obtain paid employment. The opportunities in industry are not yet as great but it is ludicrous that domestic service in Tanganyika should be the prerequisite of the male. The territory cannot afford much longer the luxury of locking up so many able-bodied men in this unproductive sphere of employment for which women are far better suited and equipped. (1957: 40, cited in Bujra 2000: 66)

The following and different argument is put forward by Lady Twining:

> The replacement of houseboys by women is an important step towards the advancement of the African . . . women in the home as housekeepers and cooks would absorb the ways of civilisation more rapidly than men and . . . they would not tend to slip back into native ways as men did once they returned to the reserves. (Quoted – without comment – in Shivji 1986: 130, cited in Bujra 2000: 161)

As Bujra (2000) noted, both arguments come to the same conclusion (that domestic work should be done by African women), the underlying rationales being very different. In the first quotation, from Molohan, the view of domestic work and women as unproductive is visible, hence African men should not waste their time on domestic work but, instead, move on to more productive tasks. The text from Lady Twining, on the other hand, views women and the home as the main carriers and spaces of civilization and, as such, as more suitable for civilizing Africa and Africans. Both texts make reference to the future –

Molohan by imagining an industrialized future where both women and men participate, Lady Twining by her future imagining of 'civilizing' the African (2000). However, despite these discourses, the change in gender distribution in the domestic-work sector did not take place until three decades later.

The colonial discourse around domestic service also evolved around expatriate women. For example, when expatriate married women tried to get the right to vote in the new elective system of local government in 1955, male colonial voices expressed in the newspapers were raised against them and used the argument 'If housewives were allowed to vote, the houseboys who lived on the premises would have to have it too' (*The Sunday News*, 8 January 1954: 4, cited in Bujra 2000: 63). The link between expatriate married women and domestic servants was here made explicit through this act of trying to maintain male European privilege. Taking a positive stance on the argument, it is noteworthy that the right for African men to be able to vote is considered. At this time only a few, mainly European, women who had inherited their property had the right to vote.

When the press took a positive stance in favour of expatriate women, it was always at the expense of African domestic servants and only for working women who contributed to provide for their family. The dominant discourse, however, was that expatriate women would be expected to have servants and to contribute to society through charitable events rather than in the monetary economy (Mhajida 2021).

The working life of expatriate women during the British colonial administration centred on family life and, when engaged in remunerated work, it was often in female-coded work as librarians or nurses or by being active in non-governmental organizations such as the Red Cross. More common was engaging with philanthropic work in combination with family responsibilities. Here the East African Women's service league and its transnational networking organization the 'Tanganyika Women's Service League' were core institutions. The president of the Tanganyika branch, Mrs Sharp, points out that 'emphasis in the League has always been on the word "Service" and that it is much more than a club which offers certain amenities to its members' (Carmichael 1965). In the same article, Mrs Sharp underlines the importance of supporting women and children 'of all races in Tanganyika' and the importance of contributing to community. This was a malleable discourse and not without tension, as this aspiration was constrained by a membership rooted in the politics of race hierarchy and race division that characterized the settler society. From this point of view, philanthropic work conducted by expatriate women challenged aspects of imperial rule and promoted what they understood as imperial welfare. At the same time, this work contributed to a moral justification of imperial power and expansion at home (van Tol 2015: 436).

As indicated in the introduction, the analysis in this chapter builds on a previous research, my analysis of archival texts *and* a fictional text. The next section digs deeper into an account of how sexual violence is intertwined with economic violence and how this intersection is articulated through relations of debt and dependency in the fictional novel.

Sexual violence, work and debt in a fictional novel

In Abdulrazak Gurnah's literary work *Paradiset* [*Paradise*] (2012), the servant Yusuf is working for the wealthy Uncle Azizi in the early nineteenth century along the coast of East Africa. What makes *Paradiset* so interesting in this chapter are the relations of migration, debt and dependency that organize Yusuf's work in the household. Yusuf was brought from the inland to the coastal area and pawned as a child labourer to pay his father's debts to a rich merchant, Uncle Azizi. In *Paradiset* we learn how relations of debt and dependency structure, how social relations are *disciplined* and managed and how they produce differentiation. Framing debt in this particular way is inspired by Lucy Cavallero and Veronica Gago's (2021) feminist analysis of debt. From this follows an emphasis on tracing the connections between different types of debt, operating at both national and household levels. Cavallero and Gago's contribution makes it possible to politicize debt and bring it out from its usual abstract and economistic framing. Following this analytical take, I here highlight the example of Yusuf to make debt visible as a concrete mechanism that works retrospectively and regulates subjects through labour.

When Yusuf is a young man, he is called to evening meetings within the household, where he is not officially permitted, by Sayyid's wife. The beautiful domestic servant Amina and the object of Yusuf's love serve as an interpreter, as she speaks both Arabic and Kiswahili. Sayyid's wife is marked by illness, spends her days isolated in the house and has become obsessed with the young servant, Yusuf. Her courtesy takes a dramatic turn as she throws herself on

Yusuf, who flees out into the garden. Yusuf is overwhelmed with shame and disgust as he oscillates between feelings of inferiority and anger and tries to calm himself while hiding in the garden:

> But he had not done anything shameful, the shameful thing was that they had forced him to live in that way, that they had forced them all to live that way. Their intrigues and their hatred and their vengeful lust had transformed even the most natural personal characteristics into the subject of barter and bargaining. (Gurnah 2012: 256 my translation)

Due to the layers of violence lived by Sayyid's wife, Yusuf and Amina are displaying different positions of vulnerability, and the episode where Yusuf reflects to himself in the garden not only is an explicit description of experiences of sexual violence but also shows how economic practices of 'barter and bargaining' have reshaped and *draw* from intimate relations. Shortly after the episode displayed in the quotation above, Sayyid returns home and blames not Yusuf but his wife for the situation, eventually giving Yusuf his freedom. After reflecting upon the nature of the freedom he will gain while continuing to work for Sayyid as a 'free' man, Yusuf decides to leave. Yusuf's get-away is the grand finale of the book and leaves the narrative open-ended for the reader; Does Yusuf run after the German colonial army to become a recruit or will he use this situation to cover for his exit? In any circumstance, the exit highlights the intersections, relations and tensions that evolve between the 'analytical' and the 'affective' narratives that are at the centre of this chapter: gender relations, domestic and care work, migration and colonialism. In addition and, as explained in the concluding section, the narrative of Yusuf add to previous research which expand the circle of cultural representation of domestic work from within and from below, hence widening the realm of the archive by unlearning colonial representations of domestic workers as passive (see also Bujra 2000, Kiaga 2007, Mbilinyi 2016 and Chapter 5 in this book).

Conclusion

This chapter makes a contribution to the ongoing work of decolonizing archival research. This is done by making a pedagogical contribution and situating the analysis of domestic work in a context of learning and unlearning. Through a learning lens, the results presented here can be understood from two different angles: learning *in* the archives and learning *from* the archives.

In this chapter, learning *in* the archives means interrogating the learning and unlearning processes displayed in various documents, letters and legislation – for example, how workers unlearn not to be pitted against each other by employers or – another example – how colonial officers learn about the growing pan-African critique of colonialism as a driving force for labour protests.

Learning *from* the archives takes place at two analytical levels – at a primary level through analysing various details and facts about how the 'division of land and labour', 'women and internal migration', 'colonial discourses on domesticity' and 'the organisation of domestic workers' are interconnected and have mutually contributed to the formation of contemporary domestic-work relations. Examples of such connections are those between 'the division of land and labour' and 'labour migration' and how 'racialized colonial discourses of domesticity' have underpinned these movements. While racialized colonial discourses of domesticity underpinned the rational for male domestic workers in colonial households and later a change from male to female occupation, other factors related to wider economic and social transformations were also important. The implementation of taxes and the circular migration that followed, the various efforts to control women's mobility as part of securing colonial labour regimes as well as how women and workers in various ways have negotiated these attempts are just such examples (see also Cooper 1996; Kaijage 2000; Mbilinyi 1988).

At a secondary level, 'learning from the archives' implies an empirically informed methodological contribution to historicizing domestic-work relations. In this chapter this is done in two steps: first, I am inspired by scholars who emphasize the need for bridging literary-informed scholarships with sociological analysis of the political economy of the history of coloniality (see also Patel 2021). From this perspective, the fictional novel is perceived as an additional layer of representation that adds to our knowledge of material relations as represented in the colonial archives or in previous historical research. In other words, the analytical method presented here expands the understanding of the archive and centres alternative narratives from within and from below. The narrative in *Paradiset* (2012) takes debt and dependency out from its usual economistic framing and analyses how capitalist labour exploitation draws from sexual violence in private households and, importantly, how Yusuf managed and responded to these labour relations. Moreover, in *Paradiset* (2012), labour relations take place between people living along the coast of Tanzania. In this context, *Paradiset* (2012) nuances race relations beyond a white–Black dichotomy and challenges representations of domestic workers who are working under conditions of debt and dependency as passive.

Secondly, I depart from global economic transformations – that is neoliberalization and privatization – during the 1990s and move back and forth in time. The focus on domestic work is the reason for choosing the 1990s instead of, for example, the years around the Second World War, which are often used in historical research into other work sectors such as mining or dockworkers (see, e.g., Cooper 1996; Kaijage 2000). During the 1990s, global structural adjustment programmes, in various ways, influenced how relations of production were going to develop in Tanzania. For example, the privatization of schools, water and electricity – currently women are responsible for producing user fees (Mbilinyi 2016). The conditions for these programmes are not arbitrary but, instead, need to be understood from the perspective of geographies of variegated social reproduction which stress how reproductive labour is hierarchically produced and unevenly distributed. Key drivers for this development can be traced back to a colonial demand for economic profit, labour and land. This chapter contributes by highlighting how domestic-work relations in Tanzania are integral to this history.

The various narratives of domestic work brought together in this chapter bring to the fore the inseparability of relations of production in societies under capitalism rather than, as the wording suggests, the existence of 'social' reproduction. This is not a new debate in social reproduction theories (Haug 2020). The results presented here add to already-existing African feminist research (Britwum 2009; Ossome 2021a) which, in various ways, has contributed to decentring debates on SR. .

5

The racial grammar of paid domestic work

'And this is the laundry area', the real-estate agent announces proudly. The colour of her lips matches the colour of her high heels. She looks at me as if she expects me to say something. It is so hot and I cannot understand why she is not sweating like the rest of us. I nod to make her happy. As we are about to leave, I see a door: 'What is in there?' I open the door and find a tiny and windowless room; it is incredibly hot and dusty. My family and the real-estate agent are waiting outside in the air-conditioned hallway. I think out loud: 'I guess if I clean it and with a fan, it could be my office'. 'So, you want to make your office, HERE?'; the real-estate agent cannot stop laughing.

We lived in the house for almost a year. I never used the tiny room as an office. I could not stand the heat, not even with a fan; we decided to use it as a storage room. Later I found out that it was supposed to be used as servants' quarter for a live-in domestic worker. Our house was located in a gated community with eight houses, four on each side of the patio. At the end of the patio was a pool. A high fence separated the pool area from the garbage area. Within the garbage area were the toilet, kitchen and resting areas for day workers – i.e., domestic workers, gardeners and guards.

'No model village [. . .] can be realized or kept presentable unless the architectural enterprise is linked with teaching, education and instruction; in short one should work with the *fellahin*. The reconstruction of the Egyptian village demands the re-education of its inhabitants, and first of all of women. We must work from the inside out'. (Mitchell 1991: 91)

While the field notes from my diary centre my encounter with the built environment, discourses, roles and relations of domestic work, this chapter will focus on the experiences of domestic workers and how they learn, cope and unlearn domestic work in expatriate households. The reason for using this field note and a quotation from Michell's (1991) research on the power of colonialism in Egypt as an introduction to this chapter is because they highlight how the built environment – hereafter, the built space[1] – is interlinked with educational relations designed to convey preferred ways of doing and organizing the everyday.[2] When the quotation from the colonial archive is read in relation to the description of the contemporary design of the house we rented during our stay as expatriates in Dar es Salaam – the work*place* for a domestic worker – the necessity of perceiving the construction of place, so-called place-making, as a historical process is highlighted (Lefebvre 1991). An understanding of place as historically produced is central in 'place-making'. This means that the ways in which places are constructed as welcoming or hostile are not arbitrary but, instead, historically produced (see also Gilmore 2022). From this it follows that it is possible to think about built space not only as resulting in the organization of materiality but also, moreover, as a continuously produced instruction, in the context of the research presented here, an instruction of labour relations and the roles and relations that follow. Descriptions of the location of kitchens and bathrooms for workers in the compound and the location of the servants' quarters in the house are inserted here to illustrate the endless pressure of racism that guides the place-making of expatriate households.[3] Here it is convenient to talk of racism as a form of grammar. The concept of grammar in the analysis of racism is used to understand how the built space and discourse mutually constitute a 'racial grammar' that regulates the conduct of subjects (Bonilla-Silva 2011). The message transmitted through this grammar is so powerful that it is often taken for granted and becomes naturalized, which makes it difficult to detect – in particular for those who are not negatively affected. In this respect, the field note points to the endless pressure of racial grammar – both in its concrete built form and in the discursive form – that domestic workers need to negotiate as they learn domestic work. In other words, the field note highlights the labour involved while learning and negotiating the racial grammar of everyday domestic work in these households. In addition, as already mentioned in Chapter 3 of this volume, a learning perspective means that instructions transmitted through discourse and the built space are possible to negotiate and implying that subjects are not mere bearers of structure or that structure determines all agency. As again pointed out in Chapter 3, agency is central for analysing learning. This chapter centres the agency of domestic workers and analyses three different but interrelated ways of learning domestic and care work – first, how domestic workers learn dominant ways of doing domestic work which involves processes of cheapening (Patel and Moore 2020). Secondly, the learning involved when domestic workers cope with – in other words, endure – oppressive labour relations and, finally, situations where domestic workers formulate a practical critique – that is they unlearn preferred ways of doing domestic work. In this respect, the analysis of coping and unlearning makes a contribution to studies of resistance.[4] Moreover, an important part of the aim of this chapter is also to analyse the continuities and changes since the British colonial era.

The workplace and work process as space

The empirical site for analysing processes of learning domestic work is expatriate households in Dar es Salaam. These workplaces are understood through feminist theories of labour (Bhattacharyya 2018; Mies 1986; Smith 1987), time–space relations (Massey 2005) and discourse (Foucault 1971) and form a multidimensional concept of internal and external practices constituting the work process – physical, social and discursive practices – and asking how they co-produce each other over time. This form of social constructivism acknowledges the materiality of practices while, at the same time, insisting that the world we experience is always already socially constructed and is continuously produced over time (Hennessy 1993). Drawing on an analytical distinction between external and internal spatial relations, the workplace of domestic workers is understood as socially constructed and continuously produced over time; taken together, these internal and external relations constitute the work process. The analytical distinction between internal and external relations will guide the structure of this chapter. Another main analytical pillar is historicizing 'place-making' (Lefebvre 1991) – that is, how internal and external spatial relations have transformed over time – which inspires the analysis in this chapter of processes of continuity and change in the structure of cheapening. Lefebvre was inspired by Marxist historical, dialectic, materialist perspectives on the continuity and change of relations of production (see Chapter 1). In addition, he added a particular emphasis on the production of space. Central in the method is a detailed investigation of a contemporary phenomenon and trace the phenomenon backwards in order to understand continuity and change and to find openings for the future, the so-called Regressive-Progressive method (for a detailed description of the method, see Hess 2000: XV; Rönnlund and Tollefsen 2016: 187; see also Arora-Jonsson 2023 for an empirical example). As I discussed in Chapter 2, this approach to historicizing is different from a more comprehensive historical analysis which would require using more and different archival data than this chapter comprises.

This chapter is structured as follows: first, the theoretical concepts of learning, coping and unlearning are outlined. Secondly, the analysis of learning about external spatial relations is examined through contracts and the built space. Thirdly, the learning of internal spatial relations is analysed through a particular relation of debt and dependency vis-à-vis the employer, which is the result of taking loans from the employer and through 'skills practices'[5] (Iskander 2021). The reason for choosing to analyse these particular internal and external spatial relations is because previous research has identified them as central for processes of cheapening labour and labourers (see Bhattacharyya 2018; Iskander 2021; Patel and Moore 2020). Finally, a concluding section presents the main results.

Learning, coping and unlearning

The divisions between processes of learning, coping and unlearning are not clear-cut but are, instead, complex and ambivalent. As pointed out in the introduction to Chapter 1 and in the theoretical Chapter 3 of this volume, a learning lens always comprises agency, first, from the perspective of *how* subjects learn and, secondly, of how subjects learn within the *context for action* (Biesta and Tedder 2007; Emirbayer and Mische 1998). From this perspective, learning is integral to analysing change, which involves but is not limited to individual processes. Learning is situated at a complex intersection between structures and individual meaning-making. Let me give an example from the field note displayed in the introduction; the structure of cheapening, here transmitted through the built space, can be learnt in terms of reproducing, as displayed by the real-estate agent's reaction, her laughter, which I interpret as a reaction to an unthinkable scenario – 'So, you want to make your office, HERE?'. The structure of cheapening can be negotiated and unlearned, for example, by my using the servants' quarters as my office – as I had initially thought to do; instead, we invited the domestic worker – who was a day worker – to dwell in the living room during her breaks. In short, unlearning involves doing, thinking and seeing things in a slightly different way (Biesta 2013) or in its collective and political form – transgression (hooks 2003). Here, I wish to add that the extent to which unlearning brings about political change is dependent on the subjects' access to power and resources; in addition to this, it is an empirical question.

Unlearning is different from learning processes, which involve coping. Coping has been used to analyse how domestic workers make meaning out of harsh working conditions (Garabiles, Mayawati and Halla 2021; Ullah 2015; Van Bortel et al. 2019). In this chapter, coping refers to processes of learning during oppressive labour relations. In this respect, the research presented here emphasizes a view of coping which is *not* standing still but, instead, involves movement (see also Kelly 1987; Kelly, Burton and Regan 1996). In other words, coping means negotiating the endless pressures of racism which have been normalized in the daily life of expatriate households. In this respect, coping becomes a powerful tool for theorizing abusive work relations without being trapped in a victim/survivor dichotomy. Such a dichotomy is problematic for a number of reasons. First, the victim/survivor is directly linked to identity formation; what is at focus here is how domestic workers negotiate a continuum of exploitative labour relations. This implies that the interviewed domestic workers' identity formations go beyond these labour relations although, at particular moments in time, identity formations that connote to that of a victim or a survivor may be very strong. From this it follows that, in accordance with Kelly, Burton and Regan (1996), I perceive the victim/survivor dichotomy to be too crude to capture nuances and complexities, and, more importantly, it prevents us from understanding how 'coping strategies connect directly to individual survival' (Kelly, Burton and Regan 1996: 93). In other words, it prevents us from seeing the labour involved when learning to cope. In this respect, I here suggest that learning to cope makes a learning contribution to theories of resistance.

Learning external spatial relations

This section is inspired by Tamale's (2020) decolonial research into legal studies which has pointed out how legal relations should be understood and researched within their historical contexts. In particular, Tamale points to the necessity of interrogating the divide between (colonial) legal text and customary practice for the production of social order.[6] In this section, I focus on the learning processes involved when domestic workers try to make sense of the contracts they are offered – or not offered – by their employers. Previous research has identified several complexities in relation to contracts – in particular, formal and informal work conditions which are often blurred (Breman 1996; Chen 2007; Hammer 2019; Steiler 2021), differences and hierarchies originating from gender or ethnicity and cast between workers (Breman 1996; ILO 2013a; Kabeer 2008; Mies 1986) and how these processes are further complicated when intersected with migration (Steiler 2021: 112). Moreover, *how* workers are labouring informally is further complicated, for example, if they are included in national labour regulations but are exposed to informality in their everyday work in practice or if they are only partly or not covered at all by labour regulations – domestic workers being a particularly contested group in these debates (ILO 2013b: 29). In Tanzania, 95.7 per cent of workers from poor households and 84.3 per cent of workers from non-poor households are in informal employment (Bonnet, Vanek and Chen 2019). The number of domestic workers is calculated to be close to two million nationwide, with many labouring under informal conditions (ILO 2016, cited in Steiler 2021: 115). In contemporary Tanzanian labour legislation, contracts between domestic workers and employers must be in writing but may include oral sections (ILO 2016: 17).[7] The age at which someone may start working in Tanzania (excluding Zanzibar) is fourteen years, provided that special conditions are met, such as the work not being physically heavy and not hindering the young person's development. If the work includes training with the employer, then young people are also allowed to perform heavy work (ILO 2016: 62–3).

Coping with informality

From a learning perspective, a contract represents a formalized instruction of how to organize work and work relations. Moreover, it is an instruction which has the potential to prevent informal labour in the domestic work sector. Against this backdrop and from a perspective of learning, it is pertinent to ask what the meaning of a written contract is in practice. In this section of the chapter I also interrogate learning processes are articulated either when domestic workers navigate contracts or when they are not offered contracts.

In many respects, the domestic workers I interviewed belong to an elite stratum of domestic workers in Tanzania. They are all working for expatriate employers and their salaries are nearly ten times higher than a live-in Tanzanian domestic worker earning a low or middle income for a Tanzanian employer. The absence of contracts was a recurring theme in the interviews with domestic workers – instead, various oral agreements were common. Many reported that they had written contracts with their previous employers. In a group interview, experiences of how a domestic worker had been made unemployed after asking for a contract were shared. During the same group interview, another domestic worker recalled how her salary was lowered after she asked for a contract. These examples reveal how domestic workers learn to cope with informality by no longer asking for contracts to keep their employment. Importantly, knowing when to ask for a contract – in other words, choosing the right moment when the employer is in a good mood or vulnerable and in need of the domestic worker's service – as well as knowing when to stop asking for one was carefully reflected upon by the domestic workers. In this respect, learning to cope highlights the labour involved when negotiating an oppressive work context that is intensified by informality, both in terms of the content of labour and the workplace. This is especially true in private households, which are characterized by the lack of possibilities to scrutinize whether and how labour regulations are followed.

The informality of domestic work is described in colonial documents and indicates that the informality of contemporary domestic work is neither new nor arbitrary. In my reading of colonial labour-regulating documents, I find that domestic workers, together with seafarers and agricultural workers, are exempt from the requirement of a written contract (The Labour Department 1945). This lack of regulation was also found in the section on the apprenticeship system, where the age rules for labour are repealed if the parent, guardian or employer can provide the apprentice with food, clothes and housing (Labour department, 1945, Apprenticeship Ordinance No. 6). While these findings point to similarities in processes of informality between the colonial and the contemporary era, it is important to underline how this informality has been transformed. The next section looks at how contemporary domestic workers negotiate the informality of domestic work in text and in practice.

Learning and unlearning 'fake contracts'

There were also situations whereby domestic workers *were* offered contracts but only once the employers had manipulated the text to suit their needs. The next section looks deeper into the learning processes involved when domestic workers negotiate what they call 'fake contracts'.

Alice has been a domestic worker for twelve years. She is a single mother of two children, both living at home. She finished secondary school and worked in a restaurant as a cook before she became a domestic worker.

> embassy they have contracts, it is modified for Tanzania. In this contract it is stipulated what we're supposed to do, what we're supposed to give. Even the loans we have are in the contract. Insurance, if you get sick, to get care, you have in the contract. So, some bosses they take that contract, they start to type a new one to try to remove what they don't like themselves. Like, 'Okay, I don't want to give her insurance, maybe "pay for hospital" I take out. I don't want to give her a loan, I take out'. You see? That is fake contract. So, there are some [domestic workers: my comment] they don't understand there is fake and . . . the real contract. Some they know, some they don't know. So, I know, a friend came to me, she got a contract, my friend got a contract, she was happy, 'Oh, Alice I got a contract'. I was, like, 'Let me see'. Then I told her, 'This is not real a contract. This is a fake contract. Don't sign'.

In this quotation, we can see how several learning processes are at work. For Alice and her friend, literacy is important both in terms of its immediate meaning – being able to read – and being able to read the contract in English. Literacy is also important in the Freirean meaning – being able to identify the work relations, hierarchies and power relations that are made possible through the contract. In line with this argument, Alice recalls that many of her friends employed as domestic workers are unsure of their contracts' legal status as these were often written in English or in the language of origin of the employer. Alice explains to me that she currently does not have a contract despite having asked for one several times; eventually she stopped asking. There are also situations which lean more towards processes of unlearning, as indicated by Alice. When domestic workers refuse to sign fake contracts, they make use of their literacy of reading 'the world through the word' – in this context, reading what is *not* stipulated in the contract. Using this knowledge, the domestic workers unlearn the subject position they were assigned to by the 'fake contract'.

Returning to the quotation again, 'fake contracts' can be understood as processes whereby the expatriate employers use 'literacy privilege' (see Švelch and Sherman 2018) to construct and reproduce class differentiation and hierarchy. This is further underlined by the fact that most middle-income or poor households in Tanzania would be less likely to offer a contract at all (Steiler 2021). The concept of 'literacy privilege' shows that the meaning of literacy goes beyond being able to read but is, instead, closer to Freire's (1998) understanding of literacy as learning the world through the word. At a different analytical level, the learning processes that emerge from negotiating a 'fake contract' point to various processes of performance. An interesting example, which also shows how fake documents require and produce particular forms of performance, can be found in research into a migration journey. Taking as an example his own migration journey to Sweden, Khosravi (2007: 330) indicates how 'border-crossing is, after all, a matter of performance'. Instructions from smugglers on how to navigate border controls and fake passports as well as how migrants adjust their bodies and body language to arrive safely represent different and diverse forms of 'border-crossing performance'. I here suggest an additional layer of interpretation of 'border-crossing performance', namely that it can be understood as a learning process that produces naturalized conceptions of race and racialized positionalities – so-called racial performativity (Inda 2000: 88). Importantly, racial performativity refers to naturalized conceptions of bodies as well as social positions. These socially constructed processes can produce both privilege and disadvantage; in addition, as I argue in this chapter, racial performativity is a learning process which can be unlearned.

> racial performativity is not a single act of bodily constitution, but a reiterative practice through which discourse brings about the effect that it names. It is only through the force of reiteration that the racialised body acquires a naturalised effect. And it is only through such reiterations that this naturalised effect is maintained. (Inda 2000: 88)

In the context of the research presented here, the focus is on *the act of reiteration and what it produces.* I here suggest that the 'fake contracts' that some expatriate employers offer to domestic workers can be understood as a text/discourse that reiterates the racial grammar that we could see in colonial texts which exempted domestic work from regulation. The outcome of this reiteration is a continuum of exploitative labour relations which produces particular subject positions. In his research, Khosravi (2007) emphasizes on how 'border-crossing performance' can be negotiated and resisted, as when he refuses to show his passport. The contribution from the research presented here shows how racial performativity – in addition to being a reiterative act – is a learning process which is coped with and, at times, unlearned: '"Let me see". Then I told her, "This is not a real contract. This is a fake contract. Don't sign"'. From this perspective, the results presented here make a contribution to theorizing how racial performativity is a learning process which can be negotiated and/or unlearned. In the context of the research presented here, unlearning racial performativity means resisting the labour exploitation produced by informal labour arrangements. Let us now turn to the second external spatial practice in this chapter – built space.

Built-in instructions of cheapening

The literature on contemporary global work relations shows that the location and design of dormitories where workers live and sleep are central for re-constituting labour relations (Burawoy 1985; Pun and Smith 2007) and that contemporary housing arrangements often recall colonial arrangements – barracks arranged in lines mirroring colonial plantations (Iskander 2021; Mezzandri 2020). Figure 5.1 shows the servants' quarters in a contemporary Nairobi compound. In 2019, I visited one of the rooms.

Despite being newly redecorated, the room was dark, and there was a distinct smell of mould in the room. It was approximately 4m^2. The entrance and window face the larger building where the employers live in their two- to four-bedroom apartments. There are three toilets and one shower at the end of the row to be shared between fourteen rooms. At the time, some of the rooms were being used as an extra storage area for the apartments, with about half of them then in use as servants' quarters for live-in domestic workers. From this image, it becomes clear how close the servants' quarters are to the main building and yet they are

Figure 5.1 Servants' quarters, Nairobi, Kenya, 2019. Photo Mårten Wallendahl.

separated and located at basement level, out of sight of the household members. This design, the location of the servants' quarters, and the separate toilets and entrances all mirror the hierarchy and segregation between domestic workers and employers (see also Ozyegin 2001 for similar examples from Turkey).[8]

The servants' quarters I visited and the ones that was described to me by domestic workers in Dar es Salaam in 2017 and 2018 varied a great deal – from being largely unfurnished with only a mattress on the floor to being fully furnished with a bed, bedside table and wardrobe. Usually, kitchen and bathroom facilities were shared among the staff. Staff facilities such as a cooking area and toilets were located next to the servants' quarters or in a remote part of the garden (as described at the beginning of this chapter). They had remarkably low standards as compared to those of the households, some examples of which were leaking toilets, leaking windows making the rooms flooded during the rainy season and walls covered with mould. While these problems could occur in the households, the difference was that members of the household could negotiate with the landlord to get these problems solved, while the domestic workers had to negotiate with their employers.

Ferro (2018) interrogates what the practice of design means for creating and maintaining labour hierarchies – in particular, the labour exploitation of construction workers. For him, design – as a representation of the separation and hierarchy of labour – is a main way of performing labour oppression as it is highly abstract; in other words, the actual drawing of the design takes place away from the construction site and, as such, it hides the labour and the various forms of labour exploitation that precede the built environment. Moreover, Figure 5.1 shows how the process of separation and the hiding of labour and labouring conditions that Ferro argued were constitutive of labour exploitation on the construction site is literally built into the bricks and walls of the servants' quarters. From this viewpoint, the design of servants' quarters and their proximity to the main house while being out of sight resonates with the organization of how domestic work is supposed to be done – that is without being seen.

The built environment of servants' quarters and the demand for the occupants to remain invisible, yet available (Figure 5.1), is remarkably similar to that in the colonial era (see Figure 5.2). Another important similarity between historical and contemporary servants' quarters is that these built spaces were and still are frequently used as storage rooms. In Figure 5.1, the rooms that were not occupied by domestic workers, guards or gardeners were used as storage rooms. We ourselves used the tiny, dusty room for storage in the house we rented. Finally, oral history reveals how the labourers' quarters in Trianon were also used as storage rooms when they were not used by labourers. I here suggest that these examples reveal how relations of cheapening are literally built into the servants' quarters and workplaces of domestic workers. In addition, there are important differences in how space is supposed to be managed in contemporary households compared to in historical expatriate households. The contemporary housing and labour conditions do not resonate well with an imaginary of a modern and emancipated household. One possible way of interpreting the instruction transmitted through the built space of servants' quarters in contemporary households is that it transmits the instruction of ignoring (through hiding) the continuing cheapening of domestic work and workers. When I visited the households of expatriates, the pool area, living room or outdoor veranda were highlighted as preferred spaces in their everyday lives and these areas were also shown to me if I conducted the interview in their households. Moreover, little attention was given to servants' quarters which were often pointed out but not described in detail: Oh, that building, that is only the servants quarters, it is their area, I never go inside was

Figure 5.2 The Old Labourers' Quarters of Trianon in 2009. *Source*: Aapravasi Ghat Trust Fund.

a frequent comment. When I asked more questions about the living conditions, comments like Oh, you don't want to go inside there were frequent.

The barracks in Figure 5.2 show Indian indentured labourers quarters in Trianon Sugar Estate, Mauritius, and date back to the 1870s. Oral history reveals how some of these barracks were also used as storage rooms (https://aapravasi.govmu.org/aapravasi/wp-content/uploads/2020/09/Trianon-1.pdf). These barracks served as workers' quarters until the 1960s.

Coping with built-in instructions of cheapening

The majority of the domestic workers I interviewed were day workers, although a majority had previous experience of live-in domestic workers. It is reasonable to believe that access to water, toilets, showers and electricity should have improved the living conditions in the servants' quarters. However, interviews with domestic workers reveal that there is no correlation between contemporary technical modernity[9] and the standard of living in most servants' quarters. The following quotation from Fatuma is just one example. Fatuma has more than thirty years' experience of domestic work. She is one of two domestic workers whom I interviewed who were currently working as live-in domestic workers for an expatriate family.[10] She also has work experience of a day worker and live-in worker for various expatriate and local families. In the following quotation, Fatuma describes her living conditions as a live-in domestic worker. It is a small room in a house at the back of the garden. She shares the toilet and shower with the *Askari* (guards).

> The room is very small and it is very, very hot. Too hot. First, she didn't give me a bed but, instead, something from a ship; it is not a bed. It is not nice, it is very bad, made from '*mbao*' (wood). [. . .] *Mbao*, a thing you can use under your fridge. [. . .] My daughter came to see me. She cried when she saw how I lived. She brought me a proper bed that I use now.

During this part of the interview, I was not sure that I understood exactly what kind of bed Fatuma was describing. As the interview continued, we agreed that she would ask her daughter to send me an email with a picture of the 'bed'. However, this soon became unnecessary. When we left the interview site – which was an outdoor cafeteria – Fatuma took my hand and led me to the garbage area just outside the cafeteria. She pointed to a wooden trolley commonly used to store crops on that was lying on the pavement: 'This is what I was given to sleep on' she explained to me. Fatuma's description of the poor housing she was offered stands in stark contrast to the comfortable and sometimes luxurious interior design of expatriate villas (as described in Chapter 3).

The quotation from Fatuma also reveals how she, with her daughter's help, negotiated the built space by putting a proper bed and personal belongings into her room – in other words, she is learning to cope with inhuman treatment and to reconstitute her dignity. In her research in Taiwan, Lan (2006) highlighted similar processes at work when domestic workers hung towels or sheets on the furniture in a bid to carve out a personal space in the household where they sleep.

Despite the efforts to separate them through built space, the proximity of servants' quarters to the main houses and the nature of domestic work which allowed and required domestic workers to dwell in the main house and in the expatriates' lives indicate how domestic workers frequently transgress these visible and invisible boundaries, creating tension (see also Cock 1984). In the research presented here and from the domestic workers' perspective, the tensions evolved around employers demanding almost unlimited access to their work. Fatuma explains how she is made to work almost around the clock:

> I work from early in the morning to very late, in the house, until 11 pm; sometimes when I go to my room for a rest in the afternoon, the child finds me, comes to me 'Ooooh no! Come ! Come!' (*Fatuma imitates a child and shows me how a child shakes her arm while she is sleeping. She explains to me that she still likes to work with children, she still likes him.*)

This interview quote from Fatuma shows how a lack of respect for her space and working hours is at the core of the process of cheapening her labour. From the perspective of social reproduction theory (see Chapter 3), the perceived differentiation between labour and non-labour is at the heart of practices of differentiation and exploitation (Bhattacharyya 2018: 42). In other words, domestic work that takes place in households is not seen as labour or seen only as very unskilled labour and, from this, follows processes of cheapening. In the situation recalled by Fatuma, the lack of respect for her working hours and her space, which represents a further lack of respect for her labour, makes her work even when she has gone to sleep. This resonates with previous research from Anderson (2002: 107): 'It is a question not simply of long hours but of permanent availability.' In the previous quotation we see how Fatuma copes with this situation by emphasizing her close relationship with the children in the family, something which is underlined in ambiguous ways in other interviews with domestic workers and in the research literature[11] (Anderson 2002; Cheever 2002). Central to Fatuma's way of coping with harsh working conditions is to make an emotional bond with the children in the family. Research into emotional labour (Hochschild 2000; Lan 2006), which is at the heart of most labour in the service sector and which is magnified for live-in domestic workers, has shown that this labour is particularly demanding and delicate. The following section digs deeper into the complexities of emotional labour: what it represents and how domestic workers learn to cope with it.

Learning internal spatial relations

This section of the chapter elaborates on how domestic workers negotiate processes of cheapening transmitted through internal spatial practices. I do this, first, by looking more closely into how domestic workers have unlearned the meaning of a particular relation of debt and dependency, resulting from loans that they have taken from their employers and continuities and changes from the system of indenture established during the colonial era. Secondly, I do so by examining how domestic workers negotiate employers' skills practices. Skills practices is an umbrella term which covers the politics of skills – for example, the distinction between the skilled and the unskilled worker in text – and how it is transmitted in practice, through the organization of labour and the value ascribed to labourers, for example (Iskander 2021). Here, skills practices are analysed through negotiations over diplomas, the learning situations when domestic workers enter new workplaces and the learning of emotional labour in everyday domestic work.

Loans – help or debt?

In the contemporary instruction books for expatriate families newly arrived in Dar es Salaam that I have examined, there is a section on loans in the chapter on domestic workers. Included here are instructions on how future employers should prepare to handle loans that they are expected to give to their employees. For example, the employer should think in advance about how much they may be willing to lend and the terms of repayment (Corona Tanzania 2009–15):

> Another important item to state is the policy on loans you wish to follow. If you will allow loans then you may want to clarify what the limits are that you will put on these loans. It is most likely that, at some point, you WILL be asked for a loan by your staff. (*Yearbooks: The Newcomers' Guide to Dar es Salaam* 2014/2015: 56)

All the domestic workers I interviewed were either in debt or had been in debt to their current or former employers. This is because the salary they are offered is not enough to survive on and even less to support a family. The loans are often informal; and the domestic worker is expected to pay off her debt by having a sum deducted from her salary each month until the loan has been repaid. Alice describes the importance of loans to me:

> **Alice**: Like, some bosses they are fine when you ask them about a loan because salary is normal but it doesn't cover everything. Like, I want to pay bill for my house rent, all bills, pay school fees for kids, make sure I'm eating, transportation, come and go home, hospital when I get sick, so, all that

stuff is not enough. So, you need to get sometimes loan, what can push you maybe to pay school fees and rent, then you can continue to work, you get some money, salary what you're getting they can cut slowly, slowly. You can do another stuff. But some boss they don't do that. They don't like it.

Paula: No, do you understand why they don't like it?

Alice: I don't know.

Paula: No? Maybe they don't want you to be, like, dependent on them.

Alice: I think so but, you need to think I'm working for you, like I'm working for only you. It's permanent. I don't have time or any place where I can get more money.

Alice also explained to me how she was unable to get a loan from a bank as she did not have a contract and was working informally. Consequently, getting a loan from her employer was pivotal for managing her everyday life. How can we understand the meaning of debt and dependency created by loans from the perspective of domestic workers? Ferguson's (2013) philosophical argument makes a contribution here. While the context of his example is different to the research context presented here, his elaboration of dependency in work relations is worth outlining at length. His example refers to the dependency that day workers in South Africa – who are getting very little payment for their work – articulate vis-à-vis potential employers. In this context, Ferguson (2013) explains the necessity of theorizing debt and dependency from the perspective of the Global South and shows how dependency needs to be theorized beyond the liberal and individualistic perspective most often applied in the Global North (for a critique of independence and male breadwinner ideals, see also Lutz 2017). Taking as his example the continuity and change in dependency relations from the colonial period to contemporary Southern Africa, he highlights the tradition of being part of social networks as a main constituency of personhood. In the context of contemporary global capitalism, which has rendered unemployed large segments of the population in Southern Africa, the workers' problem is not that they are subjected to labour exploitation but that they have become unworthy of subjection: 'To be dependent on someone is to be able to make at least some limited claims on him or her' (Ferguson 2013: 231). In other words, from the preferred subject position of a poor person being involved in dependency networks with other poor people, the alternative is not independence or autonomy but, instead, dependence on other actors with greater resources. From this perspective, Alice's perception of loans, debt and dependency on her employer as something to which she is entitled implies 'a pluralisation of truths' (Biesta 2017) of the various ways in which debt and dependency can function in practice (to secure livelihoods) and a practical critique of cheapening through debt and dependency – hence, unlearning. At a more aggregated and conceptual level, the result points to the importance of decolonizing Western and individualized understandings of dependency. The majority of domestic workers whom I interviewed negotiated loans, debts and dependency in similar ways to Alice; taking a loan from their employers was desirable and sometimes articulated as a demand, a right they considered they had. When asked what the domestic workers would do with their loan in a situation whereby they would be in conflict with their employer, a frequent answer was that they would try to pay back the loan but, if the situation became unbearable, they would simply leave. However, as Ferguson (2013) points out, what remains a challenge is not only to stop idealizing independence but to find ways in which dependency relations valorise subjects beyond labour and capital. Importantly, reworking debt and dependency at an individual level does not necessarily imply that change will take place at more aggregated levels. Thus, the analysis of learning and unlearning debt and dependency outlined here highlights the importance of analysing change as a multilayered and complex phenomenon that may or may not occur at different analytical levels.

Continuities and changes in relations of debt and dependency

Historical forms of organizing labour around debt and dependency can be found under the umbrella of indentured labour, which was applied in various parts of the world and grew in parallel to the abolition of the slave trade – which differed in various parts of the world.[12] Indentured labour was used in colonial Kenya in the early years of the twentieth century when Indian workers were brought in to build the railway to Uganda. Forms of such labour were also seen in the sisal plantations of Tanzania in the twentieth century (Mbilinyi 2023). Taking the example of indentured labour in Mauritius, large populations of Indian workers were brought in, sometimes by force, to labour on sugar plantations under the British colonial administration. The workers were 'free' because there was an employment contract but, in reality, few workers knew what they had signed and the contracts were designed to benefit the employers. The workers often got into debt through the cost of the travel to the plantation (sometimes involuntary) and the price of food and housing. Female contract workers were very few and they were mainly expected to take care of the workers' households or to work for free in the plantation owners' households (Allen 2008; Carter 2012). During the pearl-industry boom which took place along the coastal line of the Gulf area from the beginning of the twentieth century through to the Second World War, free and unfree work conditions were blurred and co-existed. So-called oriental pearls were harvested along the Gulf coast by divers who worked under a continuum of labour arrangements – enslaved men, men in debt bondage and free men whose wages were paid out as a loan (Iskander 2021: 36).

While the research presented here suggests that the practice of loans and the indebtedness of workers to their employers has not disappeared from the cultural norms of the expatriate community in Dar es Salaam, there are important differences. First, the loans and indebtedness during the colonial era of indenture were constructed and driven by the state, instead of, as revealed by the research presented here, by private actors. Moreover, the interviewed domestic workers felt that they could leave if they found the work conditions unbearable. In addition, how domestic workers unlearned a position of dependency and instead viewed a loan as something they were entitled to since the salaries they were given were too low. From this it follows that the organization, magnitude and intensity of labour exploitation produced through the system of indenture during the colonial era is not identical to the research presented here. However, the particular class position resulting from taking a loan from an employer and the relations of debt and dependency that work retrospectively to discipline the domestic workers share similarities with the colonial system of indenture (see also LeBaron 2014, for theorizing debt as a class relation and LeBaron and Ayers (2013) for the importance of historicizing debt.

Unlearning the selective (de)valuation of diplomas

During a group interview with domestic workers, I met Maria, a woman in her fifties who has worked as a domestic worker for thirty years. She is a widow and the mother of one daughter. She is also a caretaker of children from her extended family and, for this reason, she has a second profession which gives her an additional income. She recounts a personal experience which centres on diplomas. The experience is here outlined at length as it shows how domestic workers are successfully negotiating employers' skills practices.

> So, there are some . . . employers who don't want professionals. So, when you show them 'I'm a professional' they are not happy with you. But there's some people, they ask you if you are a professional, where your certificate is, then when you show them, they are happy, then they give you higher salary. That's what they do.
>
> I was telling them an example: an Expatriate was asking me to find a cook for them. And then I find . . . He said, 'I really need a professional.' So, I find a professional cook, who has been working for the diplomatic . . . for the ambassadors for long time. And he was very happy. But, after a few months, their friends told them that, 'Oh, how much are you paying for your cook?' And they said, 'Yeah, we are paying this amount, we are very happy, he's very professional . . .' 'What? Professional are not good, they are asking a higher salary' [*laughs*]. 'So, you have to find someone who is not a professional, then they are working very good. They can cook very well.' So, they made them to fire the professional, and they hired someone who is not a professional. And the next . . . the second time he asked me again to find a nanny for them. And they told me, 'Don't find a professional.' (Laughs) So, this is a big challenge. You never know. But for my view, it's better to be educated, because, you never know. It's better to learn something, to know, then you will see if someone doesn't need to see if you are professional or not then you don't show them. Yeah. So, maybe there is someone who will need to see your professional certificate, then you show them. They can pay you higher salary. From my idea, and from her idea, it is better to be educated, and it is better to do the training.

From this quotation we can see that domestic workers rework – that is unlearn – the skills practice which some employers use in order to portray domestic workers as unskilled. This is done at two analytical levels: first, by acquiring a diploma in a profession that is rarely seen as labour and, when it *is* seen as labour, it is seen as unskilled labour. Secondly, by deciding when and how to reveal to their employers that they have a diploma. This is done as a response to employers' selective (de)valuation of domestic work as skilled labour. Moreover, the quotation also reveals the delicate struggle when domestic workers cope with employers who change their skills practices – 'So, this is a big challenge. You never know' – and how the outcome of coping is directly related to securing their income: 'So, they made them fire the professional and they hired someone who is not a professional.'

As outlined previously, skills practices comprise various processes such as the evaluation of written diplomas (as outlined earlier) as well as informal processes of valuing or devaluing skills. To exemplify: an informal situation of perceiving a worker as skilled can be when an employer describes the tasks that the worker should perform as complicated, difficult and in need of training. The opposite would be to describe work tasks as simple, routine with little need for training or delicacy and workers doing this type of work as unskilled. A particular complexity is when skills are constructed as embodied, hence, naturalized. As described in Chapters 1 and 3, domestic work is constructed by cultural norms that transmit the message that it is not labour and that, when domestic work is seen as labour, it should be conducted in such a way that it is not noticed. Integral to these norms is the view that racialized and gendered bodies are naturally better disposed to conducting this labour, thus reinforcing the view of domestic work as 'non-work' and sometimes even as an instinct. The following section delves deeper into how domestic workers unlearn employers' skills practices – more specifically, how domestic workers unlearn employers' expectations of them performing invisible work.

Making the invisible visible

In her research on construction workers in Qatar, Iskander (2021) interrogated skills practices in the construction sector. In her research, she found that labelling construction workers as unskilled was the main means of dehumanizing them and, in a broader perspective, making these workers easier to exploit. Central in these processes was employers neglecting to value skills that were embodied. For example, when and how workers knew when to turn their heads and look for their work colleagues and how to hold the pipes before handing these over to their work partners was rarely thought of by foremen on construction sites as knowledge – despite this knowledge being crucial for the progress of the construction and for the safety of workers (Iskander 2021). In research, we find that skills that are separated from the body are usually ascribed more value. This is true even for tacit skills that are defined by being entangled with the body. For example, a mathematician's work, which is usually described with reference to cerebral work, is valued more highly compared to construction workers' embodied skills (Iskander 2021). The following quotations from domestic workers reveal the learning practices that they articulate when they negotiate visibility and invisibility on starting to work for new families. Invisibility is central for constructing 'good domestic work' and almost all employers praised those who could perform their work while remaining invisible; at the same time, employers rarely thought of being 'invisible' as a skill that needed to be learnt. All interviewed domestic workers had the experience of regularly changing employers as, usually, expatriate employers are residing in Tanzania on their three to five-year contracts. From the perspective of the domestic workers, learning the needs of their employers was a daunting and exhausting task. Learning and managing the needs and habits of the members of the household was done on a daily basis but was intensified when domestic workers changed employers and households.

> When you have a new family, first we sit and I ask them, because I tell them how the ex-family did, how is their way they wanted me to do, then we . . . I ask them, 'How do you want me to do?' So, I'm doing, depending what they want me to do, yeah. Because everyone has different [needs: my comment]. I am always saying that there is no, there is not expert to do the housework. Because every time when you have a new family, you are, it's like you are starting . . . again to work. Yeah. Yeah. So, for the children, I think the children it's like the same way to take care of them. Yeah, because when they have the children and I'm to look after them, you just ask how they want you to take care of their children, what kind of food they eat, what is their schedule. Yeah, that's all. And the other thing is to play, to do the activities, it's just . . . it's like the same. And, when you stay with the child, over time then you can recognise what they want. Yeah.

The foregoing interview quote, from Maria, brings to the surface the complexity of learning visibility/invisibility in private households. The first difficulty refers to how learning good domestic work – despite the cultural norms of preferred invisibility – requires visibility in terms of the knowledge transfer of general work components – for example, the care of children (in the example from Maria) or cooking (in the next example from Alice) – between workers and employers. The second complex issue refers to how domestic workers perceive that they need to negotiate this knowledge-transfer situation carefully and be careful to not exceed their status vis-à-vis the employer, as articulated by Maria: 'There is no expert in domestic work'. The third complex element refers to learning processes which extend beyond learning general work components and is related to learning the needs and desires of the employers. Alice goes further into this complexity:

> It's not easy, it's very difficult, you know? It's like you start a new job, new person, to understand each other . . . Which kind of food they like to eat, which one they don't like. Are they going to like the way I make it ? It's difficult so, I need to get time to make sure I learn how they are. [. . .] Because some boss they can say, 'Oh, you can make this food for us.' They can give you menu. In fact, they can say, 'Oh, you can make whatever what you want.' So, they give me work to think. I can make this, is she's going to like it, or not. When you make it, maybe you didn't taste, didn't eat yourself. When I come tomorrow, I find that there is a lot of food left, I was like, 'Why she didn't eat? She doesn't like it.' I start to think myself, 'Why you didn't eat when I make it?' So, I have to ask you, I used to ask. [. . .] 'Why you didn't eat maybe yesterday?' In the hotel there is no time for that. When you done work, you done. Who can ask?

In this, we can see that what is perceived as the main challenge for Alice is not related to mapping and learning the general components of domestic work but, instead, to balancing these with the employers' needs and desires – in particular, when these desires are not even spoken out loud: 'Oh you can make whatever you want'. In theories of learning (Illeris 2015) a distinction is made between assimilative learning and accommodative learning. Both types of learning are habitual in everyday life and subjects typically alternate between these forms. Assimilative learning adds to already acquired knowledge whereas accommodative learning transforms existing knowledge to accommodate new and external inputs. Generally, accommodative learning is a more challenging process than assimilative learning as, in various ways, it involves transgressive learning; particularly, it seems to be stressful to break down or abandon already acquired knowledge or practice as we do not easily abandon positions that we may have reached with great effort or, at least, that we have become used to (Illeris 2015: 65). From the learning processes articulated by Alice and Maria, we can see that these involved assimilative learning – here articulated by the desire for clear instructions on what to cook or how to clean – and accommodative learning, which implied learning the personalized and situational aspects of the family and adjusting the domestic work accordingly. Taken together, these quotations also reveal how assimilative and accumulative processes of learning are at work simultaneously in everyday domestic work and are intensified when domestic workers change families. The contribution of this analysis to research into domestic and care work is that it highlights how learning how to do domestic work in such a way that it is not noticed is a highly complex process. More specifically, it involves knowledge transfer, learning new aspects of domestic work in an assimilative manner as well as the delicate negotiation of power relations vis-à-vis the employer during these seemingly uncomplicated knowledge-transfer situations. Moreover, learning work components in an accommodative manner was a highly complicated task, in particular when the instruction was not spoken out loud.

Learning to cope with naturalization

From Alice's quote we can see how she compares the same skill of cooking, in her previous work at a hotel, with the cooking she is doing as a domestic worker in a private household. She concludes that she finds it more challenging in a private household: 'In the hotel there is not time for that. When you done work, you done. Who can ask?' What become visible through Alice's comparison is the close and sometimes even intimate relations that domestic work in a private household has, both in terms of physical closeness and also by learning the needs, likes and dislikes of various family members. The following quote looks deeper into how domestic workers negotiate the demand for emotional labour. As Alice says:

> Sometimes when I go to work, I feel stress. 'I don't know how madame will be feeling today, what she will be like today'. You find your boss, she is angry, she has stress. And you, you have stress too. And because it's your boss, you need to force, to make sure your tempo, your everything, your mood come good. it's not easy to make your mood okay. It's difficult. [. . .] I will be quiet. [. . .] I will not approach her, if she is watching a movie in her room I will not come knocking on the door and ask questions.

Central in emotional labour (Hochschild 1983) is adjusting emotions according to the demands from the organization or customer and being invisible. In this way, learning emotional labour is, in many ways, contrary to the understanding of learning specific qualifications which depart from the knowledge that learning specific skills is separate from the body.[13] From the examples outlined here, we can conclude that emotional labour, which is at the core of domestic work and performing domestic work in a preferred way, 'is supposed to be done without being noticed'; it is also at the core of processes of naturalization articulated earlier by Alice: 'You need to force, to make sure your tempo, your everything, your mood come good.' Importantly emotional labour is also that which, in important ways, distinguishes domestic work from the example of construction work outlined previously, or from more instrumental aspects of domestic work in a private households – such as knowing which cleaning product to use for the bathroom or dishwashing. The emphasis on the emotional labour necessary for performing 'good domestic' work in private households indicates the labour involved when domestic workers learn to cope with and, when possible, unlearn processes of cheapening in their everyday. In this respect and more specifically by analysing the labour involved in learning to cope with naturalization, the research presented here makes a contribution to resistance studies. This is further underlined when considering the context of this research; insecure working conditions where domestic workers without contracts could lose their job on the spot because they cooked food 'the wrong way', a particularly delicate task since the domestic workers often were unfamiliar with the dishes they were assigned to cook and did not know how these dishes were supposed to taste 'maybe you didn't taste, didn't eat your self', or because they did not get the blessing of the children they are assigned to look after.

Conclusion

This chapter has analysed how domestic workers learn, learn to cope and unlearn processes of cheapening. The results have been presented along the analytical distinctions of internal and external relations that constitute the workplace and the work process and continuities and changes. The results reveal the labour involved when domestic workers learn to labour under the endless pressure of a normalized racial and colonial grammar. Through the lens of place-making, the results demonstrate how relations of the cheapening of domestic labour are literally incorporated into the built space of their workplaces and in the variations in contracts. The analysis of place-making reveals how domestic work is being constructed through a continuum of informality which takes different shapes over time. In this vein, the relations of debt and dependency that contemporary domestic workers experience are not identical to those produced under the system of indenture. There are, nevertheless, similarities in the class position and disciplining functioning that taking loans from an employer produces. The chapter makes a learning contribution to theories of racial performativity by highlighting how processes of citation are learnt and how they can be unlearned.

By analysing how domestic workers learn to cope with harsh working conditions, this chapter produces an empirically informed theoretical contribution to theories of resistance. In other words, the nuances and complexities of learning how to cope with the built space, with expatriate employers' selective (de)valuation of labour or with processes of naturalization all stress the agency and labour involved in coping. In this respect, these results make a contribution to theorizing a political economy of survival in the everyday from the standpoint of domestic workers in expatriate households.

6

Can the oppressor be oppressed?

The concrete fences enclosing the school area are high, painted white and covered with drawings in bright colours. The cheerfulness of the drawings stands in stark contrast to the electrified barbed wire on the top of the fences. By coincidence, we meet at the car park as we are about to pick up our children from school.

- *I got an invitation to a reception with the diplomatic spouses' group.*[1]
- *Aaa, you mean the nail polish group?*

  '... and we should not forget partners and families supporting our work here at the embassy. Here is a toast for them'.

These field notes from my diary are chosen as an introduction to this chapter as they exemplify the dissonance between, on the one hand, formal discourses of appreciation of domestic and care work, as articulated in a speech by an ambassador at an embassy reception in Dar es Salaam, and the everyday, on the other hand – as articulated through the labelling 'the nail polish group', which suggests that the group members only care about their physical appearance. At the centre of dissonance is the hierarchy between those who are producing remunerated labour and those producing non-remunerated labour and the related processes of valorization. From this it follows that the variegated relations of production under scrutiny in this chapter refer to those of privileged expatriate women's unpaid care and domestic work, indicating their dual and complex position of privilege and subordination. The description of the walls enclosing the school area is chosen as it highlights one of many built and discursive barriers that are present in expatriate lives. There are, for example, electrified walls around most private houses, shopping centres, recreation areas and so on. In addition, the discursive boundaries are perhaps even more prominent when compared to the built walls – relating, for example, to visa requirements, citizenship and work permits. Here, expatriate women's residence is often covered by their husband's visa, which produces a situation of graded citizenship – making it difficult, for example, for them to get a work permit, open a bank account or set up a phone account. The immediate message from built and discursive boundaries is processes of dividing at a secondary level – boundaries simultaneously separate and connect those inside from those outside, pointing to the liminality of boundaries. In this respect, boundaries are important sites for interrogating processes of learning the complex and sometimes contradictory relations of privilege and disadvantage that are involved in learning domestic and care work and for transgressing these boundaries. This does not mean that boundaries are easily subverted or even unlearned for that matter. Taking the standpoint of privileged expatriate women, the aim of this chapter is to analyse how intersecting circles of inclusion and exclusion, privilege and subordination shape the contours of how expatriate women learn, cope with and at times unlearn domestic work in the everyday. Moreover, an important part of the aim of this chapter is also to analyse the continuities and changes since the British colonial era.

The chapter is structured as follows. First, I provide a note on the analytical lens in this chapter. This involves introducing the theoretical argument for analysing oppression and privilege as processes of learning. Secondly, the empirical sections are presented in four steps: the re-enrolment of class and the colonial state through the professionalization of domestic work; ambivalent processes of learning gender; learning who are unable to learn; and learning to cope with being an oppressor and an exploiter. Finally, the concluding remarks are presented.

The analytical lens

The title of this chapter is inspired by Paul Gilroy's critique of the idea that victims of racism cannot be racist and, moreover, how this view often slides into 'the proposition that only white people could be racist became confused with the different notion that black people could not be racist' (Gilroy 2000: 220). Of bearing for this chapter is Gilroy's insistence on analysing the complexities and nuances of what racism produces, rather than departing from the idea of race and analysing what race produces (2000: 219). When this theoretical argument is applied to the research presented here, it demonstrates the necessity of interrogating what interlinked systems of oppression – such as racism, sexism and capitalism (in all their plural, complex and variegated dimensions) – produce in the context of expatriate households in Dar es Salaam, rather than deciding beforehand who can be victims of oppression and who can become the oppressors.

The learning processes of non-remunerated labour analysed in this chapter are shaped by processes of migration, graded citizenship, gender power dynamics in expatriate households and, from a broader perspective, the regulations and cultures of international diplomacy and international business. In other words, the learning processes that are under scrutiny here depart from how expatriate women learn everyday domestic work but do not end there (see also Enloe 2014; Mies 2010; Smith 2005 for similar approaches to theorizing the everyday). Here, the analysis of learning domestic and care work involves examining pedagogies and their content – in other words, the ways in which educational relations are practised and what they produce. This involves analysing formal and informal instructions and using different types of data[2] on how to perform domestic work in the way preferred by the employer. Moreover, the shape of these instructions, the content and what these pedagogical practices produce are also analysed. Finally, I interrogate the messy and often contradictory process of negotiating and occasionally transgressing established ways of learning domestic work. As described previously in this book (see Chapters 3 and 4), unlearning means doing, thinking and seeing in slightly different ways and, as such, transgressing established orders. Closely related to unlearning is coping with these established orders; in this volume, I therefore also argue for a more nuanced understanding of coping which goes beyond an understanding of it as merely a passive act of preserving a situation of oppression. Instead, as elaborated on in Chapter 5, when coping takes place under oppressive conditions it involves labouring (see also Kelly, Burton and Regan 1996).[3] Therefore, I here suggest that learning to cope can be understood as a process of learning resistance.

Colonialism and housewifization

As we could see in the introduction chapter under the heading variegated social reproduction, reproductive work is unevenly and hierarchically produced.

This means that reproductive work is not produced in identical ways across the globe. This merits attention to different – yet connected histories – of colonialism which has evolved differently in different parts of the world. Moreover, the nuances, hierarchies and complexities within different societies and households change over time. In these processes, Bhattacharyya (2018) pinpoints how social reproductive labour, which involves the maintenance and reproduction of life and the means of life, becomes a distinguishing factor based on racialized differences. It is for this reason that this book refers to social reproduction as Life's Work (Mitchell, Marston and Katz 2004) as it captures various forms of labour which extends beyond wage labour. Here, Maria Mies' (1986) theory on the connection between patriarchy, capitalism and colonialism merits our attention. In particular, Mies' understanding of the importance of non-wage labour for the development of capitalism:

> In contrast to Marx, I consider the capitalist production process as one which comprise both: the superexploitation of non-wage labourers (women, colonies, peasants) upon which wage labour exploitation then is possible. I define their exploitation as superexploitation because it is not based on the appropriation (by the capitalist) of the time and labour over and above the 'necessary' labour time, the surplus labour, but of the time and labour *necessary* for people's own survival or subsistence production. (Mies 1986: 48, Italics in original)

In the context of this chapter, it is important to consider how processes of exploitation are interlinked. More specifically, Mies points at how colonial demand for profit coexists with processes of 'housewifization' (the expectation for women to perform unpaid domestic labour). It is through these parallel processes that non-wage labour is utilized for accumulation:

> [. . .] housewifization means the externalization, or ex-territorialization of costs which otherwise would have to be covered by capitalists. This means women's labour is considered a natural resource, freely available, like air and water. (Mies 1986: 110)

This quotation is highlighted here as it points to the importance of analysing unwaged work or very poorly paid work for understanding exploitation (see also Chapter 3 in this volume and Mezzadri 2020) . As this chapter will show, these are not straightforward processes but instead full of complexities and ambivalences. Before we delve into the empirical sections, let us have a look at the role and functioning which expatriate women in diplomatic circles and in multinational business corporations – the so-called trailing-spouses – have had historically and, to some extent, still have today.

From marriage diplomacy to the incorporated wife

The role of woman in a successful expatriation is well documented in research (Davoine et al. 2013; McCarthy 2014). While a successful expatriation can be conceptualized from various perspectives, a dominant understanding is that it means being able to 'remain in the assignment to the end of the term, adjust to living conditions in the host country and perform well professionally' (Aycan and Kanungo 1997: 251). In this context, the role of diplomatic spouses has received particular attention. The reason for this is twofold and refers to the nature of diplomatic work as well as to the particular conditions which diplomatic spouses have faced historically and still, to some extent, face today. On the one hand, international diplomacy can be conceptualized as craftsmanship conducted by representatives of states who act according to state interests. On the other hand, networking and social gatherings play an important part and are considered by some as a defining feature of diplomatic relations. As Lord Palmerston, prime minister of Britain in the nineteenth century, once declared, 'Dining is the soul of diplomacy!' (quoted from Domett 2005: 291). In this context, diplomatic spouses become important actors as they often hosted and still do host these events – being in charge of the location of events, the private household or the residence where private and public spheres merge (Domett 2005: 291). Before the formation of modern states in Europe, diplomatic spouses played an important role in foreign affairs through so-called marriage diplomacy. During this period, marriage was a way of consolidating political power that would ensure the continuity of empires. The importance of marriage diplomacy declined in Europe as the modern state emerged, and the professionalization of a diplomatic corps began, although many were still recruited from the aristocracy (McCarthy 2014). Despite these changes, marriage remained central in diplomatic circles through representations of the embassy as a 'family'. Here, junior bachelors resided at the residence, and ambassadors and their spouses were supposed to take a parental interest in these young men. In those days, the main obligations of the diplomatic spouse were to offer domesticity and hospitality to this 'official family'. From this perspective, it is worth noting that hospitality and domesticity are also key components of Western bourgeois femininity (Wood 2005). During the early nineteenth century, marriage took on a new role compared to the earlier era of 'marriage diplomacy' and, instead, became a means by which to strengthen embassies abroad – and households were part of the colonial administration. In these households, the role of expatriate women was to contribute to the empire by protecting racial hierarchies in the household and by giving birth to white children (Hall 2007).

Feminist sociologists have labelled the role played by wives in organizations and career-building as processes of 'incorporation' (Finch 1983). From this perspective, women are incorporated into their husband's career through their unpaid domestic labour. In the context of foreign services, Callan and Ardner's seminal text from 1984 discusses how the 'incorporated wife' provided the foreign services with valuable sources of free labour. The position of a spouse is that she is offered political protection at a posting as the dependant of the posted officer. This means receiving an allowance for furnishing the house and for purchasing evening dresses (!) (Black 1995: 197). From this followed a duty to entertain and be entertained – whatever their individual opinions or preferences might be, the spouse is duty- and honour-bound to represent the embassy and ultimately the empire (Black 1995: 197). While states have taken advantage of diplomatic spouses' unpaid labour, there has been and still does not exist an official contract or job description, so the duties remain open-ended, undefined and therefore also unlimited (Callan 1975). Cynthia Enloe (2014: 184–5) has pointed out how states are limiting spouses' possibilities for employment elsewhere while simultaneously not including them on the embassy's payroll, indicating the ambiguities and paradoxes of privileged expatriate women's lives, particularly in diplomacy. When processes of migration and graded citizenship are taken into account, it is worth talking of processes of being semi-incorporated instead of being fully incorporated in the foreign service and in the host and the home community (Black 1995).

The foreign services are not acting in a social vacuum. When changes occurred in gender relations in societies during the 1960s and 1970s, women's protests also spread to foreign ministries and diplomatic set-ups; hence, diplomatic spouses began to protest against the expectation of unpaid labour (Enloe 2014). Diplomatic spouses demanded recognition of their roles and compensation for what they sacrificed while following their husbands on their missions (McCarthy 2014). This has led to political changes – for example, in Sweden, diplomatic spouses negotiated successfully for direct payment from the government for their loss of income and, in the United States, women are less likely to carry out unpaid labour in the residences (McCarthy 2014; Standfield 2020). Despite these changes, the representational functioning of diplomatic spouses persists, mainly through reproduction, giving birth to children and home-making (Yuval-Davis 1997). Against this backdrop, which has outlined the role of expatriate women in general with a particular focus on diplomatic spouses, the next section looks into the details of how contemporary expatriate women learn the division of labour in diplomatic households and in households of international business men. The former are – households that are directly produced and funded by the state.

The re-enrolment of class and the colonial state through the professionalization of domestic work

When I first arrived in Tanzania, I found a glossy pamphlet in most shops, hairdressers or cafés that I visited. This immediately caught my attention as one of the headings was '*The Newcomers' Guide to Dar es Salaam*'; moreover, it also advertised social gatherings. The sender of the pamphlet was a group called Corona Tanzania, which is 'A friendly international organisation which helps people all over the world to adapt to new countries and cultures' (cited from the pamphlet). Corona Tanzania organizes social gatherings and supports community projects, sometimes in collaboration with the diplomatic spouses' group. They also publish a yearbook. In many aspects, the yearbook can be viewed as something between a magazine – as the content revealed photos in bright colours displaying beaches and restaurants – and a handbook, as it contains detailed information on how to get by in Dar es Salaam. The contemporary handbooks analysed for this chapter devote significant space to lifestyle reports. These suggest where expatriate families could spend their weekends – such as the yacht club – their vacations – in exclusive villas along the coast of Zanzibar – or in restaurants in Dar es Salaam and even where to shop for exclusive interior designs for their houses. Moreover, they also included advice on how to get by on a daily basis – such as where to shop for daily groceries, organize childcare and find pharmacies and health clinics. In other words, how expatriate families should navigate the space. Other areas to which significant space is devoted are information about domestic workers' terms of employment, work tasks and contracts,[4] together with a detailed section on how expatriate families should manage staff who ask for loans.[5] These written accounts are directed at expatriates and explain the preferred ways of organizing public spheres of life as well as how to organize domestic work in the household.

From my interviews with privileged expatriate female employers, I could see how the racialized division of labour articulated in the glossy lifestyle magazines in many ways overlaps with how domestic work is done in everyday life. This is done through racialized distinctions of domestic work where expatriate women instruct domestic workers to perform instrumental domestic work – such as how they should clean floors or bathrooms. Expatriate women explained to me that they themselves focus on other work tasks, such as spending more time with their children and helping them with their school work, decorating the house, cooking or laundry. Doris, a woman from the West who has three small children at home, has employed an additional domestic worker so she can home-school her oldest child. 'I love home schooling! I even employed an additional nanny so we would not be disturbed'. This finding connotes with Anthias' (2001) perspective on the cultural and symbolic meanings of gender and processes of racialization and class in the production of work stratification and skills. She points out that gender and processes of racialization intersect with the division of labour, influencing how certain types of work are perceived and valued. Domestic work serves as an example, as different household tasks are assigned varying values along racialized lines. In this context, Lundström's (2013) research becomes relevant as well, highlighting how Swedish expatriate women prioritize certain tasks – such as focusing on schoolwork with their children – while transferring tasks like cleaning floors and toilets to domestic workers. This further demonstrates the racialized coding and value ascribed to the different household chores.

From the interviews with privileged expatriate women I here present another example, from Josephine, which points to the pedagogical processes involved when privileged expatriate women instruct their domestic workers. In a broader perspective, the work of instructing domestic workers influences privileged expatriate women's meaning-making, hence learning, of domestic work in their everyday. Josephine has spent five years as a trailing-spouse. She has two grown-up children and a childhood experience of growing up in an expatriate household in various non-Western countries. During our interview, she explains to me that she has learnt to do domestic work and to manage staff from her mother, for whom she expresses admiration. Here Josephine tells me how she learnt from her mother to respect staff and to value people more than things; she underlines to me that 'They are human. They are peers'. Before the description of how Josephine learnt to manage staff (from her mother), she talked about the division of labour between the domestic worker and herself as well as the relationship she has had with the various domestic workers who have worked with her over the year.

Josephine: They are now my children . . . because you develop a relationship with them. Some of them you have to be careful, to develop boundaries, because they will ask for too much and others you trust them and . . . and . . . and you literally get to the point where, well, my children are in my home country but this young person, I want her do well and I want her to succeed and, you know, her daughter is having a birthday so I give them the cake and, and [. . .].

Paula: Are you saying you are expecting less from them?

Josephine: Oh, yes ! (*emphasizes*)

Paula: Less than other people?

Josephine: Yes and yet, if they know you care about them, they will try more. They really do work harder to please you. And you know, if you are really fortunate to find the ones that are motivated, you know, some of that is cultural, some of that is individual, but if you find the people who really want to make you happy, it is like raising children. You know, they want to please you, they really want to make you happy so, even if they did not do a particularly good job, you say 'Yes! Wow! Yeay you!' It is about cultivating their sense of satisfaction, cultivating their sense of excitement. Anyway, sometimes it is really like dealing with children. I hope I do not sound patronising.

I am keen to understand what Josephine is describing to me and I want to respect her wish to not sound patronizing. For this reason, when our interview comes to an end, I return to her comparison between domestic workers and children so she will have plenty of space to elaborate and to avoid misunderstandings:

Paula: What did you mean by comparing domestic workers to your children?
Josephine: I meant that in terms of positive motivation, in terms of how you cultivate a child's willingness to take initiatives, to do things and not crush them if they make a mistake. So that was what that conversation was about.

From this long interview quotation we can see that Josephine had learnt from her mother to conceptualize domestic workers as humans and as peers. Moreover, I here suggest that the necessity to establish that domestic workers are humans points to how a colonial discourse which suggests that domestic workers may be less than human is lingering in the background. In addition, we see how the comparison of adult domestic workers (many being highly experienced as we could see from Chapter 5) with children suggests that for Josephine, it is not domestic workers' skills which need training/improvement but instead their motivation and to cultivate them. It is also clear that Josephine expects less from domestic workers than from other workers. In the context of the whole interview where Josephine frequently mentions to me how much work she devotes to train her domestic workers – not only in domestic work but in life skills – I interpret this as a discourse which connotes a colonial discourse of naturalization which implies that subaltern domestic workers are in a state of becoming cultivated and motivated, hence, preferred naturalised workers. Finally, the link between racism, mode of instruction and exploitation: 'If they know you care about them they will try more.' Taken together I here suggest that what Josephine articulates to me is that she has developed a pedagogical method for instructing the domestic workers. Core in this method is a link between domestic work, racism and paternalism in order to increase the work output of the domestic worker. This is done by learning to know the domestic worker and to create a bond of a caring parent, where the 'mother' is in control of the material and discursive boundaries of the relation. In this respect, the establishment of this pedagogical method is closely aligned with the professionalization of domestic work articulated in glossy magazines outlined earlier. The link between professionalization, racism, paternalism and exploitation is not isolated in this interview but was instead visible in various interviews with expatriate women. More specifically through the various efforts to instruct domestic workers beyond the immediate household chores. These areas included gender relations in the domestic workers' households, the education of their children as well as the planning of their household economy. In one interview, one expatriate woman spoke of giving advice on reproductive health and menstruation to the domestic worker in her household[6]. While the quotation from Josephine lies at the extreme end of racist and paternalistic discourses within the group of interviewed expatriate women, the discourse of the necessity to care for or help domestic workers was strong among the privileged expatriate women; this will be further elaborated on in the final section. In the next section, the continuities and changes in these pedagogies – that is both the content and the form of instruction – from the colonial era will be examined.

Continuities and changes in how expatriate women learn to reproduce the colonial state

In *Kilimanjaro Tales: The Saga of a Medical Family in Africa* (Latham and Latham 1995)[7] we can follow the experiences of Gwyneth Latham, who resided with her husband Donald – who worked as a medical doctor – in colonial Tanganyika during the 1920s and 1930s. Different chapters of the book are written from the perspective of Gwyneth and her son Michael. We can see how a broad range of servants were part of the expatriate household:

> At Kilosa we had no piped water so, added to our string of servants, cook, cook's boy, washerman, headboy, assistant, children's toto and gardener, we had a water carrier. He spent all his working days toiling backwards and forwards to the river, which was about half a mile away and some 50 meters below our house, carrying water in two paraffin tins lashed to each end of a pole and slung on his shoulders. (Latham and Latham 1995: 63)

This extract shows in detail how domestic work was organized and how different categories of workers performed different tasks. In important ways, this involved organizing domestic work into small units. At the top of the hierarchy was the expatriate woman who was meant to lead the work and at the bottom were those whose main skill was their body, such as the water carrier. Blackett (2019) notes how a significant element of cookbooks during the early 1900s in the United States was devoted to describing how privileged white women should instruct their domestic workers, thus creating a division of labour between the white woman and the (mostly Black) former enslaved women, in a bid to create and maintain order in the household. This resonates well with what I found in Bradley's (1948) *A Household Book for the Tropical Colonies*, which was particularly directed at women and bachelors in the British colonies. In this book, the importance of how to 'direct your staff' was underlined (1948: 12–13) and there were plenty of instructions as regards cooking, cleaning, storing food and even packing for moving to the colonies and furnishing colonial houses:

> Perhaps I should add that the amounts of materials for furnishing, and the ingredients in recipes, represent normal requirements in normal times. Supplies of fabrics and food vary enormously from place to place and from time to time. (Bradely, 1948, Preface to the second edition viii).

The quotation above not only highlights the scope and detail of instructions but also, moreover, reveals how learning domestic work implies learning to view the colonized land as *empty spaces*. In other words, learning to set up an imperial household on colonized land meant that expatriate women should learn to erase the lives and livelihoods that already existed and learn to fill the land with imperial lives. The next extract looks more closely into the details of the everyday – and, more specifically, into instructions as to why expatriates should closely monitor domestic workers:

> It is silly to be careless about stores. The worry about expenses far outweighs the 'worry' of keeping the key to your store and then taking minutes in the morning to direct your households. If you take a little care, the staff will respect it – and you. *Verb Sap.* (Bradley 1948: 13, Italics in original)

> You can obtain an extra pair of hands (but you will not necessarily get a head as well) to help with the heavy work. Others like to take advantage that here servants can be obtained and enjoy a more leisurely day than they can have otherwise. (Housewifes Kenya 1960: 6)

These reasons for monitoring domestic workers reveal a preferred division of labour in households; the expatriate is expected to lead and instruct the workers or to enjoy some leisure time while the workers are expected to perform heavy work under surveillance. The close monitoring of labour is legitimized by two different reasons: first, by a view of domestic workers as being likely to steal and, secondly, by the view that they are naturalized, less human. Both the reasons for monitoring are profoundly racist.

The monitoring of staff is not restricted to their labour in the expatriate household. From Gwyneth Latham's (1995) diary we find how she instructed her staff not only about domestic work but also about intimacy, hygiene and social relations in the domestic worker's family.

> [. . .] Africans were like our children. We trusted them and they trusted us. No woman left alone on the loneliest farm, surrounded by African servants and labourers, had the slightest fear for her safety; she had perfect confidence in her staff and could sleep in peace with this knowledge [. . .] we acted *in loco parentis* to our young staff and they and the older ones discussed their troubles with us – marital, financial and others. (Latham and Latham 1995: 146–7)

Taken together, I find that there are areas of continuity in how expatriate women learn domestic and care work as well as areas that have been transformed. One area of continuity is the level of detail in how to organize expatriate lives outlined in the colonial and contemporary handbooks. I here suggest that the level of detail produces an overall view of the colonial land as empty, ready to be filled with imperial lives. Another continuity is the division of labour within the expatriate and colonial household, where expatriate women are supposed to take care of work tasks which connote purity and development – such as taking care of furnishing and decorating the household and providing an education for their children; they are also expected to direct domestic workers who will carry out household chores which, historically, have been constructed as dirty or low-skilled. Another continuity refers to how expatriate women become involved in the domestic workers' private lives, as was stipulated in the colonial handbook and in Gwyneth's diary (Latham and Latham 1995) and was part of the colonial project. The discourse of naturalization, that is constructing domestic workers as less than human, was blatant in the colonial texts and less visible, yet lingering in the background, for example, as displayed in the interview with Josephine. These instructions nevertheless resonate with how contemporary expatriate women discuss and give advice to their domestic workers about intimate spheres of life. These instructions are given from various perspectives ranging from racist and demeaning to benevolent and with good intentions, sometimes with a desire for friendship.

The section on domestic workers' contracts and rights in today's manuals is a novelty, which can be understood in two ways. On the one hand, this section can be seen as a professionalization of domestic work and the domestic worker, which could lead to an increase in the status of the work. On the other hand, the professionalization of domestic work can be understood as a re-enrolment of colonial hierarchies of power; here, the expatriate women will learn to become employers for the Tanzanian women who will carry out the heavy and dirty part of domestic work in the household. Despite these differences, I here interpret these written and informal instructions as crucial pedagogical components that in different, complex and sometimes in contradictory ways reproduce a colonial state through the intertwining of discourses of racism, paternalism and professionalism.

Ambivalent processes of learning gender

As pointed out in previous research (Lundström 2013; Lutz 2011), closely related to doing class through domestic work are processes of doing gender. In contemporary households where ideals of dual income, gender equality and equality as such are all dominant, the doing of gender and class often involves highly complex relations of privilege and subordination – more specifically between spouses and between the domestic worker and expatriate women employers (Lundström 2013). Ambivalence has been used to describe tensions and contradictions in how women negotiate gender relations – and expectations of doing gender in particular – in relation to managing work life and family relations, particularly parental relations such as motherhood.

> The learning content that our reflections on social learning are about [family life and motherhood: my comment] relates to the reality of women, with the conflicts in the female lifecourse that are a necessary result of the way in which gender relations are socially organised. (Becker-Schmidt 1987: 9, cited in Illeris 2015a: 201, my translation)

The conflicts that Regina Becker-Schmidt centres on refer to situations when femininity is idealized and simultaneously devalued. Taking care work in Western contexts as her example, Becker-Schmidt notes how women often take on caring responsibilities at work and in families and how this work is not valued or remunerated in comparison to men's work, thereby creating ambivalence. From a social-psychological perspective, ambivalence can be traced to individual behaviour and reactions such as denial, repression, reversal or substitution. These reactions are manifest through 'opposing affective orientations toward the same person, object or symbol' (Smelser 1998: 5). From this perspective, ambivalence can comprise simultaneous and opposing affects such as love and hate, attraction and repulsion. In migration research, ambivalence has been used as an analytical entrance for understanding how migrants make meaning of new, complex and contradictory situations (Tazreiter 2019). Here, ambivalence is proposed as a suitable concept for understanding the relations of temporariness that are significant for the migration process. More specifically it has been used to analyse how subjects make sense of complex and changing everyday lives that characterize moving between social and geographic contexts, sometimes by force. From this backdrop, ambivalence is understood as a 'rational choice' of humans in complex social situations rather than as messy or irrational behaviour (Tazreiter 2019: 96). In the context of a migration process, ambivalence is expected to occur and can provide 'evidence of a healthy level of self-reflexivity' (Tazreiter 2019: 96) when migrant or marginal subjects negotiate changing and complex migration regimes. The expatriate women who are the focus of this chapter have not moved by force but, instead, made transnational mobility into a privileged lifestyle that nevertheless involves frequent change. Against this backdrop, this section of the chapter probes into the ambivalences involved in learning gender during transnational mobility, processes of graded citizenship and intra-households' gender dynamics resulting from transnational mobility, especially the complexities, overlappings and non-overlappings of processes of learning (gender, race and class) between contemporary and colonial times. The interview with Karen sheds light on these complex and ambivalent processes of learning.

Karen – a white woman from the West and a mother of two children who she takes care of – and her husband had been working in non-Western countries before they had children. At the time of our interview, Karen was working part-time on a contractual basis in Tanzania and tells me that she enjoys working outside of the household very much. During our interview, Karen emphasized that she has enjoyed being able to spend more time with her children and that venturing abroad as a family in many ways has been a positive and exciting experience. For example, they have been able to travel as a family and she has had more time for herself as she has been relieved of some work tasks which have been transferred to the domestic worker. Nevertheless, she describes how she experienced tensions in her role as a trailing-spouse:[8]

> It may be due to our upbringing that we are expected to contribute to society. After all, we are here to accompanying our husbands and to take the main responsibility for home and children but I was still not prepared for it to be so heavy and take so much time, that my life would be so associated with the home [. . .]. My husband has travelled a lot and I have had to cancel work trips and remain at home because the children are ill. I have had the main responsibility.

In the interview quote above, Karen describes how the expectations on her as the main person responsible for family life affected her room for manoeuvre both within and outside the family. We can also see how Karen articulates surprise over her new situation as a part-time so-called tspouse: 'I was still not prepared for it'. I here interpret this as an ambivalent situation of learning in which Karen discovers that the taken-for-granted knowledge on how to organize everyday expatriate life, which she had gained from her previous expatriate residence, did not function in her new situation. Instead, her new role as a part-time 'trailing spouse' was found to be more difficult and demanding than she had expected and more demanding than displayed in the lifestyle reports found in the glossy magazines of Corona Tanzania. I here suggest that Karen needs to learn to negotiate three ambivalences: first, to juggle her gender-equality ideals which originate from her upbringing and her previous experiences of dual-income-no-children expatriate life. The second ambivalence refers to her perceptions of the dominant discourse of domestic and care work as being the opposite of contributing to society. I here argue that this discourse produces a view of domestic work as labour which has low value, which should be understood in relation to how time-consuming domestic and care work was for Karen and that this labour was considered so important that it was given priority over her paid work. Moreover, we can also see how Karen articulates a desire to perform paid work – because it gives her a sense of belonging and being able to take control of her own time and space – and how this clashes with her new role as a part-time spouse. All in all, this indicates a paradox where domestic and care work involves a great deal of time but are not recognized as real or valued work. The invisibility of domestic work has been explored in previous research, which showed how this process produces the simultaneous processes of privilege (i.e. the expatriate woman gains a privileged position by distancing herself from this work) and of the subordination of expatriate women (vis-à-vis the male breadwinner) (Lundström 2013). Finally, the invisibility of domestic work masks the privileges of the (often male) breadwinner (Lan 2006; Lutz 2011). While a paid domestic worker is praised for being invisible, the privileged expatriate woman plays a crucial role not only in constructing gender and heterosexual relations in the family but also in representing the nation, particularly in the diplomacy *milieu,* as we could see from the incident at the beginning of this chapter and from the overview of previous research. From this perspective, for Karen to reach the desired subject position she needs to learn to be visible but circumscribed, which represents the third ambivalence and has a spatial dimension to it. The following paragraph looks further into how Karen learns to negotiate mobility and immobility in space in her new life.

In the remaining part of our interview, Karen shared with me that the first year of their stay had been extremely stressful, and explains how she has remained for days, even weeks, when her children have been unwell. This resulted in a micro-level experience of navigating space characterized by not leaving the household. When it comes to navigating space within the household, being available implied increased responsibilities. These involved waiting, seemingly immobile but alert – hence the opposite of relaxing. Karen described setting alarms every hour throughout the night, constantly waking up to check her child's temperature. She expressed her fear that her children would contract malaria and recounted numerous instances of fever. From this perspective, navigating space through immobility made her work even when she was supposed to sleep (see also Chapter 5 for discussions of how domestic workers, from a vastly different position of precarity, describe similar though not identical situations). While this may seem like an ordinary situation of parenting work when a child is unwell, Karen underlines that the expatriate situation has magnified her domestic and caring responsibilities, which were more equally shared with her husband during their stay in their home country:

> For sure my life has become smaller, I have spent a lot more time at home with the children [. . .] we have had a lot of family time here but I'm not sure it is quality time, I'm not sure it is a good thing for a family to spend so much time in the house.

In answer to my question as to whether and how her relationship with her husband has changed, she states: 'Well how can I put it? There has been a lot of tension in the family. We are going back [*to our home country; my comment*] soon, so let's hope it will change back to what it was (*laughs*)'.

In my interviews with contemporary expatriate women, several accounts revealed how they coped with and at times transgressed this expected role of remaining at home. They achieved this by engaging in charity work, pursuing further studies or working in international consultancy, which, according to them, were tasks that were possible to combine with their responsibilities as main caregivers. What are the continuities and changes from the colonial era? The following section looks more closely into this.

Continuities and changes in learning gender

In Gwyneth's diary from 1920s to 1930s' colonial Tanzania, descriptions of paid domestic work are merged with descriptions of an expatriate woman's life; moving between different postings, packing and unpacking household items, making new friends, organizing parties and vacations, and managing staff.

> Whenever we went it was always exciting. Usually, a house different from the last one, a new hospital, new outlook and new people. [. . .] Settling in at a new station, getting the house in order, receiving visitors and returning calls (for those were the days of visiting cards) naturally took a considerable time. Once we had completely settled in, we began looking forward to our next leave! (Latham and Latham 1995: 135–7)

This section of the diary describes how the expatriate woman is in charge of furnishing and decorating the household, as well as for establishing and maintaining social relations outside of the family, something which was underlined in previous research into the role of the expatriate spouse (McCarthy 2014). While this section of the diary describes a privileged lifestyle articulated in a cheerful tone, it needs to be contextualized in relation to previous historical research, which shows expatriate women during the British colonial era living unfree lives and being socially and economically dependent on their husbands.[9]

> The role of women in racist societies is always the same, it is to be the bearers of purity, to be the repositories of whiteness. [. . .] The European woman had to be very feminine – anyone who thinks about Michaela Dennis in her khaki drill has got us wrong. We were wearing stiletto heels and bouffant

> hairstyles and 30-yard petticoats and fluttering around, because it was a very male-dominated society. It was male-dominated in the sense that it was the men who had all the power and prestige in society. [. . .] We lived these tiny circumscribed – geographically circumscribed, socially circumscribed – lives. (Dr Pamela Shermer-Smith in OSPA 2016: 80-81)

Dr Pamela Shermer-Smith was one of the few critical voices during a workshop which aimed to interrogate the experiences of British women during the British colonial empire. Emphasizing women's unpaid labour both within and outside the household, Shermer-Smith notes how women become 'the incorporated wife'[10] serving as a 'handmaiden of empire'. Moreover (as we see in the quotation), she explains how this labour involved adjusting expatriate women's bodies and their entire persona at the service of their husbands.[11]

In various ways this image has been contested by expatriate women, who insist on their agency and the many ways in which they perceive that they had contributed to the settler societies. They underlined that their contributions had not only been by supporting their husbands on their missions for the British colonial administration but also through their unpaid labour in education, health and social work in the societies where they were based.

> I do not recognise Pamela Shermer-Smith's picture of Northern Rhodesia. I served all my time hundreds of miles away from any railway line and it was quite different from that. I do have very fond memories of some of the remarkable ladies I met early in my career in Northern Rhodesia. (D'Arcy Payne, OSPA 2016: 93)

While the pattern of learning to be available and navigating space by restricting their movements – and the subsequent increased responsibilities that followed from being available – persisted across different texts and times, I also encountered instances where women negotiated these demands, as displayed in the quotations above. Similarly, in the colonial texts (supported by archival research in Chapter 3), Gwyneth Latham (Latham and Latham 1995) managed the expectations of availability by working at her husband's medical clinic and engaging in charitable endeavours.

In both contemporary interviews and colonial texts, learning preferred gender performance meant to take care of domestic and care work which connoted purity and development rather than instrumental and heavy work and work tasks that connoted dirt. In addition, doing gender often entailed not venturing outside far from the household for extended periods. Maintaining physical proximity remained crucial for women and their families to establish a desired availability, that is one which aligned with dominant ways of understanding the role and functioning of expatriate women and, in particular, diplomatic spouses (see, e.g., McCarthy 2014). Importantly, this view has remained despite advances in technology – for example, the use of smartphones for Skype or Facetime – or gains in gender equality in the foreign ministries. In other words, colonial and contemporary approaches to learning gender intersected in the sense that women, without warning or preparation, learnt to limit their movements in space. Taken together, these results point to the complex nature of learning gender within the lives of privileged expatriate women. In short, learning gender becomes a means of navigating gender norms of subordination vis-à-vis a male breadwinner, being available and spatially circumscribed, while upholding the privileges associated with race and class.

One important narrative reveals the differences between how privileged expatriate women make meaning of domestic work in colonial and in contemporary households – with the focus on gender equality – and how dual-income households create a new form of ambivalence that they needed to negotiate. I have not included interviews with men in this book, this does not mean that men and men's role as breadwinners are not important for how expatriate women learn to do gender through domestic and care work. Men's role was more explicit in the colonial texts, yet lingering in the background in the contemporary interviews. In this context it is worth underlining that the male breadwinner role has remained remarkably intact and is constructed as both hard-working and meaningful.

The subsequent discussion explores the co-existence of a gendered, subordinate position alongside a racialized and class-based position of privilege.

Learning who is unable to learn

Miles and Brown (2003) have been central in the theoretical development of research into racism through the theory of processes of racialization. In particular, they have explored how racism involves separation and a hierarchical structure where whites are privileged over Blacks. This world view contributes to the creation of divisions and institutions that maintain this hierarchical order, hence processes of racialization. Mählck (2016) complements Miles and Brown's work by emphasizing how racialization processes are ongoing and vary between the different geographical and postcolonial contexts. These processes operate at multiple levels within society, shaping everyday interactions, institutional dynamics and structural inequalities. This understanding helps us recognize how racialization is embedded in various aspects of social life, including domestic work, which becomes unevenly distributed along racialized and gendered lines.

Drawing on the above discussions, Gerrard, Sriprakash and Rudolph (2022) shed light on processes on the significance of educational institutions in shaping and perpetuating racist world views in the way they extract value from labour processes – and, more specifically, how colonial governmental instructions have worked through institutions and through the division of labour to reinforce racial hierarchies within society. By analysing the pedagogical processes of teaching and learning inherent in these instructions, it is possible to uncover how racism is transmitted and sustained through educational practices. The next section probes the interviews with expatriate women and analyses the form and content of the instructions that expatriate women give to their domestic workers and the continuities from and changes compared to the colonial era.

Maya has resided in Tanzania for a year. She has long-standing experience of expatriate life, and Tanzania is her third residence. She takes care of three children at home and is from the West. Speaking of her domestic worker, she says:

> I don't know why, but it seems impossible for her to learn not to mix coloured shirts with white shirts when she does the laundry. I gave up and I do it myself now.

From this quote we can see that, when Maya decides to take over from the domestic worker, she also transmits the view that domestic work is something which anybody can do, hence unskilled work.

From the following quote by Sabina, this pedagogy comprises further complexities that go beyond skilled or unskilled labour and are interlinked with how domestic workers are perceived by some expatriate women.[12] Sabina has a long-standing experience of living life as an expatriate woman, and Tanzania is her second posting. She takes care of her two children and is from a non-Western context. During our interview she frequently stressed, 'I'm a person who likes to explain, I like to talk to them, I want them to learn'; however, she also admits that she finds this frustrating. While a focus on learning domestic and care work has the potential to raise the value of such work, as skilled work, this is not what Sabina has in mind when she refers to the educational processes of what she perceives that the domestic worker can learn and how the domestic worker should be instructed:

> She says 'Yes' to everything but, when I come down, nothing has happened or something completely different has happened. [*laughs*] My friends tell me I spend too much time giving instructions: 'Don't explain too much, it will just confuse her, just tell her'.

Taken together, these quotations reveal a pedagogy which separates and hierarchizes between subjects who are seen to be either able or unable to learn (in the example from Maya) and how they can learn (in the example from Sabina). I here suggest that the difficulty and even impossibility of giving instructions to domestic workers that the expatriate women articulate are important for understanding how learning to view domestic work as unskilled involves learning racism and sexism. Central to my argument are processes of naturalization. Scholarship on racism at work as well as feminist labour studies have shown how a main constituency of lowering the value of labour conducted by subalterns is founded on the view of skills being integrated in their bodies, as instinct (Bhattacharyya 2018; Patel and Moore 2020). The result of this exercise is not only tremendous human suffering by the workers but also the construction of a workforce whose main skill is being a labouring body and, as a consequence, a non-human and disposable body (Iskander 2021). While Iskander's (2021) research focuses on workers in the construction industry, the following analysis of the interview with Sabina can provide some insights into the pedagogical practices of learning the naturalization of domestic workers.

In the interview with Sabina, we find that she makes a distinction between the different household chores on the grounds of their complexity and how this becomes an argument for the distribution of household chores between herself and the domestic worker. Following this line of thought, Sabina explains to me that she does the cooking herself as she anticipates that cooking would be too complicated for the domestic worker. Instead, what she values the most is the feeling which the domestic worker invokes in her: 'I just want to have somebody in the house who gives me peace'. This example highlights the emotional labour produced by domestic workers and how this is more valued compared to more instrumental domestic labour (which, according to Sabina, domestic workers are seen as unable to learn). Yet, emotional labour is rarely acknowledged as a skill by expatriate employers (see also Chapter 5). Importantly, naturalized knowledge is not always devalued. In fact, there exists a hierarchy between the different embodied skills, where skills that are seen as more cerebral – such as, for example, the work of mathematicians – are more highly valued compared to tasks performed by construction (Iskander 2021) or domestic workers – in particular, their emotional labour, as described in this chapter and from the perspective of domestic workers in Chapter 5.

Taken together, the examples highlighted above suggest that the processes of hierarchy and separation that are central for the production of processes of racialization are also central in the pedagogical methods – that is in the forms and content of instructions conveying this world view. The central components here being processes of naturalization: 'Don't explain too much, it will just confuse her, just tell her'. So what are the continuities from colonial times?

Next is an extract from Bradley's (1948) household book, which is chosen because it displays a preferred way of giving instructions in the colonial household: 'The most competent cook will need a good deal of coaching until you are sure that he can be trusted to do things as you like them done, without constant reminding and correction.' Here, cooks are seen as having the potential to learn, albeit slowly: 'If you can find a boy who understands two-thirds of the above [list] take him on and gracefully set about bringing the other third up to standard' (Bradley 1948: 19–20). From Blackett's (2019) research we know that cooks had a higher labouring status compared to other servants – for example, domestic workers. In her analysis of cookbooks, Blackett (2019) notes how giving instructions to domestic workers compared to cooks is more complicated as the needs of the employer may vary. Moreover, it is impossible to provide information about every aspect of mundane domestic work. This results in a situation whereby 'very little instruction can be given' (2019: 108). The instructions in the household books therefore convey that a main part of the domestic worker's labour is to maintain a respectful manner in relation to the expatriate woman and to 'remain in attendance until she is dismissed' (2019: 108).

The contemporary interview quotes from Maya and Sabina resonate with how domestic work and domestic workers have been constructed in the colonial household books described above. Central sections of overlapping are the construction of a subject who is not only unskilled but also unable to learn: for example, 'I gave up' and 'it seems impossible for her to learn' resonate with the instructions found in the colonial cookbook, 'If you find a boy who understands.' These experiences and perceptions of domestic workers are central for the pedagogical method that the women developed; 'Don't explain too much, it will just confuse her, just tell her.' Along this line of thought, we can see an overlapping between the divisions of labour in the colonial household which, at the bottom of the hierarchy, produced a labourer who is described in dehumanizing language. Examples here are the water carrier: 'He spends all his working days toiling backwards and forwards to the river' (Latham and Latham 1995: 63): the description of the domestic worker in Blackett's research whose main skill is 'to remain in attendance until she is dismissed' and Sabina's contemporary desire for 'somebody who can move smoothly in the house' but who is unable to take instructions. While the pedagogies outlined here indicate blatant racism, the interviewed women also spoke of situations where they have experienced complexities and dilemmas and where they have struggled to make interventions to improve the work conditions and livelihoods for the domestic workers. What follows looks more closely into this.

Learning to cope with being an oppressor and an exploiter

Loans and how they were to be handled were a recurrent theme in my interviews with female employers and domestic workers.[13] In fact, giving loans to workers is so well established in mundane expatriate life that instructions on how to give them were outlined in the handbooks for contemporary expatriates that I have analysed for this research[14] (see also Chapter 5). The following quote digs deeper into the complexities of loans. Lilian has resided in Tanzania for more than ten years and has employed various domestic workers. She is one of the few expatriate women I interviewed who worked full-time; she has two children and her husband also works full-time. The following exchange describes her relationship to loans. Her response is given as an answer to my question on how she balances friendship, intimacy and more formal worker and employer relations with the domestic employee working in her household:

> **Lilian**: We [Lilian and her husband] have made the decision that we choose to support her child through primary school . . . it was a relationship that lasted well beyond the years she worked for our family. We also gave smaller loans so she could start a small business. But of course, we could not agree every time she or her relatives asked us for a loan. [. . .]
>
> **Paula**: But don't you think giving a loan is problematic, that a loan will increase the inequality between you?
>
> **Lilian**: But if they need a loan you must help. Otherwise, they may have to take a loan from somebody on the street, not a bank but a private person – a professional money lender – and they [the domestic worker] will have to pay a really high interest rate. So, you really must give them a loan. But it depends on what they are going to do with the money, so it is very informal and fluid – for example we don't give anyone a loan if they have already borrowed money from us. [. . .] But they also know that if they are seriously ill, we will take care of them and pay for the hospital.

Our conversation reveals how loans are an integral part of the conditions for employment. Prior to this answer, Lilian had described the salary she gave to her previous live-in domestic worker as 'pocket money', as her other expenses were paid for and also comprised a 'gift' which would cover the domestic worker's daughter's school fees. The salary for Lilian's current live-out domestic worker was very low but still within government recommendations (150,000–200,000 shilling for part-time work).[15] The salary was legitimized by Lilian's informal arrangements of loans and promises of future help in case of illness or accidents. Gifts, loans and promises of covering expenses for hospital treatment were very common among the expatriate women I interviewed. These gifts involved paying large amounts of money over several years to cover the cost of the construction of domestic workers' houses or their children's school fees, for example. Complex and mixed feelings of responsibility and repulsion and even anxiety about their position vis-à-vis the domestic worker were dominant themes in the interviews: 'Yes, sometimes it strikes me that this is a very involuntarily position we are in; of course we want to help but where are the limits, what if she needs an ambulance helicopter to South Africa? That simply would not work', states Vera.

To understand the role of loans, debt and dependency, we need to revert back to the system of indenture described more closely in Chapter 5. Under this system, workers were legally bound to their employers, and the setup was directly initiated and driven by the colonial state. The system was built on debt and dependency, where workers were expected to work off their debts to their employers (Allen 2008). The loans and relations of dependency, in the context of the research presented here, are informal, articulated between private actors and transmitted within a complex web of exploitation and help that is channelled through relations of interdependence between the domestic worker and the employer, albeit occupying very different and hierarchical positions. Against the backdrop of analysing layers of debt and dependency among migrant workers in the United States, LeBaron (2014) theorizes contemporary relations of debt between workers and the state and between workers and employers who benefit from state regulations or a lack of regulations as a class relation. This class relation works through disciplining workers retrospectively – and, moreover, it is highly gendered. In the context of the research presented here, loans can be understood through primary and secondary levels of analysis on which I now expand.

At a primary level of analysis, the loans given by the privileged expatriate women are producing a class position on the grounds of debt and dependency similar to that described by LeBaron (2014). At a secondary level, the frequent use of loans can be understood as micro-level learning processes of how expatriate female employers learn to balance oppression, guilt, intimacy and appreciation of the domestic employees' work performance within an overall structure of economic and symbolic privilege (resulting from exploitation). Importantly, the result from these learning processes is not a change in oppressive work relations; instead they serve as remedial work for injuries originating from a systemic level. Having said this, it is worth underlining that an overall ambition of loans was change and not help. Common statements were:[16] 'Before we leave, we would like to pay for a cooking course so that, when we leave, she can find another and better job'. We support her with her children's school fees, so that the next generation can find better opportunities or We help her to build her house so she can have a plot where she can grow vegetables and secure a livelihood. From a pedagogical perspective, learning to normalize the organization of labour around loans and debts and to rephrase this as 'help to change' can be viewed as, albeit ambivalent, pedagogical practices of reproducing the colonial state despite good intentions at an individual level. This pedagogy is produced from and draws from a continuum of erasure of the colonial history of exploitation of land and labour and a culture of erasing established ways of living. This erasure results in the necessity to help to produce that land and ways of living. Sometimes, as for Josephine, this extends in helping to produce the entire persona of the domestic workers – 'to cultivate'.

Concluding remarks

The overall question posed in this chapter was 'Can the oppressor be oppressed?' With a particular focus on learning processes, I set out to interrogate how expatriate women in diplomatic households and in the international business sector learn domestic work and the related processes of racism, sexism and coloniality in their everyday lives, together with the continuities and changes over time. The results make a contribution to the growing research debates on variegated social reproduction as it takes place in expatriate households and over time. This involves interrogating how expatriate women negotiate boundaries, both concrete and discursive, as well as processes of coping with and at times unlearning power relations involved in learning domestic work and the positions that result.

Through probing professionalization of domestic work, gender relations in the household, skills practices and finally loans between employers and workers – areas which are central for doing domestic work in expatriate households – I find a number of continuities between contemporary and colonial times. In particular, continuity can be found in the pedagogical practices involved in transmitting preferred ways of doing domestic work. More specifically, these pedagogies are built on separation and hierarchy when it comes to the content of learning, how instructions are supposed to be followed and between those who are seen as being able to learn and those whose main labouring contribution is their body. In other words, we can see a continuation of naturalization, sexism and racism in the pedagogical enterprise of teaching preferred ways of carrying out domestic work in expatriate households; here we note that diplomatic households are directly funded by the state. In addition, this chapter also points at how privileged expatriate women through teaching the domestic workers learn to reproduce racism and exploitation. This is interesting considering the emphasis on contracts and workers' rights in the contemporary written instructions for expatriates.

There are also differences in how privileged expatriate women learn to live expatriate lives. Contemporary discourses on gender equality – and equality in general – are novelties that impact on how privileged expatriate women navigate gender relations in contemporary households. This has brought new layers of complexity to expatriate women's processes of learning, revealed here by the layers of ambivalence that are produced from the position of staying at home in households with a dual-income ideal. We also see how expatriate women coped with and at times unlearned the subject positions they were offered by engaging with charity work, consultancies or education – or by enjoying staying at home, as was the case for Doris. While these processes of ambivalence are new, the imaginary of a Western male breadwinner has been continuously produced and reproduced through the intertwined histories of colonialism and diplomacy.

7

Imagining differently

The research presented in this book can be likened to a journey, starting with a series of questions about how to better understand and examine domestic work, both paid and unpaid, in expatriate households in Dar es Salaam. The aim has been to explore domestic work as a means of learning, coping with or unlearning – which implies challenging circumstances – and confronting and dismantling racism, sexism and colonialism. As outlined previously in this book, the work of unlearning involves learning from transgression and formulating a practical critique. This requires thinking. In his philosophical work 'The Principle of Hope' Bloch (1986) understands thinking as hopeful journey of 'venturing beyond'; the capacity to link what is desired and what is known (1986: 1). In other words, it means dreaming of and working for a future we do not know – it means imagining differently. From this perspective, unlearning has an element of hope in it. Hope is not passive. For Bloch, hope is a pedagogical relation; 'It is a question of learning hope' (1986: 1). In other words, hope is a pedagogical relation which is simultaneous, practical, emotional and cognitive. Dinerstine's (2022:48) interpretation of Bloch's philosophy emphasizes that hope is not a passive expectation, fantasy or paralysing ideology but, rather, the driving force behind action and the active process of exploring the world. Moreover, learning hope is rooted in a perspective which conceptualizes the everyday as a process which lies as much in the future as in what is, and what has been. Here Bloch draws from Marx's historical material dialect method for analysing change or non-change. More specifically and as outlined in Chapter 1, this is a methodological approach which moves away from treating history as the emergence or retreat of entities and instead can be applied to understand processes of change and non-change. Bloch (1986) notes how all freedom movements are driven by utopian aspirations. What distinguishes a passive and inward looking utopia or daydream from movements that are active is a focus on knowledge, 'only knowledge as a conscious theory-practice confronts Becoming and what can be decided within it' (1986: 8). Another distinguishing feature in Bloch's philosophy on hope is a focus on labour and envisioning 'a life of fulfilling work free of exploitation, but also a life beyond work' (1986: 19). Moreover, a distinguishing feature of Bloch's philosophy of hope is a focus on pedagogical method. In particular, repetition becomes a way of learning on a new level; in other words, this means the possibility of learning which may allow the identical thing to be learned anew (1986: 21). This hopeful-driven work involves constantly discovering new possibilities. For these reasons, the concluding chapter in this book discusses the main research findings, with a particular focus on unlearning, from the perspective of the diverse field of prefigurative politics (Monticelli 2022).

Prefigurative politics have been conceptualized in various ways as 'practiced by social movements that embody, in the here and now, the future society they desire' (Piccardi 2022: 161); a new and holistic orientation of being in the world – 'this means prefiguration has an ontological dimension: it is about creating "alterative worlds" – other ways of being, knowing and doing' (Escobar 2022: xxiv); and, from a perspective of critical pedagogy, the different ways 'of envisioning social relationships that the system of power cannot assimilate or suppress' (De Vita and Vittori 2022: 82). Moreover – and linking the routines of the everyday with prefigurative politics – 'Everyday practices can thus demonstrate that alternatives are not distant dream but can be considered in the here and now' (Forno and Wahlen 2022: 124). From an ambition to decolonize prefigurative politics, Dinerstein (2022) draws from Bloch's philosophy of the multiverse to theorize diverse prefigurative struggles that emerge from 'a multiplicity of situations, oppressions and relations *in, against and beyond* the violent ongoing process of abstraction, homogenisation and synchronisation that underpins the accumulation of capital' (2022: 49; italics in the original). Drawing from scholarships of hope (among others Bloch) and a critical reading of intersectional theory as it has evolved in Sweden, de los Reyes and Mulinari (2019) point at how scholarships of hope entangle with traditions in Black feminism. In particular, de los Reyes and Mulinari (2019) point at the necessity of theorizing beyond the academy and how in the tradition of Black feminism intellectual practices refer to thinking and labouring with and a commitment to others (2019: 192). This resonates with – but is not identical to – the argument made in Pereira's seminal article 'Between Knowing and Imagining: What Space for Feminism in Scholarship on Africa?' which draws from various African feminisms. Pereira (2002) situates her discussion on imagining differently – a central aspect of the scholarship of prefiguration – in the knowledge politics of the academy and discusses the violent restructuring of life which took place across the continent as a consequence of the structural adjustment programmes put in place as IMF's increased pressure on developing countries during the 1980s and 1990s. Moreover, she points at how a shared history of colonialism constructs particular complexities for African feminists as they negotiate Eurocentrism, racism and gender blindness in the academy. Against this backdrop Pereira points at the relationship between how scholarships are imagined and how this impact on the knowledge that is produced therefrom, 'Looking forward and outward, African feminists must continue to produce scholarships that engage with the possibilities and practices of re-imagined futures' (2002: 33). This philosophy is taken up in Amir Curry's (2021) scholarship. Here the plurality of vision and practice is underlined:

> Ensuring the collective vitality and life force of Africa requires a vision and imagination to see the liberation of every member of that community, so we must include all that face a particular oppression: African women, children, queer and trans folks, non-binary folks, and so forth. (2021: 3)

Against this backdrop, the main results and an emphasis on unlearning are presented and discussed with regard to what they can contribute to prefigurative politics. This is done in two steps – first, the methodological contributions from this volume are outlined, followed, secondly, by the empirical and theoretical contributions.

Methodological contributions

The methodological approach in this book is influenced by Marx's perspective on historical material dialectics, which focuses on explaining continuities and changes in how capitalist relations and forces shape our everyday lives (Marx 2018:

13). It is also influenced by Lefebvre (1991), who draws from this methodology to analyse how we can understand contemporary situations and even make suggestions on how to change our futures through tracing phenomena backwards in history (see Chapters 5 and 6). I also draw from feminist sociological research into the everyday, rendering it a feminist 'research problematic' (Smith 1987) and African feminism's decolonial critiques of historicizing which underline the necessity to recognize the ideological dots of racism, colonialism and patriarchy while underlining power and resistance (Tamale 2020). In addition, the methodological contribution involves broadening the understanding of the archive, which I refer to as 'learning from the archive'.

Learning from the archive

Swaby and Frank's (2020) article proposes experimental and future-oriented methodologies to decolonize the archive. They argue for challenging linear notions of time and place by dwelling on and lingering in the archives and exploring the processes that make events possible. This requires considering events from a non-linear historical perspective and examining the interconnectedness of various processes, continuities and changes.

In this book, I have adopted a non-linear approach to historicizing domestic work. I started by describing the global economic transformations in the 1990s that influenced relations of production in Tanzania. I then investigated these processes in a non-linear way, bringing together narratives of domestic work from different time periods. This allowed me to highlight how colonialism and capitalism operated through the economy, education and law at different times to accomplish a narrative which produces the view of domestic work as poorly valued, low-skilled labour and which, in large segments, has made the agency of domestic workers invisible.

Learning from the archive also involves examining the co-existing narratives within the 'colonial matrix' (Tlostanova and Mignolo 2012). Tlostanova and Mignolo (2012) remind us that there is no perspective completely outside of the colonial matrix, as we are all, in some way, situated within it. In the context of this book, it means considering silences or subaltern narratives in the archive. It requires rethinking the archive and incorporating memories, identities, communities and homes into its landscape (Sawyer and Osei-Kofi 2020; Swaby and Frank 2020). In this book (in Chapter 4), I have expanded our understanding of the archive by drawing from historical research, archival sources and fictional literature. This approach bridges literary-informed scholarship with sociological analysis and challenges simplistic white–Black dichotomies in systems of oppression. For example, in Chapter 4, the novel *Paradiset* (Gurnah 2012) adds another layer of representation to historical research into domestic-work relations. From this, it follows that it is possible to explore relations of debt and dependency and how capitalism *draws* from intimate relations. In addition, it can highlight the plurality of forms of resistance in the non-West which are often not at the centre of narratives of social reproduction in scholarships in the West or in the colonial archives. The methodology of learning from the archives developed here contributes to prefigurative politics by interweaving different texts, from the colonial archives and from the fictional novel. From here, we can attempt to unlearn dominant narratives into domestic work from within and from below. For example, narratives from the archives which display how domestic workers have organized in Tanzania for better work conditions or historical research which point at how rural women have challenged local and colonial efforts to control their mobility and livelihoods. Learning from the archives means to draw together narratives of migration and labour: from the perspective of domestic workers from rural-to-urban Tanzania and that of privileged expatriate women from various countries in the West who lived imperial lives in Tanzania. This involves analyzing the connections and discontinuities between these narratives and acknowledging differences and contradictions. At the core is an examination of capitalism, colonialism, patriarchy, and racism. The contribution to prefigurative politics is to spark a dialogue on the archive as memory. Here memory can make a contribution to research into resistance and a possibility for change, re-membering.

Unlearning through analytical autoethnography

Another methodological contribution from this book is a constant and ongoing critical reflection on my positioning and participation in this research. This means reflecting on how my journey is not separate from dominant narratives and power asymmetries. It means being self-critical of how I am complicit with colonialism (in my position as an expatriate and 'trailing spouse' and as a researcher from the West conducting research in non-Western contexts) while also being critical of the same.

I have chosen to outline these dual positionalities of translocational privilege and disadvantage (see also Anthias 2008) in a series of autoethnographic situations outlined at the beginning of each chapter. The episodes are chosen specifically because they represent complex feminist problematics (Smith 1987) which, when analysed, resist simplistic interpretations and single stories and have no simple solutions. From the perspective of prefigurative pedagogies, critically analysing autoethnographic situations entails writing about a situated self-awareness as part of our relationship with the world:

> People, as beings 'in a situation', find themselves rooted in temporal-spatial conditions which mark them and which they also mark. They will tend to reflect on their own 'situationality' to the extent that they are challenged by it to act upon it. Human beings *are* because they *are* in a situation. And they *will be more* the more they not only critically reflect upon their existence but critically act upon it. (Freire 2000: 109, emphases in the original, cited in De Vita and Vittori 2022: 76)

Sharing autoethnographic situations which illustrate power relations, complexities and dilemmas in everyday expatriate lives means highlighting not only areas which need change. In addition, I here make these situations explicit as part of a critical interrogation of dilemmas involved in everyday expatriate lives as well as a contribution to critical self-awareness in research methodology, particularly when researchers from the West do research in the non-West. Here, Mama (2017: 1) reminds us how 'Conscientisation is a dynamic dialectic relationship between radical thinking and action [. . .] Feminists writing and publishing is a key route to conscientisation'.

Moreover, the practice of sharing these research dilemmas connotes to pedagogies applied within social movements, aiming to unlearn collectively through 'affinity for affinity'. Affinity for affinity means engaging in transformative work based on non-universalizing, non-hierarchical, non-coercive relationships grounded in mutual aid and shared ethical commitment (De Vita and Vittori 2022: 82). Having said this, it is important to keep in mind that researchers are acting from a different subject position as compared to activists or subalterns. This means that researchers work with different 'tools' moreover, the power imbalances and hierarchies in the research process are under constant negotiation. Here Said (1996) reminds us of the role of the intellectual, which should be to communicate research results in a non-elitist way; intellectuals should break down simplistic categorizations which are hampering thought and communication. Moreover, intellectuals need to recognize their limited possibility of bringing about direct change. For this reason, observing and analysing processes that otherwise would have been unnoticed remains at the core of work tasks for the intellectual. For future, it is worth exploring how a pedagogy of analytical autoethnography can be applied in methodological discussions in other research areas and contexts.

Empirical and theoretical contributions

In this section of the chapter, I will outline the empirical and theoretical contributions with a particular focus on unlearning. The presentation is guided by the main themes outlined in Chapter 1: continuities and changes; analysing connections between learning domestic and care work in everyday life and wider institutions. Finally, I analyse theoretical connections with a particular focus on moving towards a decolonial take on SRT.

Unlearning what colonialism produces

Examining the learning process of domestic and care work with a particular focus on continuity and change leads to a reflection on the impact of colonialism. To illustrate this, in Chapter 6, I observed detailed descriptions in colonial household books of what to bring to the colonies, how to pack these items as well as how to decorate the new household and to instruct staff – and the reasons for these instructions. In contemporary handbooks I found lifestyle reports which convey preferred ways of living expatriate lives, advising where to shop, eat or go on holiday. In addition, I found continuities in the areas of instructions as well as the form of instruction that expatriate women are supposed to learn when they direct their staff. Taken together, I here suggest that these results represent a continuing view of the non-West, here Tanzania, as an empty space – ready to be filled with lives and cultures from the metropole – and Tanzanian domestic workers in need of training in a preferred and Western way of living.

Importantly, there were also differences, in particular those around contracts and labour regulations, which were a novelty, as well as gender-equality discourses which add new and ambivalent processes of learning to live privileged expatriate lives. At a different analytical level, these results point to the necessity of interrogating change as a complex, multilevel and multidimensional phenomenon. This means that change taking place in policy does not necessarily indicate that change is taking place in practice.

Furthermore, in Chapter 5, I discovered that the architectural design of expatriate households reflects the patterns seen in colonial households. This design segregates domestic workers and privileged household members into separate spaces, intended for leisure or work respectively. Leisure spaces such as dining rooms and bedrooms, meant for the household members, are conveniently and lavishly decorated, highlighting social distinctions. On the other hand, spaces designated for domestic work, such as laundry areas and servants' quarters, are deliberately placed away from the main entrance, sometimes in basements or distant corners of the household. Often, these spaces are clustered together in a small house located at a distance in the garden, hidden from view.

This arrangement signifies that areas of domestic work and servants' quarters are designed to keep the domestic worker close to the household members, ready to service them, yet to be kept out of sight. By analysing colonial texts such as household handbooks and an expatriate woman's diary and contemporary handbooks and interviews, it becomes clear that the location and design of built spaces align with a colonial discourse of hiding regarding domestic work – extending sometimes to the overall perception of domestic workers. Let me elaborate on this result: colonialism's objective, beyond economic gain, was to replace existing ways of life. Thus, through the analysis of the temporal it is possible to show how colonialism operates through repetitive narratives in the economy, education, law and built space, obscuring domestic work as skilled labour and negating the agency of workers, persistently. Overall, this analysis emphasizes the need to challenge prevailing narratives around domestic and care work, recognizing their expertise and the agency of workers. The next section outlines the results from my historicizing analysis – and, in particular, the contribution from alternative narratives.

In Chapter 4, it becomes clear that domestic workers in Tanzania have a rich history of organizing themselves against oppressive working conditions, even predating the organization of many other labour groups in the country. In addition, pedagogies of unlearning were also identified in previous historical and feminist research which depart from Tanzanian women's everyday lives (see, e.g., Mbilinyi 1988; Tripp 1997). In this literature, women's various negotiations of structures of dominance are here interpreted as prefigurative politics which co-exist with formal work complaints observed in the archives. These narratives of organization and unlearning are evident in how contemporary domestic workers challenge traditional notions of loans, debt and dependency in relation to their employers. Specifically, these workers unlearn the mindset of being in a position of debt and, instead, view loans from their employers as a rightful entitlement due to their low salaries. They perceive their employers to be part of their extended network of dependency and, therefore, expect them to provide loans when needed. Another example is the findings in Chapter 5 which indicate that domestic workers often experience employers rewriting contracts to suit their own interests, which aligns with historical patterns of the exclusion of domestic workers from legal protection. Additionally, the same chapter reveals how domestic workers cope with and sometimes manage to unlearn when some employers attempt to selectively devalue – hence to cheapen – their labour (Patel and Moore 2020). In particular, this was done through choosing if, when and how to reveal to the employers that they had diplomas.

These findings contribute to prefigurative politics by expanding the realm of the everyday work and worldviews to include the co-existing narratives of subaltern workers' agency in their everyday contemporary and colonial lives. The narratives of subaltern workers , displayed in in interviews, the archival research done for this volume, in previous historical research and in a fictional novel challenge colonial efforts aimed at erasing workers' agency. They underscore the significance of recognizing and amplifying the voices and experiences of subaltern workers who have been actively resisting and fighting for their rights alongside colonial and postcolonial forces.

Pedagogies of unlearning of the everyday

In this book, I have interrogated how domestic work is learnt and unlearned at the intersection of everyday life and broader societal structures. I approached this by considering the state as the individual's relationship to the state in his or her everyday life, taking into account gender, race and class, as well as examining the absence or weakness of connections.

To analyse how colonialism has operated through societal relations, such as economy, law and education and moreover how the effects of colonialism at times is undone through subjects negotiations in their contemporary everyday lives, is well established in African decolonial feminisms (Tamale 2020). Such broad understanding of educational relations resonates with Freire's (1998) idea of 'learning the world through the word'. This pedagogical philosophy demonstrates how educational relations extend beyond educational institutions and manifest in social relations in the everyday. These theoretical insights are used to frame the analysis in the empirical chapters and is presented next.

Chapter 6 highlights the expectation that privileged expatriate women will engage in diplomatic duties or in business representation on a short notice. An important part of these duties means being the main responsible for domestic and care work in the households. From this follows that women learn to limit their movements in space, for example, by learning to be available and remaining close to the household. Furthermore, it explores expatriate women's ambivalent learning of gender, from a position of class privilege – and how they navigate being complicit with the oppression and exploitation of domestic workers simultaneously with their own relative subordination. The various ambivalent ways in which expatriate women envision change within their own families and in the domestic workers' lives point to how pedagogies of unlearning are at work at the level of their everyday lives and how experiences from the everyday is in tension with wider institutional and discursive contexts. For example, Karen juggle with experiences of not living according to gender-equality ideals in her current life and envisions a more equal division of labour in the household when she and her husband will return to their home country; Doris enjoys staying at home despite a dual-income ideal operating at a discursive level. Another example, Chapter 5 reveals how domestic workers challenge the understanding of domestic work as unskilled work by acquiring a diploma and carefully navigating if and how they reveal to their employers that they have a diploma. Another example of unlearning refers to how domestic workers make domestic work visible as they navigate the expectations from new families. This involves discussing formal aspects of domestic work with their new employers as well as managing unspoken expectations from their employers. Here, domestic workers transgress established ways of doing and learning domestic work by naming domestic work and outlining different dimensions and aspects of domestic work to their employers. It also involves coping with naturalization. In this book, the understanding of coping draws from previous feminist research into gender-based violence. I suggest here that learning to cope makes a pedagogical contribution to studies in resistance. This is the opposite of being passive but instead involves labouring to survive: hence, a political economy of survival from the standpoint of domestic workers.

As emphasized in Chapter 4, it is crucial to approach labour from a perspective that examines the tensions between dominant narratives at the state level and individual beliefs, social relations and everyday practices. It is through this perspective that the results presented here contribute to imagining change. Let me expand on this line of thought – actors in the everyday, whether they are individuals or institutions, are neither completely empowered nor fully constrained in their actions or in the consequences of their actions (Cooper 2022: 234). In this argument lays the prefigurative potential of the processes of unlearning from the everyday presented here.

Pedagogies of unlearning – Towards a decolonial take of SRT

Prefigurative politics emphasizes the necessity of imagining differently and making space for it, even without knowing the explicit outcome. It also recognizes that the practices shaping our dreams are grounded in the everyday as they unfold in the present. Naming and fighting for change today, even if the desired goal seems far away, is an integral part of prefigurative politics. The conversation between intersectional research on SR and critical education presented in Chapter 3 in this volume contributes to prefigurative politics through the development of an ontology of transgressions and pedagogies of unlearning. Central here is contextually sensitive worldviews and theoretical contributions from decolonial African feminisms, Black feminisms and feminist geography: in particular, contributions which focus on land and livelihoods and the connections between human and nature, subjective and objective, local and global and the West and the non-West. These theoretical contributions place knowledge which emerges from liminality, subalternity, materiality and spirituality/hope at the centre. In this respect, pedagogies of unlearning make explicit the relation between unlearning and undoing. This ontology and pedagogies of unlearning challenge global capitalist relations – regardless of their diversity – and call for alternative organization of the Life's Work from below and from within. Taken together, this ontology and pedagogies of unlearning contribute to the ongoing work of developing a decolonial take on SRT.

Furthermore, pedagogies of unlearning acknowledge the everyday work involved when subjects resist change or solidarity. They emphasize the importance of *care*ful transgressions as we unlearn in solidarity. To imagine ontological and pedagogical change implies departing from the everyday and holding onto a radical vision while engaging in the messy daily practice of Life's Work (Davis et al. 2022: 16).

Concluding remarks

The research presented here is a journey but it does not take us full circle. Over the course of six years, significant political changes have taken place which have, in various and variegated ways, impacted on the conditions for Life's Work. For example, in Tanzania. President John Magufuli's isolationist policies have been replaced by those of President Samia Suluhu Hassan, who has pursued a different direction. The global Covid-19 pandemic has further exacerbated existing vulnerabilities, particularly in non-Western regions. Moreover, the increasing militarization worldwide coupled with devastating conflicts – among others, in Ukraine, Gaza and Ethiopia – has greatly influenced and continues to shape our understanding of Life's Work. In Stockholm, Sweden, where I am currently writing this final chapter, there has also been a shift in political leadership. A conservative coalition now holds power, with the support of a right-wing party with roots in neo-Nazism. To liken the research in this book with a journey that does not go full circle means that, while the social and political contexts have changed, the underlying mechanisms that uphold oppressive relationships, such as capitalism, racism and patriarchy, continue to influence Life's Work. In this respect the research results presented here are part of an ongoing conversation rather than indicators of the end of a journey. Consequently, this chapter concludes with an invitation to readers to collectively, in various ways, engage with the ongoing work of imagining differently, as advised in the following African proverb:

> *If you want to go fast, go alone. If you want to go far, go together.*

Notes

Chapter 1

1 Note on language: *Dada* is the Kiswahili name for sister. This is how domestic workers are usually labelled in Dar es Salaam (see Kiaga 2007 for a critical discussion around the labelling '*Dada*', which she suggests is obscuring inequality in the work relationship). In this book I use the label of dada because this is how the domestic workers themselves prefer to be labelled. Private information. In this book I use Tanganyika when this is the formal labelling, as in the example of the 'International school of Tanganyika'. I also use Tanganyika when I refer to the timeperiod when the country was called Tanganyika. I use Tanzania when I refer to the timeperiod after 1964. I use the concept of trailing-spouse in this book. The concept is used in research to describe women and men that follow their partner on his or her international work mission (see for example McNulty 2012). Trailing-spouses often leave their careers in their country of origin and take care of household shores in the new country. I am aware that the concept signal beeing passive – this was explained to me by the interviewed privileged expatriate women. I hope that the analysis of their agency in this book can nuance the understanding of so-called trailing-spouses. I also use the terminology of privileged expatriate female employers to describe the women that I have interviewed. I am aware that the terminology expatriate is contested for its colonial and racial connotations (see Kunz 2020). I use the concept here to illustrate that the women are non-Tanzanians, sometimes white but not always, they are transnational migrants and are following their husband on his work mission to Tanzania. They belong to a global mobile elite and are privileged (see for example Kunz, 2020).

2 In this book, unpaid domestic work is performed by privileged expatriate women. The Tanzanian domestic workers interviewed for this research are all being paid, albeit low wages.

3 Here the Human Development figure for Tanzania is 0.528 compared to countries in Southern Africa at 0.541. The index measures development along the lines of 'life expectancy', 'years of schooling among the adult population' and 'standard of living' (Human Development Report 2019).

4 The gender inequality index for Tanzania is 0.539 compared to countries in Southern Africa at 0.573. The index measures development along the lines of 'reproductive health', 'empowerment' and 'economic activity' (Human Development Report 2019).

5 Waged and salaried workers (employees) are those workers who hold down the type of job defined as 'paid employment', where the incumbents hold explicit (written or oral) or implicit employment contracts that give them a basic remuneration not directly dependent upon the revenue of the unit for which they work (World Bank 2020a).

6 Vulnerable employment includes family workers and self-employed workers as a percentage of total employment. According to World Bank Development Indicators, 88 per cent of the women, out of the total group of women in employment, are in vulnerable employment (World Bank 2020b).

7 See Tlostanova and Mignolo (2012) for a different focus on unlearning. At the centre here is a discussion focusing on epistemologies and ontologies.

8 For an overview of non-learning, see Illeris (2015). For empirical examples of non-learning, see Langström (2017).

9 Recognizing that African feminisms' decolonial perspectives are diverse (for a discussion and overview, see Sylvia Tamale 2020), I here highlight examples that are particularly important for critically discussing SR.

10 When paid domestic work is contrasted with other practices, in particular home-making (see, e.g., Boccagni 2018; Young 2005, who use the concept in their research into domestic work), various forms of domestic work become visible. Home-making should be understood as something that includes domestic and care work but does not necessarily include *paid* domestic work or servitude.

11 Within the diverse field of african feminisms, Tamale 2020 point at how sometimes feminist intersectional debates reproduce western conceptions of gender.

12 I have received invaluable help to search the archive by Dr Samwel Mhajida, University of Dar es Salaam. The responsibility for the analysis of historical documents rest on me. This is further expanded on in the Appendix.

Chapter 2

1 The name is a pseudonym. The names and some personal data of the interviewed domestic workers and expatriate women employers have been changed to anonymize their identity.

2 The diary extract from Chapter 2 is the only extract which has the potential of revealing the identity of the person involved. Here I have specifically asked for a written consent to narrate the incident in this book and in the way that I have interpreted the situation.

Chapter 3

1 The name is a pseudonym.
2 This information was later verified in several interviews that I conducted with domestic workers and privileged expatriate employers. The extract from my diary that introduces this chapter is the only diary extract displayed in this book that has the potential of revealing the identity of the person involved. For this reason, I have collected a written consent from the domestic worker which allows me to renarrate my personal experience of this scene in this book.
3 In interviews with domestic workers and expatriate women in contemporary private households in Dar es Salaam, Tanzania, paid and unpaid domestic work is analysed as processes of learning and unlearning gender, race and class. Integral to analysing contemporary interviews are analysing information pamphlets, research from the archives, a fictional novel and an expatriate woman's diary to map and explore the continuities and changes from the British colonial era (from the 1920s to the 1960s) in processes of learning domestic and care work and possibilities of unlearning. The results are presented in Chapters 4, 5 and 6 respectively.
4 In this respect, the dialogue in this chapter resonates with recent theoretical research in the field of sociology of education, more specifically a dialogue between the Global South and North (Peruzzo et al. 2024). The authors of this project argue that their intention is not to replace sociology of education from the Global North with the Global South. Here they use these divisions to highlight the coloniality of power and recognize that the Global South can be found in the Global North and the authors' ambition is to expand the epistemic imagination and 'make it global but not universal' (Peruzzo et al. 2023: 1241). In this chapter, the ambition is more modest, and I initiate a dialogue (between intersectional research on SR and critical education) and identify connections with the ambition to move towards a decolonial take of SRT.
5 The everyday as a research problematic is outlined later in this chapter.
6 See two empirical examples which theorize educational relations from below and from within; Garcia-Arias,Corbetta and Baronnet (2023), which focuses on formal and informal education from schools, communities and households in

Argentina and Mexico. At the centre of analysis is a critique of Western-centred discourses in SDG's educational frameworks and an empirically driven theoretical contribution to re-imagining education. Another empirical contribution from Zambia focuses on the necessity to broaden the sociology of education currently taught in Zambia to also encompass literature and empirical areas that are locally grounded alongside with dominant and Western-centred classical sociological literature such as Mead, Marx and Mills (Thomas, Serenje and Chipindi 2023).

7 See also a similar critical note in Graness (2019).

Chapter 4

1 The villagization programme was central in President Julius Nyerere's vision of African socialism – that is *Ujaama*, which comprised locally administered villages. Populations were transferred from small to larger villages, sometimes involuntarily (see also Coulson 2013: 23).

2 Master and servant ordinances. Consolidated and amended on 31 December 1945. *Employment of Women and Young Persons* (1945: 85). Printed and published by the Government Printer in Dar es Salaam.

3 Ibid.

4 Labour office provincial administration. Tanga ref: Bo 254/41/4:no 58.

5 Mbilinyi's (1988) research focuses on the Rungwe area, which is part of the Tanzanian Highlands. During the post-war years, this area was constructed as a labour reserve for the colonial administration. It was a period when men were increasingly drawn into forced labour, were 'recruited' to the Tanga sisal plantations and into mining and, later, during the 1940s, as forced labour to the military defence. By 1954, 25 per cent of all men had been absent from the Rungwe area and 85 per cent of all young men (17–35-year-olds) had worked as migrant labourers at least once.

6 See Nyanto (2019) for a discussion of the role of missionaries in the division of land and processes of education and, importantly, for a perspective from below – that is, ways in which communities challenged these land-grabbing aspirations.

7 In particular by creating wage labour and enacting the House and Poll Tax Ordinance 1912, Hut and Poll Tax Ordinance No. 13 of 1922, together with Involuntary Servitude (Abolition) Ordinance, No. 13 and House Tax Ordinance, No. 26 both of the same year.

8 Section 2 of the Master and Native Servant (Recruitment) Ordinance 1946 Cap 80.

9 In this context it is worth noting prior research which emphasizes how women, in various ways, objected to this rule and sometimes travelled, disguised as men, to find work and livelihoods (see also Giblin 2005).

10 There were also discordant voices in the colonial administration during this period. Here is an example from Colonial officer Frederick Pedler who, in 1942, tried to increase the wages of workers significantly, from 15 shillings per month to 15 shillings per *week* (Cooper1996: 117). The underlying rationale for Pedler's proposal was the ambition to make it possible for migrant workers to bring their families to their workplace, hence to stabilize the workforce. Thus, Pedler put the worker's family at the centre of the labour issue, insisting 'that the orderly reproduction of a labor force was a necessary condition to increasing production' (Cooper 1996: 117).

11 After the Second World War, the Colonial Office in Britain also prepared for a withdrawal from the empire. Bujra's (2000: 67) archival research shows how international bodies such as the United Nations, under whose mandate Britain ruled, as well as its under-department, the International Labour Organization (ILO) were all protesting against the super-exploitation of workers and claiming that the work of women and children should also be counted and their rights protected. From the archives, these bodies also advocated for workers' rights to be more organized. In the colonial files, a separate file (UN, Visiting Commission 1951: Petition: African Cooks . . . etc.' (V22/37681) which collected the activities, letters and petitions from the domestic workers' union, was gathered – cited in Bujra (2000: 67). Other laws passed in the1950s were the Factories Ordinance, Cap 297, and Workmen's Compensation Ordinance, Cap 263, Accidents and Occupational Diseases (Notification) Ordinance, Cap 381. Some of the above Ordinances, amended from time to time, are still in force today.

12 NO/97/16/8; Ref 9/15/102. April 1960, Extract from a monthly report from Senior Labour Officer Iringa.

13 NO 97/16/8.

Chapter 5

1 In accordance with feminist geographers (Gilmore 2022; Massey 2005) I understand place and space as mutually constituted and therefore I use them interchangeably. Integral to this is the understanding of place–space as continuously produced and therefore place–space *is* also always temporal, hence time–place–space.

2 As described in Chapter 3, this volume departs from the view that the everyday is a social construct which is crucial for understanding any process of continuity and change (Smith 2005). Importantly, continuity and change are always graded processes that can only be separated at an analytical level.
3 The terminology 'Endless Pressure' is inspired by the title of the book *Endless Pressure: A Study of West Indian Life-Styles in Bristol* (1986) by Ken Pryce.
4 See, for example, Katz (2001b), for different elaborations on resistance.
5 Skills practices and how they are used in this chapter are described under the heading 'Learning internal spatial relations'.
6 Tamale (2020: 84) uses the concepts State Customary Law vs Living Customary Law.
7 In this context, we note that Tanzania is among those countries which have not ratified the UN Convention 189 for Domestic Workers' Rights, despite several initiatives to raise awareness of the conditions of this workgroup. To contextualize, we note that several countries in the West, among them Sweden, only ratified the convention in 2018, indicating how domestic work, globally, remains a contested work sector; the main areas of controversy being the blurring of private and public relations that emerge while domestic work is taking place in private homes. Another contested area is the role of paid domestic work for gender equality; Taking the example of Sweden, for mostly white, for white, well-educated and economically privileged women, paid domestic work is seen as a gender-equality tool which would release privileged women from the burden of domestic work. For, mostly, low-educated migrant or racialized women, domestic work is constructed as a way of finding employment, albeit poorly paid. In this respect, domestic work is articulated as a way of increasing their emancipation. These gender-equality arguments rarely tap into the role of men or the economic and social hierarchies that are reproduced through this labour, both between women and between women and men.
8 At a different scale, the separation between servants' quarters and private residences also mirrors the spatial separation between living areas for domestic workers and those for expatriate employers in the city at large.
9 For example, the use of smartphones, communication and economic transactions via M-pesa was put in practice and used long before the Swedish system, Swish.
10 Janet, another domestic worker I interviewed, also worked as a live-in domestic worker. Janet's experiences resonate with those of Fatuma, except that she does not reside in the servants' quarters, as the employers she is working for live in an apartment. Instead, she sleeps on the floor next to the baby she is taking care of.

11 For examples of how live-in domestic workers choose to distance themselves from the children they take care of, see Parreñas (2001).

12 The East African slave trade was formally outlawed in 1873 when the British and the Sultan of Zanzibar signed a treaty prohibiting the transport of enslaved persons anywhere along the coast of East Africa (Iskander 2021: 36). The slave trade was a feature of the Omani control of Zanzibar and the coastal regions in the precolonial period; slave labour was also drawn on to work the clove plantations in Zanzibar.

13 The latter originating from industrial sociology. Instead, learning emotional labour is closer to competence learning, which departs from a position that merges labour and labouring bodies – more specifically, the view that a person can merge skills and draw from their personality to fulfil their work. In addition, competence learning emphasizes flexibility and the ability to learn and adjust to unknown situations (see also Illeris 2015).

Chapter 6

1 The diplomatic spouses' group is an informal group that meets on a regular basis to discuss and organize social gatherings aimed at strengthening the diplomatic as well as the local community. Such activities include raising fund for local hospitals, schools or women's shelters as well as supporting new expatriate families finding their way in Dar es Salaam. Personal information.

2 For this chapter, I have analysed contemporary interviews with expatriate women and contemporary handbooks for expatriate families: Corona Tanzania (2009–2015); United Nations Tanzania (2014). The colonial texts include *The Kenya Handbook, 1960*; Bradley (1948); Latham and Latham (1995); OSPA (2016).

3 Importantly, Kelly, Burton and Regan (1996) focus on a different research area, namely how women cope with sexual violence. As explained in detail in Chapter 4, I draw from this research as the claim for a more nuanced discussion around victims, who are often portrayed as the opposite to survivors, resonates with my argument here.

4 The *UN Tanzania Welcome Booklet* is more formal in its representation, with fewer photos and lifestyle reports compared to Corona Tanzania.

5 This text extract is outlined in Chapter 4.

6 The advice on sexual education, menstruation and abortion was revealed in an interview which was not recorded and therefore cannot be transcribed. This means that no direct citation could be made.

7 In the preface, we also find a cautionary note on how to understand the language which is reproducing derogatory imaginaries of Africans and of African servants.

8 Important to note here is that I have also interviewed privileged expatriate women who were more satisfied with staying at home compared to Karen. In particular they were satisfied if they had small children. The reason for highlighting Karen's experiences here is because this is a very clear example of how doing gender is not straightforward but is, instead, a complex and ambivalent process of learning which shifts across different geographic locations. To exemplify the ambivalence: the women expressed more satisfaction with their current lifestyle compared to Karen and also said that they had felt ambivalence when they had paid work, which most of them had before embarking on an expatriate journey. Taken together this means that, for women, balancing paid work and unpaid domestic and care work is ambivalent regardless of whether women prefer to perform unpaid domestic work before paid work. At the centre of these ambivalent discussions that the women shared with me was conditions for doing mothering, which is a main way of performing femininity.

9 The quotation, which has been transcribed, is from a historical research project and a workshop. In this workshop, former expatriate women or their relatives (if they had died) met and discussed the role of expatriate women during the British colonial empire (OSPA 2016).

10 See Callan and Ardener (1984).

11 See also Gwyneth Latham's diary (Latham and Latham 1995), particularly chapter 12, 'The Lupa Goldrush', for similar examples – articulated, however, in a cheerful tone.

12 In my contemporary interviews with expatriate women, their perception of domestic work implies them giving plenty of instructions to the domestic workers in their household while, at the same time, bemoaning the impossibility of giving instructions – which is articulated as cumbersome. 'Oh, it becomes easier for me to do the work rather than to explain it to her' is a common statement. The reason for this varies from being about care and respect for the domestic worker and about the work she is doing: 'I don't want to interfere with her work, I don't want to be somebody who is telling her what to do.' Other comments lean more towards demeaning accounts, as articulated in the interview with Maya. I interpret these accounts as representations of perceptions of the women who perform paid domestic work where the former signals respect and appreciation and the latter devaluation and at times naturalization.

13 See Chapter 4 for an analysis on how loans are perceived by domestic workers.

14 In the 1914–1915 yearbook of Corona Tanzania, we can read the following:

> Another important item to state is the policy on loans you wish to follow. If you will allow loans, then you may want to clarify what the limits are that you will put on these loans. It is most likely that, at some point, you WILL be asked for a loan by your staff. (Corona Tanzania 2009–15: 56)

15 The majority of employers paid between 300,000 and 600,000 Tanzanian shillings for a full-time domestic worker per month. One Tanzanian shilling is 0.00037 Euros as of 21 August 2023.

16 Some of these statements appear in the interviews and some are retrieved through follow-up personal information. For this reason some of the statements are not cited as direct quotations.

Appendix

Research method and participants' profiles

The research presented here is the result of a multilayered approach to analysing interviews, archival research, fictional texts, educational texts as well as built space and built space displayed in photos (see Hall 1997 and Chapters 2 and 5 in this book). The interviews, which I conducted, took place on the Msasani Peninsula, Dar es Salaam, from March to June 2018. When necessary, I contacted domestic workers and expatriate women again later, for follow-up interviews or clarifications. In total, thirty-five individual interviews and four group interviews have been made.

The group interviews were arranged in a location that was suggested by the participants. This could be a public space or in a private house. The majority of those interviewed in a group were not interviewed individually. The group interviews lasted between 1.5 and 2.5 hours and centred around themes such as work conditions, work experiences, recruitment situations, training and contracts. These themes are similar but not identical to those of the individual interviews, which also dwelt on the work-life history of the expatriate women and of domestic workers. The group interviews, two with domestic workers and two with expatriate women, had between five and ten participants respectively, which made the group big enough to stimulate a conversation between participants but small enough to eliminate the risk of some voices being overruled by others. In a group interview, there is always a risk that participants will hold back or adjust their personal views to fit with what they perceive to be the dominant perceptions. For this reason, some questions that were posed in the group interview were followed up in individual interviews. The results from this triangulation showed that answers in both types of interviews pointed in the same direction.

One of the domestic workers, Rusi Samweli Kabinga (the name is a pseudonym) who worked with me in my household together with two of her closest work colleagues were of tremendous importance for arranging the group interviews with domestic workers. The language spoken in the group interviews made with domestic workers oscillated between Kiswahili and English. During the group interviews, the domestic workers who were more skilled in English translated my questions in English to Kiswahili and the domestic workers' answers from Kiswahili to English. I realized that the fact that we were all non-native English-speakers and that I knew some basic words in Kiswahili created a bond between us when we communicated and this helped to diminish power hierarchies during the interviews. Nevertheless – and as explained in the introductory chapter – power relations are inevitable in a research situation and can never be completely overcome. What can be done, as I did, is to make efforts to upset these power hierarchies.

Twenty individual interviews with domestic workers were conducted. Again, the trio of women who helped me to organize the group interviews with domestic workers were of tremendous importance for facilitating contact with individual domestic workers. The interviewed domestic workers were all Tanzanians. The interviews were organized in themes. I discussed the themes that I had found in the previous literature on research on domestic work and domestic workers with Rusi and made adjustments according to her recommendations. These began with the view of what she thought would be the most important for researchers and other stakeholders to know about domestic workers' lives and working conditions and that would have the potential to improve domestic workers' working lives in the future.

The individual interviews with domestic workers lasted between 30 minutes and 1.5 hours. One reason for the variation in length is because the interviews were loosely organized using themes. Organizing interviews in themes instead of a detailed questionnaire is because I wanted the interview to take the form of a conversation. My view is that a conversation rather than a questionnaire functions better in creating the ambiance of a meeting between the interviewer and the interviewee, which is important for building trust. Trust is essential for creating a situation where nuances, reflections and uncertainties can be outlined more freely. I let the participants choose how much they wanted to expand on each theme, eventually asking follow-up questions but being sensitive to the participants' wishes. Other aspects that have impacted on the length of the interviews were language barriers or individuals' work-life schedules which sometimes put limits on the time that could be spent on interviews.

When I interviewed a domestic worker individually and we found language barriers, we would try to use Google Translate. If the internet connection was bad or if we could not get the right answer, we would try to call somebody who was skilled in both English and Kiswahili and who could help us to get round the obstacle. I would first ask the domestic worker if she wanted to contact somebody she trusted. If she preferred me to call someone, I would call Rusi, the domestic worker who was employed in my household and who was knowledgeable of this project, and often whom we both knew and trusted.

The domestic workers were aged between twenty-five and fifty-five. All were mothers and the vast majority were single mothers, either following a divorce or by being widowed. Their education levels ranged from middle school to high school. The majority of domestic workers had migrated from surrounding areas, such as Iringa, Moshi, Arusha or Dodoma, to find work in Dar es Salaam. Frequently, a relative had helped them to migrate to Dar es Salaam, and this was also where the vast majority had their first experience as a domestic worker. Their work experience ranged from three to thirty years. The majority of them worked full-time, but a third were employed part-time. One domestic worker was employed by the hour. Their salaries were between 300,000 and 600,000 Tanzanian shillings for a full-time job. Two were a so-called live-in domestic worker, who earned 400,000 shillings, with accommodation and food included.

Fifteen individual interviews with expatriate women were conducted in either English or Swedish when this was their mother tongue. Three of the females interviewed individually were not diplomats and had followed their husband on his international business career. Their ways of organizing and doing domestic work were very similar to the diplomatic spouses.

The expatriate women's age ranged between thirty-five and sixty years. Their education ranged from a high-school level to a PhD degree. The majority were from European or North American contexts, with just three originating from non-Western contexts. All the expatriate women I interviewed had experiences of mothering. Their expatriate experience ranged from one to fifteen years. Some also had experience of growing up in expatriate households in various parts of the world. I have particularly strived to interview women who had followed their husbands or partners on this mission because I have been interested in how domestic work is experienced from the standpoint of so-called 'trailing-spouses'. This means that the majority of women whom I interviewed were not performing salaried work, although three were doing part-time salaried work. Two were working full-time. During one group interview, a male spouse participated. His experiences have not been included in the analysis as they were outside the scope of this book, which focuses on domestic work as a process of learning the standpoint of women.

The individual and group interviews with the domestic workers were transcribed by a professional who is knowledgeable in both English and Kiswahili. Both Kiswahili and English were transcribed. The sections of interviews with expatriate women which have been quoted in this book were transcribed by me.

As explained in the first chapter, the overall methodological framework in this book is inspired by oral history and analysis of work-life interviews. This methodological entrance was operationalized as follows: the interviews were coded and analysed according to themes such as 'the content of domestic work', 'instructions and instructing', 'worker–employer relations', 'the household workplace', 'gender equality/inequality' and 'aspirations for the future'. These themes have been further analysed and sub-themes have been constructed. For example, 'the content of domestic work' creates the sub-theme of 'the difference between domestic work and work in general', which then extends into sub-themes on the cheapening of domestic work and domestic workers. Another example, the theme of 'Instructions and instructing' extends into the sub-theme of 'making the invisible visible', which lays the ground for an analysis of how domestic workers unlearn processes of cheapening of their work by negotiating processes of knowledge transfer or diplomas. Finally, the themes generated through the interviews have been analysed in relation to the total number of interviews within the respective groups. This way of analysing the data is inspired by a hermeneutical thematic method which implies working in and out from the data and theory in order to produce a thick understanding of a particular phenomenon (Kvale 1997). Importantly, while the themes for the interviews with domestic workers were discussed with Rusi, the domestic worker working in my household, the responsibility for the analytical work in this book rests on me.

In the context of the research presented here, the themes that resulted from the interview analysis are related to the historical context of research using other sources of texts such as cookbooks, handbooks and historical work. This is done by tracing the contemporary theme found in the interviews backwards and by analysing how the theme has transformed or not, with the aim of finding openings for the future. The texts that are included here are chosen on the grounds that previous research has pointed out that cookbooks (Blackett 2019) and literary novels (Jansen 2019) are particularly useful for understanding the organization of lives and gender, race and the class complexities that exist between privileged women and domestic workers. There are numerous texts which display similar narratives to those analysed here. The reason for including these particular texts – that is, these particular household handbooks, a fictional novel and a diary – is that they display particularly clear narratives of domestic and care work in everyday expatriate lives under the British colonial administration of East Africa, in particular in Tanganyika between 1920 and 1960.

Dr Samwel Mahjida from University of Dar es Salaam have helped me to search the archives. The search have been guided by the words 'domestic work', 'expatriate women's work', 'subaltern domestic workers', 'labour' and 'labour regulations during the British colonial period of the 1920s–1960s'. The responsibility for analysing the documents and for Chapter 4 lays on me. In the historicizing chapter I was inspired by decolonial feminist and archival research. This means that I have strived to connect different narratives of domestic work from various positionalities and in differing periods in time (Swaby and Frank 2020). To accomplish this task, I have chosen to include a novel which displays a narrative from a subaltern domestic worker. Importantly, the novel *Paradiset* reflects an earlier era – Tanganyika during the beginning of the nineteenth century – but is included here as it provides a narrative of how a subaltern domestic worker negotiate relations of debt and dependency in the everyday life, a theme which has been central in the contemporary interviews, archival research and handbooks analysed in this book.

References

Allen, R. B. (2008), 'Capital, Illegal Slaves, Indentured Labourers and the Creation of a Sugar Plantation Economy in Mauritius, 1810–60', *The Journal of Imperial and Commonwealth History*, 36 (2): 151–70. https://doi.org/10.1080/03086530802180569

Ally, M. (1992), 'Time for a Multi-Party System', *Daily News*, 19 February.

Amadiume, I. (1987), *Male Daughters, Female Husbands: Gender and Sex in an African Society*, London: Zed Books.

Amnesty International (2021/22), *Amnesty International Report 2021/22: The State of the World's Human Rights*. https://reliefweb.int/report/world/amnesty-international-report-202122-state-worlds-human-rights-enar (accessed 18 June 2023).

Anderson, B. (2000), *Doing the Dirty Work?* London: Zed Books.

Anderson, B. (2002), 'Just Another Job? The Commodification of Domestic Labour', in B. Ehrenreigh and A. R. Hochschild (eds), *Global Woman: Nannies, Maids and Sex Workers in the New Economy*, 104–14, New York: Metropolitan Books.

Anderson, B. (2015), 'Migrant Domestic Workers: Good Workers, Poor Slaves, New Connections, Social Politics', *International Studies in Gender, State & Society*, 22 (4): 636–52. https://doi.org/10.1093/sp/jxv040 (accessed 18 June 2023).

Anderson, L. (2006), 'Analytic Authoethnography', *Journal of Contemporary Ethnography*, 35 (4): 373–95.

Anthias, F. (2001), 'The Material and Symbolic in Theorising Social Stratification: Issues of Gender, Ethnicity and Social Class', *British Journal of Sociology*, 52 (3): 367–90.

Anthias, F. (2008), 'Thinking Through the Lens of Translocational Positionality: An Intersectionality Frame for Understanding Identity and Belonging', *Translocations: Migration and Social Change*, 4 (1): 5–20.

Arora-Jonsson, S. (2023), 'The Sustainable Development Goals: A Universalist Promise for the Future', *Futures*, 146 (2023): 103087. https://doi.org/10.1016/j.futures.2022.103087

Aruzza, C., T. Bhattacharya and N. Fraser (2019), *Feminism for the 99 Percent: A Manifesto*, New York: Verso.

Aycan, Z. and R. N. Kanungo (1997), 'Current Issues and Future Challenges in Expatriation Research', in D. M. Saunders and Z. Aycan (eds), *New Approaches to Employee Management*, 245–60, Greenwich: JAI Press.

Bakker, I. and S. Gill (2019), 'Rethinking Power, Production and Social Reproduction: Toward Variegated Social Reproduction', *Capital and Class*, 43 (4): 503–5023.

Becker-Schmidt, R. (1987), 'Dynamik Sozialen Lernens. Geschlechterdifferenz und Konflikte aus der Perspektive von Frauen', in R. Becker-Smith and G. A. Knapp (eds), *Geschlechtertrennumung-Geschlechterdifferenz-Suchbevegungen Sozialen Lernens*, 13–24, Bonn: J. H. W. Dietz.

Best, A. (2003), 'Doing Race in the Context of Feminist Interviewing. Constructing Whiteness through Talk', *Qualitative Inquiry*, 9 (6): 895–914.

Bhabha, H. (1994), *The Location of Culture*, New York: Routledge.

Bhambra, K. G. (2007), *Rethinking Modernity. Postcolonialism and the Sociological Imagination*, New York: Palgrave Macmillan.

Bhambra, K. G. (2014), *Connected Sociologies*, London: Bloomsbury Collections.

Bhattacharya, T. (2017), *Social Reproduction Theory. Remapping Class, Recentring Oppression*, London: Pluto Press.

Bhattacharyya, G. (2018), *Rethinking Racial Capitalism. Questions of Reproduction and Survival*, London: Rowman and Littlefield.

Biesta, G. (2013), 'Interrupting the Politics of Learning', *Power and Education*, 5 (1): 4–15.

Biesta, G. (2017), 'Interrupting the Politics of Learning', in K. Illeris (ed.), *Contemporary Theories of Learning. Learning Theorists .... In Their Own Words*, 2nd edn, 243–59, New York: Routledge.

Biesta, G. and M. Tedder (2007), 'Agency and Learning in the Lifecourse: Towards an Ecological Perspective', *Studies in the Education of Adults*, 39 (2): 132–49.

Black, A. (1995), 'The Changing Culture of Diplomatic Spouses: Some Fieldnotes from Brussels', *Diplomacy and Statecraft*, 6 (1): 196–222. https://doi.org/10.1080/09592299508405959

Blackett, A. (2019), *Everyday Transgressions: Domestic Workers' Transnational Challenge to International Labor Law*, Ithaca: Cornell University Press/ILR Press.

Bloch, E. (1986), Introduction. *The Principle of Hope*. https://www.marxists.org/archive/bloch/hope/introduction.htm (accessed 26 January 2024).

Boccagni, P. (2018), 'At the Roots of Home, Away from It: Meanings, Places and Values of Home through the Biographic Narratives of Immigrant Care Workers in Italy', in K. Davis, H. Gorashi and P. Smets (eds), *Contested Belonging: Spaces, Practices, Biographies*, 313–32, Bingley: Emerald Publishing.

Bonilla-Silva, E. (2011), 'The Invisible Weight of Whiteness: The Racial Grammar of Everyday Life in Contemporary America', *Ethnic and Racial Studies*, 35 (2): 173–94.

Bonnet, F., J. Vanek and M. Chen (2019), *Women and Men in the Informal Economy. A Statistical Brief*, Manchester: Wiego.

Bradley, E. G. (1948), *A Household Book for Tropical Colonies*, London: Oxford University Press.

Breman, J. (1996), *Footloose Labour: Working in India's Informal Economy*, Cambridge: Cambridge University Press.

Britwum, A. O. (2009), 'The Gendered Dynamics of Production Relations in Ghanaian Coastal Fishing', *Feminist Africa*, 12: 69–84.

Bujra, J. (2000), *Serving Class. Masculinity and the Feminization of Domestic Service in Tanzania*, Edinburgh: Edinburgh University Press.

Burawoy, M. (1985), *The Politics of Production: Factory Regimes Under Capitalism and Socialism*, London: Verso.

Callan, H. (1975), 'The Premiss of Dedication: Notes Towards an Ethnography of Diplomats' Wives', in S. Ardener (ed.), *Perceiving Women*, 87–104, London: Dent & Sons.

Callan, H. and S. Ardener (1984), *The Incorporated Wife*, London: Croom Helm.

Carmichael, L. (1965), 'Aunts Need to Boost Morale', *The Sunday News*, 8 December.

Carpenter, S. and S. Mojab (2017), *Revolutionary Learning. Marxism, Feminism and Knowledge*, London: Pluto Press.

Carter, M. (2012), *Women and Indenture. The Experiences of Indian Labour Migrants*, London: Pink Pigeon Press.

Cavallero, L. and V. Gago (2021), *A Feminist Reading of Debt*, London: Pluto Press.

Chakrabarty, D. (2000), *Provincializing Europe. Postcolonial Thought and Historical Difference*, Princeton and Oxford: Princeton University Press.

Cheever, S. (2002), 'The Nanny Dilemma', in B. Ehrenreich and R. Hochschild (eds), *Global Women: Nannies, Maids and Sex Workers in the New Economy*, 31–8, New York: Henry Holt.

Chen, M. A. (2007), *Rethinking the Informal Economy: Linkages with the Formal Economy and the Formal Regulatory Environment*. New York: UN/DESA, Working Paper 46. http://www.un.org/esa/desa/papers/2007/wp46_2007.pdf (accessed 18 June 2023).

Chin, C. B. N. (1998), *In Service and Servitude: Foreign Female Domestic Workers and the Malaysian 'Modernity' Project*, New York: Columbia University Press.

Cock, J. (1984), *Maids and Madams: A Study in the Politics of Exploitation*, Johannesburg: Ravan Press.

Colen, S. (1995), 'Like a Mother to Them: Stratified Reproduction and West Indian Childcare Workers and Employers in New York', in F. D. Ginsburg and R. Rapp (eds), *Conceiving the New World Order: The Global Politics of Reproduction*, 78–102, Berkeley: University of California Press.

Constable, N. (2007), *Maid to Order in Hong Kong: Stories of Migrant Workers*, 2nd edn, Ithaca: Cornell University Press.

Cooper, D. (2022), 'Afterword', in L. Monticelli (ed.), *The Future is Now. An Introduction to Prefigurative Politics*, 230–41, Bristol: Bristol University Press.

Cooper, F. (1996), *Decolonization and African Society: The Labor Question in French and British Africa*, Cambridge: Cambridge University Press, E-book. https://hdl.handle.net/2027/heb.02578.

Corbin Dwyer, S. and J. L. Buckle (2018), 'Reflection/Commentary on a Past Article: "The Space Between: On Being an Insider-Outsider in Qualitative Research"', *International Journal of Qualitative Methods*, 17 (1): January–December 2018. https://doi.org/10.1177/1609406918788176

Corona Tanzania (2009–2015), *Yearbooks. The Newcomer's Guide to Dar es Salaam*, Dar es Salaam: Jamala.

Cotter, J. (2020), 'The "Flat Ontology" of Neoliberal Feminism', in K. Fakier, D. Mulinari and N. Räthzel (eds), *Marxist-Feminist Theories and Struggles Today*, 51–69, London: Zed Books.

Coulson, A. (2013), *Tanzania: A Political Economy*, Oxford: Oxford University Press.

Crenshaw, K. (1991), 'Mapping the Margins: Intersectionality, Identity Politics, and Violence against Women of Color', *Stanford Law Review*, 43 (6): 1241–99.

Curry, A. (2021), *Extending the Imagination of African Gender Thought*. https://hoodcommunist.org/2021/02/18/extending-the-imagination-of-african-gender-thought/ (accessed 20 July 2023).

Davis, A., G. Dent, E. Miners and B. E. Richie (2022), *Abolition. Feminism. Now*, London: Haymarket Books.

Davis, Y. A. (1983), *Women, Race and Class*, New York: Vintage Books.

Davoine, E., C. Ravasi, X. Salamin and C. Cudré-Mauroux (2013), 'A "Dramaturgical" Analysis of Spouse Role Enactment in Expatriation: An Exploratory Gender Comparative Study in the Diplomatic and Consular Field', *Journal of Global Mobility*, 1 (1): 92–112.

de los Reyes, P. and D. Mulinari (2019) 'Hegemonic Feminism Revisited: On the Promises of Intersectionality in Times of the Precarisation of Life', *Nora – Nordic Journal of Feminist and Gender Research*, 28 (3): 183–96.

De Vita, A. and F. Vittori (2022), 'Prefiguration and Emancipatory Critical Pedagogy: The Learning Side of Practice', in L. Monticelli (ed.), *The Future is Now. An Introduction to Prefigurative Politics*, 76–90, Bristol: Bristol University Press.

Dinerstein, A. C. (2022), 'Decolonizing Prefiguration: Ernst Bloch's Philosophy of Hope and the Multiverse', in L. Monticelli (ed.), *The Future is Now. An Introduction to Prefigurative Politics*, 47–64, Bristol: Bristol University Press.

Domett, T. (2005), 'Soft Power in Global Politics? Diplomatic Partners as Transversal Actors', *Australian Journal of Political Science*, 40 (2): 289–306. https://doi.org/10.1080/10361140500130014

Du Bois, W. E. B. (1998), *Black Reconstruction in America, 1860–1880*, New York: Free Press (originally published 1935).

Emirbayer, M. and A. Mische (1998), 'What Is Agency?', *American Journal of Sociology*, 103 (4): 962–1023.

Enloe, C. (2006), 'Just Like One of the Family: Domestic Servants in World Politics', in M. K. Zimmerman, J. S. Litt and C. E. Bose (eds), *Global Dimensions of Carework and Gender*, 118–23, Stanford: Stanford University Press.

Enloe, C. (2014), *Bananas, Beaches and Bases. Making Feminist Sense of International Politics*, Berkeley: University of California Press.

Escobar, A. (2022), 'Foreword', in L. Monticelli (ed.), *The Future is Now. An Introduction to Prefigurative Politics*, xxii–xxx, Bristol: Bristol University Press.

Fakier, K. and J. Cock (2009), 'A Gendered Analysis of the Crisis of Social Reproduction in Contemporary South Africa', *International Feminist Journal of Politics*, 11 (3): 353–71.

Farahani, F. (2015), 'Home and Homelessness and Everything in Between: A Route from One Uncomfortable Zone to Another', *European Journal of Women's Studies*, 22 (2): 241–7.

Farahani, F. (2018), *Gender, Sexuality and Diaspora*, New York: Routledge

Federici, S. (2012), *Revolution at Point Zero*, Oakland: PM Press.

Ferguson, J. (2013), 'Declarations of Dependence: Labour, Personhood, and Welfare in Southern Africa', *Journal of the Royal Anthropological Institute*, 19 (2): 223–42.

Ferguson, S. (2016), 'Intersectionality and Social-Reproduction Feminisms: Toward an Integrative Ontology', *Historical Materialism. Research in Critical Marxist Theory*, 24 (2): 38–60.

Ferguson, S. (2020), *Women and Work. Feminism, Labour and Social Reproduction*, London: Pluto Press.

Ferro, S. (2018), 'Concrete as Weapon', *Harvard Design Magazine*, 46: 8–30.

Finch, J. (1983), *Married to the Job: Wives' Incorporation in Men's Work*, London: Allen & Unwin.

Forno, F. and S. Wahlen (2022), 'Prefiguration in Everyday Practices: When the Mundane Becomes Political', in L. Monticelli (ed.), *The Future is Now. An Introduction to Prefigurative Politics*, 119–29, Bristol: Bristol University Press.

Foucault, M. (1971), 'Orders of Discourse', *Social Science Information*, 10 (2): 7–30.

Foucault, M. (1984), 'What is Enlightenment?', in P. Rabinow (ed.), *The Foucault Reader*, 32–50, New York: Pantheon Books.

Foucault, M. (1989), *Truth and Power. Power/Knowledge: Selected Interviews and Other Writings 1972–1977*, trans. Gordon, C. et al., Hemel Hemstead: Harvester Press.

Foucault, M. (1991), 'Questions of Method', in G. Burchell, C. Gordon and P. Miller (eds), *The Foucault Effect: Studies in Governmentality*, 73–86, Chicago: University of Chicago Press.

Freire, P. (1998), *The Paulo Freire Reader*, New York: Continuum.
Freire, P. (2000), *A Pedagogy of the Oppressed*, 30th anniversary edn; trans. M. B. Ramos, New York and London: Continuum.
Garabiles, M. R., E. H. Mayawati and B. Halla (2021), 'Exploring Resilience Processes of Filipino Migrant Domestic Workers: A Multisystemic Approach', *Journal of Community Psychology*, 50 (7): 3122–40.
Garcia-Arias, J., J. Corbetta and B. Baronnet (2023), 'Decolonizing Education in Latin America: Critical Environmental and Intercultural Education as an Indigenous Pluriversal Alternative', *British Journal of Sociology of Education*, 44 (8): 1394–412. https://doi.org/10.1080/01425692.2023.2234088
Geiger, S. (1982), 'Umoja wa Wanawake wa Tanzania and the Needs of the Rural Poor', *African Studies Review*, 25 (2/3): 45–65.
Geiger, S. (1987), 'Women in Nationalist Struggle: Tanu Activists in Dar es Salaam', *The International Journal of African Historical Studies*, 20 (1): 1–26. https://www.jstor.org/stable/219275
Gerrard, J., A. Sriprakash and S. Rudolph (2022), 'Education and Racial Capitalism', *Race Ethnicity and Education*, 25 (3): 425–42. https://doi.org/10.1080/13613324.2021.2001449
Giblin, J. L. (2005), *A History of the Excluded: Making Family a Refuge from State in Twentieth-Century Tanzania*, Ohio: Ohio University Press.
Gilmore, W. R. (2022), *Abolition Geography: Essays towards Liberation*, London: Verso.
Gilroy, P. (2000), *Against Race: Imagining Political Culture Beyond the Color Line*, Cambridge, MĀ: First Harvard University Press.
Glenn, E. N. (1992), 'From Servitude to Service Work: Historical Continuities in the Racial Division of Paid Reproductive Labor', *Signs*, 18 (1): 1–43.
Gore, E. and G. LeBaron (2019), 'Using Social Reproduction Theory to Understand Unfree Labour', *Capital and Class*, 43 (4): 561–80.
Gramsci, A. (1971 [1929–35]), *Selections from the Prison Notebooks of Antonio Gramsci*, trans. G. N. Smith and Q. Hoare, New York: International Publishers.
Graness, A. (2019), 'Ubuntu and Buen Vivir: A Comparative Approach', in J. Ogude (ed.), *Ubuntu and the Reconstitution of Community*, 150–75, Bloomington: Indiana University Press.
Gregoratti, C. and S. Tornhill (2023), 'The Making of a Business Case for Unpaid Care and Domestic Work in the Global South: New frontiers of Corporate Social Responsibility?' *Antipode,* 0 (0): 1–18. https://doi.org/10.1111/anti.12995
Gurnah, A. (1994/2021), *Paradiset*, Lund: Celanders Förlag.
Gutierrez-Rodriguez, E. (2021), 'Temporal – Spatial Entanglements of Global Inequalities: On Care and Domestic Work in Western Europe', in E. Gutierrez-Rodrigue and R. Reddock (eds), *Decolonial Perspectives on Entangled Inequalities. Europe and the Carribean*, 77–94, London: Anthem Press.

Hall, C. (2007), 'Of Gender and Empire: Reflections on the Nineteenth Century', in P. Levine (ed.), *Gender and Empire*, 46–76, Oxford: Oxford University Press.

Hall, S. (1997), *Representation: Cultural Representations and Signifying Practices*, London: Sage.

Hammer, A. (2019), 'Comparative Capitalism and Emerging Economies: Formal-Informal Economy Interlockages and Implications for Institutional Analysis', *Review of International Political Economy*, 26 (2): 337–60.

Haraway, D. (1996), 'Situated Knowledges: The Science Question in Feminism and the Privilege of Partial Perspectives', in E. F. Keller and H. E. Longino (eds), *Feminism and Science*, 249–64, Oxford: Oxford University Press.

Haug, F. (1997), 'The Neoliberal Project, The Masculine Concept of Work, and the Overdue Renewal of the Gender Contract', *The South Atlantic Quarterly*, 96 (4): 896–908.

Haug, F. (2020), 'Contradictions in Marxist Feminism', in K. Fakier, D. Mulinari and N. Räthzel (eds), *Marxist-Feminist Theories and Struggles Today*, 27–39, London: Zed Books.

Hennessy, R. (1993), *Materialist Feminism and the Politics of Discourse*, New York: Routledge.

Hess, R. (2000), 'Avant-Propos à la Quatrième Édition Française. Henri Lefebvre et la Pensée de l'Espace', in H. Lefebvre (ed.), *La Production de l'Espace*, v–xvi, Paris: Anthropos.

Hochschild, A. R. (1983), *The Managed Heart: Commercialization of Human Feeling*, Berkeley: University of California Press.

Hochschild, A. R. (2000), 'Global Care Chains and Emotional Surplus Value', in A. Giddens and W. Hutton (eds), *On the Edge: Living with Global Capitalism*, 130–46, London: Jonathan Cape.

Hondagneu-Sotelo, P. (2001), *Doméstica: Immigrant Workers Cleaning and Caring in the Shadows of Affluence*, Berkeley: University of California Press.

hooks, b. (1989), 'Choosing the Margin as a Space of Radical Openness Framework', *The Journal of Cinema and Media*, 36 (1): 15–23.

hooks, b. (1994), *Teaching to Transgress. Education as the Practice of Freedom*, New York: Routledge.

hooks, b. (2003), *Teaching Community. A Pedagogy of Hope*, London: Routledge.

Housewives (Kenya) (1960), *The Kenya Handbook*, Nairobi.

Human Development Report (2019), *Inequalities in Human Development in the 21st Century*, Inequalities in Human Development in the 21st Century (modernghana .com) (accessed 18 June 2023).

Human Development Report (2020), *Human Development Insights: United Republic of Tanzania*. http://hdr.undp.org/en/countries/profiles/TZA (accessed 18 June 2023).

Human Rights Watch (2019), *Tanzania: Events of 2019*. https://www.hrw.org/world-report/2020/country-chapters/tanzania-and-zanzibar (accessed 18 June 2023).

Illeris, K. (2015a), *Lärande*, Lund: Studentlitteratur.

Illiffe, J. (1979), *A Modern History of Tanganyika*, Cambridge: Cambridge University Press.

ILO (2013a), *Women and Men in the Informal Economy: A Statistical Picture*, 2nd edn, Geneva: International Labour Organization.

ILO (2013b), *Transitioning from the Informal to the Formal Economy: Fifth Item on the Agenda. Report V(1)*, Geneva: International Labour Organization.

ILO (2015), *Global Estimates on Migrant Workers. Results and Methodology. Special Focus on Migrant Domestic Workers*. https://www.ilo.org/wcmsp5/groups/public/---dgreports/---dcomm/documents/publication/wcms_436330.pdf (accessed 18 June 2023).

ILO (2016), *A Situational Analysis of Domestic Workers in the United Republic of Tanzania*, Dar es Salaam, Tanzania: ILO Country Office.

Imam, A. (1988), 'Rethinking the Household: Where Are We Now?' Paper presented at CODESRIA/UNESCO/AWORD Seminar on Changing Household, Kinship and Gender Relations in Africa, Dakar, 25–28 April 1988.

Inda, J. X. (2000), 'Performativity, Materiality, and the Racial Body', *Latino Studies Journal*, 11 (3): 74–99.

Ingram, D. (1992), 'Africa's Eventful Year', *Daily News*, 1 January.

Iskander, N. (2021), *Does Skill Make Us Human? Migrant Workers in 21st Century Qatar and Beyond*, Princeton: Princeton University Press.

Jansen, E. (2019), *Like Family. Domestic Workers in South African History and Literature*, Johannesburg: Wits University Press.

Kabeer, N. (2008), *Mainstreaming Gender in Social Protection for the Informal Economy. New Gender Mainstreaming Series on Development Issues*, London: Commonwealth Secretariat.

Kaijage, F. J. (2000), 'War of Clubs: Life, Labour and Struggles of the Tanga Dockworkers', in S. Davies, C. J. Davies, D. de Vries, L. Heerma van Voss, L. Hesselink and K. Weinhauer (eds), *Dock Workers: International Explorations in Comparative Labour History, 1790–1970*, 290–319, Burlington: Ashgate.

Kapoor, I. (2004), 'Hyper-Self-Reflexive Development? Spivak on Representing the Third World "Other"', *Third World Quarterly*, 25 (4): 627–47.

Katz, C. (1991), 'Sow What You Know: The Struggle for Social Reproduction in Rural Sudan', *Annals of the Association of American Geographers*, 81 (3): 488–514.

Katz, C. (2001a), 'Vagabond Capitalism and the Necessity of Social Reproduction', *Antipode*, 33 (4): 709–28.

Katz, C. (2001b), 'On the Grounds of Globalization. A Topography of Feminist Political Engagement', *Signs*, 26 (4): 1213–34.

Keene, D. E. and M. B. Padilla (2010), 'Race, Class and the Stigma of Place: Moving to "Opportunity" in Eastern Iowa', *Health & Place*, 16 (6): 1216–23.

Kelleher, F. (2019), 'Africa: Why the World Needs an African Eco-Feminist Future', *African Arguments*, 12 March. https://africanarguments.org/2019/03/why-world-needs-african-ecofeminist-future/ (accessed 7 August 2023).

Kelly, L. (1987), 'The Continuum of Sexual Violence', in J. Hanmer and M. Maynard (eds), *Women, Violence and Social Control. Explorations in Sociology*, 46–60, London: Palgrave Macmillan.

Kelly, L., S. Burton and L. Regan (1996), 'Beyond Victim or Survivor: Sexual Violence, Identity and Feminist Theory and Practice', in L. Adkins and V. Merchant (eds), *Sexualizing the Social: Power and the Organization of Sexuality*, 77–101, London: Palgrave Macmillan.

Keyl, S. (2017), 'Subaltern Pedagogy: A Critical Theorizing of Pedagogical Practices for Marginalized Border-Crossers', *The International Journal of Critical Pedagogy*, 8 (1): 173–94. http://libjournal.uncg.edu/ijcp/article/view/1095

Khosravi, S. (2007), 'The "Illegal" Traveller: An Auto-Ethnography of Borders', *Social Anthropology/Anthropologie Sociale*, 15 (3): 321–34.

Kiaga, A.-M. (2007), *Blaming the Other Woman. Rural Housegirls and Urban Employers. On Identity, Labour and Migration in Tanzania*, Minneapolis: University of Minnesota, PhD thesis.

Killias, O. (2018), *Follow the Maid: Domestic Worker Migration In and From Indonesia*, Copenhagen: Nias Press.

Kunz, S. (2020), 'Expatriate, Migrant? The Social Life of Migration Categories and the Polyvalent Mobility of Race', *Journal of Ethnic and Migration Studies*, 46 (11): 2145–62. https://doi/10.1080/1369183X.2019.1584525

Kvale, S. (1997), *Den Kvalitativa Forskningsintervjun*, Lund: Studentlitteratur.

Labour Department (1945), *Apprenticeships Ordinance 1940*, Dae es Salaam: Tanganyika Government Printer.

Lan, P. (2006), *Global Cinderellas. Migrant Domestics and Newly Rich Employers in Taiwan*, Durham: Duke University Press.

Langström, C. (2017), *Lärande i Professionaellt Samtalsstöd. Villkor för Vuxna Arbetssökandes Karriärprocesser*, Stockholm: University of Stockholm, Department of Education, PhD thesis No. 54.

Latham, G. and M. Latham (1995), *Kilimanjaro Tales: The Saga of a Medical Family in Africa*, London: Radcliff Press.

LeBaron, G. (2014), 'Reconceptualizing Debt Bondage: Debt as a Class-Based Form of Labor Discipline', *Critical Sociology*, 40 (5): 763–80.

LeBaron, G. and A. J. Ayers (2013), 'The Rise of a "New Slavery"? Understanding African Unfree Labour Through Neoliberalism', *Third World Quarterly*, 34 (5): 873–92.

Lee, C. K. and Y. Kofman (2012), 'The Politics of Precarity: Views Beyond the United States', *Work and Occupations*, 39 (4): 388–408.

Lefebvre, H. (1991), *The Production of Space*, Cambridge: Blackwell.

Lugones, M. (2010), 'Toward a Decolonial Feminism', *Hypatia*, 25 (4): 742–59. https://doi.org/10.1111/j.1527-2001.2010.01137.x

Lundström, C. (2013), '"Mistresses" and "Maids" in Transnational Contact Zones: Transnational Wives and the Intersection of Differences and Intimacy in Swedish Domestic Spaces in Singapore', *Women's Studies International Forum*, 36: 44–53.

Lupatu, M. (1992), 'NEC Proposes Multi-Party System', *Daily News*, 21 January.

Lutz, H. (2011), *The New Maids: Transnational Women and the Care Economy*, London: Zed Books.

Lutz, H. (2017), 'Care as a Fictitious Commodity: Reflections on the Intersections of Migration, Gender and Care Regimes', *Migration Studies*, 5 (3): 356–68.

Lutz, H. (2018), 'Care Migration: The Connectivity between Care Chains, Care Circulation and Transnational Social Inequality', *Current Sociology*, 66 (4): 577–89.

Luxton, M (2018), 'The Reproduction of Life Itself: Gender, Social Reproduction and IPE', in *Handbook on the International Political Economy of Gender*, 37–47, Cheltenham: Edgar Elgar.

Mählck, P. (2012), 'Differentiering och Excellens I det Nya Forskningslandskapet Om Kön, Tystnad och Performativa Vithetshandlingar', *Tidskrift för Genusvetenskap*, 1–2: 25–48.

Mählck, P. (2013), 'Academic Women with Migrant Background in the Global Knowledge Economy: Bodies, Hierarchies and Resistance', *Women's Studies International Forum*, 36: 65–74.

Mählck, P. (2016), 'Academics on the Move? Gender, Race and Place in Transnational Academic Mobility', *Nordstep*, 2: 29784. http://dx.doi.org/10.3402/nstep.v2.29784

Mama, A. (2011), 'What Does It Mean To Do Feminist Research in African Contexts?' *Feminist Review*, 98 (1_suppl): e4–e20.

Mama, A. (2017), 'The Power of Feminist Pan-African Intellect', *Feminist Africa*, 22: 1–15.

Marx, K. (2018), *Capital. A Critique of Political Economy. Volume 1. Book 1. The Process of Production of Capital*, Mission: Modern Barbarian Press.

Massey, D. B. (2005), *For Space*, London and Thousand Oaks: Sage.

Mbilinyi, M. (1988), 'Runaway Wives in Colonial Tanganyika: Forced Labour and Forced Marriage in Rungwe District 1919–1961', *International Sociology of Law*, 16: 1–29.

Mbilinyi, M. (1994), 'Restructuring Gender and Agriculture in Tanzania', in U. Himmelstrand and K. Kinyaknjui (eds), *African Perspectives on Development: Controversies, Dilemmas and Development*, 166–82, London: James Curry.

Mbilinyi, M. (2016), 'Analyzing the History of Agrarian Struggles in Tanzania from a Feminist Perspective', *Review of African Political Economy*, 43 (1): 114–29.

Mbilinyi, M. (2023), 'Women in Tanzania (Tanganyika & Zanzibar)', in P. Scully and K. Sheldon (eds), *Oxford Encyclopedia of African Women's History*, Oxford: Oxford University Press.

McCarthy, H. (2014), 'Women, Marriage and Work in the British Diplomatic Service', *Women's History Review*, 23 (6): 853–73. https://doi.org/10.1080/09612025.2014.906844

McCoy, K., E. Tuck and M. McKenzie (2016), *Land Education: Rethinking Pedagogies of Place from Indigenous, Postcolonial and Decolonizing Perspectives*, London: Routledge.

McNulty, Y. (2012). 'Being dumped in to sink or swim': an empirical study of organizational support for the trailing spouse. *Human Resource Development International, 15*(4), 417–434. https://doi.org/10.1080/13678868.2012.721985

Mendoza, B. (2018), 'Can the Subaltern Save Us?', *Tapuya: Latin American Science and Technology Society*, 1 (1): 109–22.

Mezzadri, A. (2020), 'The Informal Labours of Social Reproduction', *Global Labour Journal*, 11 (1): 156–63.

Mhajida, S. (2021), 'Motherhood, Career Development and Modernization: Experiences of Early Post-Colonial Tanzanian Women', *Journal of Education, Humanities and Sciences*, 10 (2): 1–16.

Mies, M. (1986), *Patriarchy and Accumulation on a World Scale. Women and the International Division of Labour*, London: Zed Books.

Mies, M. (2010), *The Village and the World*, Victoria: Spinifex Press.

Miles, R. and M. Brown (2003), *Racism*, 2nd edn, London: Routledge.

Mitchell, K., S. A. Marston and C. Katz (2003), 'Introduction. Life's Work: An Introduction, Review and Critique', *Antipode*, 35 (3): 415–42.

Mitchell, K., S. A. Marston and C. Katz (2004), *Life's Work: Geographies of Social Reproduction*, Hoboken: Wiley Blackwell.

Mitchell, T. (1991), *Colonising Egypt*, Oakland: University of California Press.

Mohanty, C. (1991), 'Under Western Eyes: Feminist Scholarships and Colonial Discourses', in C. T. Mohanty, A. Russso and T. Lourdes (eds), *Third World Women and the Politics of Feminism*, 51–80, Indianapolis: Indiana University Press.

Mohanty, C. T. (2003), *Feminism Without Borders. Decolonizing Theory, Practicing Solidarity*, Durham: Duke University Press.

Molohan, M. J. B. (1957), *Detribalization*, Dar es Salaam: Tanganyika Government Printer.

Monticelli, L. (2022), *The Future is Now. An Introduction to Prefigurative Politics*, Bristol: Bristol University Press.

Motta, C. S. (2013), 'Teaching Global and Social Justice as Transgressive Spaces of Possibility', *Antipode*, 45 (1): 80–100.

Mulinari, P. (2020), 'The Best Thing I Have Done is to Give Birth; The Second is to Strike', in K. Fakier, D. Mulinari and N. Räthzel (eds), *Marxist-Feminist Theories and Struggles Today*, 124–43, London: Zed Books.

Nyanto, S. S. (2019), '"The Empire Strikes Back": Communities, Catholic Missions, and Imperial Authority in Western Tanzania, 1934–1960', *The Catholic Historical Review*, 105 (1): 139–56.

Nyerere, J. (1966), *Freedom and Unity*, Dar es Salaam: Oxford University Press.

OSPA (2016), *The Role and Experiences of Expatriate Women in the Last Phase of Empire and After*, London: University of London, Institute of Commonwealth Studies.

Ossome, L. (2021a), 'Land in Transition: From Social Reproduction of Labour Power to Social Reproduction of Power', *Journal of Contemporary African Studies*, 39 (4): 550–64.

Ossome, L. (2021b), 'Pedagogies of Feminist Resistance: Agrarian Movements in Africa', *Agrarian South: Journal of Political Economy*, 10 (1): 41–58.

Oyěwùmí, O. (1997), *The Invention of Women: Making an African Sense of Western Gender Discourses*, London: University of Minnesota Press.

Ozyegin, G. (2001), *Untidy Gender: Domestic Service in Turkey*, Philadelphia: Temple University Press.

Parreñas, R. S. (2001), 'Mothering From A Distance: Emotions, Gender and Intergenerational Relations in Filipino Transnational Families', *Feminist Studies*, 27 (2): 361–90.

Parreñas, R. S. (2015), *Servants of Globalization: Migration and Domestic Work*, 2nd edn, Stanford: Stanford University Press.

Parreñas, R. S., K. Kantachote and R. Silvey (2020), 'Soft Violence: Migrant Domestic Worker Precarity and the Management of Unfree Labour in Singapore', *Journal of Ethnic and Migration. Studies*, 47 (20): 4671–87. https://doi/org/10.1080/1369183X.2020.1732614

Patel, R. and J. Moore (2020), *A History of the World in Seven Cheap Things. A Guide to Capitalism, Nature and the Future of the Planet*, London: Verso.

Patel, S. (2021), 'Colonialism and its Knowledges', in D. McCallum (ed.), *The Palgrave Handbook of the History of Human Sciences*, 1–24, Singapore: Palgrave. https://doi.org/10.1007/978-981-15-4106-3_68-1

Pattanaik, B. (2020), 'Will Human Trafficking Increase During and After COVID-19?' https://gaatw.org/blog/1059-will-human-trafficking-increase-during-and-after-covid-19 (accessed 19 June 2023).

Pereira, C. (2002), 'Between Knowing and Imagining: What Space for Feminism in Scholarship on Africa?' *Feminist Africa*, 1: 9–33. https://www.jstor.org/stable/48726056

Peruzzo, F., S. Joiko, J. Allan and M. T. Rojas (2023), 'Other Sociologies of Education: Providing Critical Perspectives from the Global South and North', *British Journal of Sociology of Education*, 44 (8): 1239–48. https://doi/org/10.1080/01425692.2023.2296008

Phyfer, J., K. Durrheim and A. J. Murray (2020), 'Buttressing Whiteness by Confessing Guilt and Rejecting Racism: A Study of White-Talk about Paid Domestic Labour', *South African Review of Sociology*, 51 (1): 3–16. https://doi/org/10.1080/21528586.2020.1741442

Piccardi, E. G. (2022), 'Prefiguring Post-Patriarchal Futures: Jineoloji's Matristic Praxis in the Context of Rojava's Revolution', in L. Monticelli (ed.), *The Future is Now. An Introduction to Prefigurative Politics*, 161–76, Bristol: Bristol University Press.

Portelli, A. (2009), 'What Makes Oral History Different', in L. D. Giudice (ed.), *Oral History, Oral Culture, and Italian Americans*, 21–30, New York: Palgrave Macmillan.

Pryce, K. (1986), *Endless Pressure: A Study of West Indian Life-Styles in Bristol*, Bristol: Bristol Classical.

Pun, N. and C. Smith (2007), 'Putting Transnational Labour Process in its Place: Dormitory Labour Regime in Post-Socialist China', *Work, Employment and Society*, 21 (1): 7–25.

Räthzel, N. (1997), 'Gender and Racism in Discourse', in R. Wodak (ed.), *Gender and Discourse*, 57–80, London: Sage.

Räthzel, N. (2018), '*…the Experience of Acting in the Organization: There's Nothing Equal to it'. A Discursive Approach to Understanding Life-Histories*. https://www.researchgate.net/publication/328261790_%27_the_experience_of_acting_in_the_organization_there%27s_nothing_equal_to_it%27_A_discursive_approach_to_understanding_life-histories (accessed 19 June 2023).

Rodríguez-Rocha, V. (2021), 'Social Reproduction Tehory: State of the Field and New Directions in Geography', *Geography Compass*, 15 (8): 1–16. https://doi.org/10.1111/gec3.12586

Romero, M. (1992), *Maid in the USA*, London: Routledge.

Romero, M. (2018), 'Reflections on Globalized Care Chains and Migrant Women Workers', *Critical Sociology*, 44 (7–8): 1179–89.

Rönnlund, M. and A. Tollefsen (2016), *Rum: Samhällsvetenskapliga Perspektiv*, Stockholm: Liber.

Roy, A. (2021), 'We are Witnessing a Crime against Humanity', *The Guardian*, 28 April. https://www.theguardian.com/news/2021/apr/28/crime-against-humanity-arundhati-roy-india-covid-catastrophe \ (accessed 19 June 2023).

Said, E. (1996), *Representations of the Intellectual*, New York: Vintage Books.

Santos, B. (2014), *Epistemologies of the South: Justice against Epistemicide*, Boulder: Paradigm.

Sawyer, L. and N. Osei-Kofi (2020), '"Listening" With Gothenburg's Iron Well: Engaging the Imperial Archive Through Black Feminist Methodologies and Arts-Based Research', *Feminist Review*, 125 (1): 54–61. https://doi.org/10.1177/0141778920913555

Scully, B. (2016), 'Precarity North and South: A Southern Critique of Guy Standing', *Global Labour Journal*, 7 (2): 160–73.

Shivji, I. G. (1976), *Class Struggle in Tanzania*, London: Heineman.

Shivji, I. G. (2019), *Good Governance, Bad Governance and the Quest for Democracy in Africa: An Alternative Perspective*, Dar es Salaam, HakiElimu, Working Paper No. 8. http: wwww.hakieleium.org

Smelser, N. (1998), 'The Rational and the Ambivalence in the Social Sciences', *American Sociological Review*, 16: 1–6.

Smiley, S. L. (2010), 'Expatriate Everyday Life in Dar es Salaam, Tanzania: Colonial Origins and Contemporary Legacies', *Social & Cultural Geography*, 11 (4): 327–42.

Smith, E. D. (1987), *The Everyday World as Problematic: A Feminist Sociology*, Boston: Northeastern University Press.

Smith, E. D. (2005), *Institutional Ethnography: A Sociology for People*, Oxford: AltaMira Press.

Soja, E. (2010), *Seeking Spatial Justice*, Minneapolis: University of Minnesota Press.

Spivak, G. C. (1988), 'Can the Subaltern Speak?', in C. Nelson and L. Grossberg (eds), *Marxism and the Interpretation of Culture*, 271–314, Urbana: University of Illinois Press.

Standfield, C. (2020), 'Gendering the Practice Turn in Diplomacy', *European Journal of International Relations*, 26 (S1): 140–65.

Steiler, I. (2021), 'The Intersectionality of Informal Employment: Insights from Street Vending and Domestic Work in Tanzania', *Journal of Labor and Society*, 24 (1): 107–32.

Stoler, A. (2010), *Along the Archival Grain: Epistemic Anxieties and Colonial Common Sense*, Princeton: Princeton University Press.

Stewart, A. (2021), 'Feminism for the 99% or Solidarity in the House of Difference? Intersectionality and Social Reproduction Theory', *Femina Politica–Zeitschrift für feministische Politikwissenschaft*, 30 (2): 23–35.

Švelch, J. and T. Sherman (2018), '"I See Your Garbage":Participatory Practices and Literacy Privilege on "Grammar Nazi" Facebook Pages in Different Sociolinguistic Contexts', *New Media and Society*, 20 (7):2391–410.

Swaby, N. A. and C. Frank (2020), 'Archival Experiments, Notes and (Dis) Orientations', *Feminist Review*, 125: 4–16. https://doi.org/10.1177/0141778920931874

Tamale, S. (2020), *Decolonization and Afro-Feminism*, Wakefield: Daraja Press.

Tazreiter, C. (2019), 'Temporary Migrants as an Uneasy Presence in Immigrant Societies: Reflections on Ambivalence in Australia', *International Journal of Comparative Sociology*, 60 (1–2): 91–109.

The Labour Department (1945), *A Handbook of the Labour Laws of Tanganyika Territory Together with an Explanatory Note*, Dar es Salaam: Government Printer.

Thomas, M. A. M., J. Serenje and M. F. Chipindi (2023), 'Reconsidering and Teaching Sociologies in Zambian Teacher Education: Seeking Mbuyi, Mulenga, and Munkombwe', *British Journal of Sociology of Education*, 44 (7): 1199–215. https://doi.org/10.1080/01425692.2023.2295993

Tlostanova, M. V. and W. D. Mignolo (2012), *Learning to Unlearn. Decolonial Reflections from Eurasia and the Americas*, Columbus: The Ohio State University Press.

Tripp, A. M. (1997), *Changing the Rules: The Politics of Liberalization and the Urban Informal Economy in Tanzania*, Berkeley: University of California Press.

Ullah, A. A. (2015), 'Abuse and Violence Against Foreign Domestic Workers. A Case from Hong Kong', *International Journal of Area Studies*, 10 (2): 221–38.

UNECA (1975), 'Women and National Development in African Countries: Some Profound Contradictions', *African Studies Review*, 18 (3): 47–70.

United Nations Tanzania (2014), *UN Tanzania Welcome Booklet*, Dar es Salaam: United Nations Tanzania.

Van Bortel, T., S. Martin, S. Anjara and L. B. Nellums (2019), 'Perceived Stressors and Coping Mechanisms of Female Migrant Domestic Workers in Singapore', *PloS ONE*, 14 (3): e0210717. https:// doi.org/10.1371/journal.pone.0210717

Van Tol, D. (2015), 'The Women of Kenya Speak: Imperial Activism and Settler Society, c.1930', *Journal of British Studies*, 54 (2): 433–56.

Vogel, L. (2013), *Marxism and the Oppression of Women: Toward a Unitary Theory*. Brill.

Webster, E., A. O. Britwum and S. Bhowmik (2017), 'A Conceptual and Theoretical Introduction', in E. Webster, A. O. Britwum and S. Bhowmik (eds), *Crossing the Divide: Precarious Work and the Future of Labour*, 1–32, Epworth: University of KwaZulu-Natal Press.

Webster, E. and K. Van Holdt (2005), *Beyond the Apartheid Workplace: Studies in Transition*, Petermaritzburg: University of KwaZulu-Natal Press.

Weiner, M. F. (2018), 'Decolonial Sociology: W.E.B. Du Bois' Foundational Theoretical and Methodological Contributions', *Sociology Compass*, 12 (8): 1–16.

Wood, M. M. (2005), 'Diplomatic Wives: The Politics of Domesticity and the "Social Game" in the U.S. Foreign Service, 1905–1941', *Journal of Women's History*, 17 (2): 142–65.

World Bank (2020a), *Development Indicators: Tanzania*, Washington DC: The World Bank. https://tradingeconomics.com/tanzania/wage-and-salaried-workers-total-percent-of-total-employed-wb-data.html (accessed 19 June 2023).

World Bank (2020b), *Development Indicators: Vulnerable Employment*, Washington DC: The World Bank. https://tradingeconomics.com/tanzania/vulnerable-employment-female-percent-of-female-employment-wb-data.html (accessed 19 June 2023).

Yeats, N. (2012), 'Global Care Chains: A State-of-the-Art Review and Future Directions in Care Trans-Nationalization', *Global Networks*, 12 (2): 135–54.

Young, I. M. (2005), 'House and Home: Feminist Variations on a Theme', in I. M. Young (ed.), *Throwing Like a Girl and Other Essays*, 123–54, Oxford: Oxford University Press.

Yuval-Davis, N. (1997), *Gender and Nation*, Thousand Oaks: Sage.

Index

www.ingramcontent.com/pod-product-compliance
Ingram Content Group UK Ltd.
Pitfield, Milton Keynes, MK11 3LW, UK
UKHW020818290926
15470UKWH00003B/1223

9 781350 277038